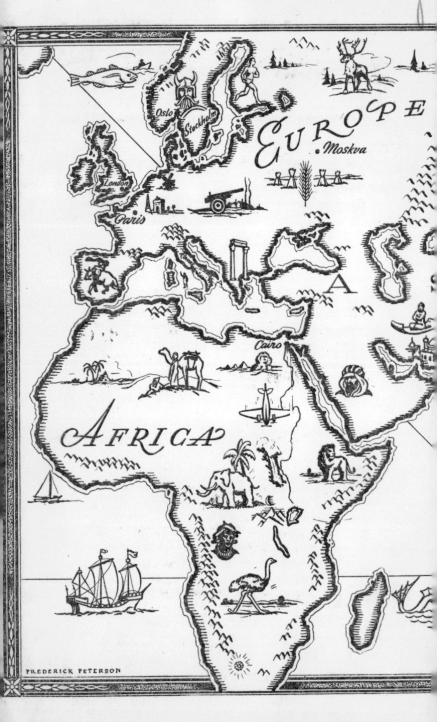

EUROPE

Oslo

Stockholm

•Moskva

London

Paris

A

Cairo

AFRICA

FREDERICK PETERSON

# DECISION IN KOREA

by

Rutherford M. Poats

*With an Introduction by*
*Major George Fielding Eliot*

THE McBRIDE COMPANY
NEW YORK

Library of Congress Catalog Card Number:
54–7378

Printed in the United States of America

Published Simultaneously in Canada by

McClelland & Stewart, Ltd.

Toronto

# Contents

*Contents*

## MAPS

# Introduction

To many Americans, the Korean armistice has brought a feeling of frustration, not untinged with the bitterness of defeat. We have stopped fighting without having brought about a clear-cut military victory. We have not made the enemy cry "enough." There has been no "unconditional surrender" to offset our 137,000 casualties. We are, therefore, all too ready to salve our injured pride by readily accepting partisan assertions that we have been "betrayed," that our policy and strategy have been mismanaged, that firmer purpose, better judgment, and clearer vision on the part of those in high places could have found for us some magic key to victory.

To these distressed imaginings, Mr. Poats offers a much-needed antidote of realism. He makes clear the central point that the Korean conflict was not just a war waged by the American nation in pursuit of a purely American objective, but rather the first test in arms of the validity of the concept of collective security against centralized aggression. To the burning question—was Korea worth the cost?—he answers without qualification, Yes. Not only did our resistance stop Soviet aggression and roll it back for the first time, but it warned the men in the Kremlin of the risk involved in future aggressions of similar nature. Writing with his emphasis on light rather than heat, and with ad-

mirable objectivity, Mr. Poats provides the reader with a
calm and analytical account of the origins and events of
the war in Korea which is the more valuable because it ap-
pears in print while many of the issues arising from the
Korean armistice are still in the area of public debate and
discussion. His book should prove a most useful yardstick
to troubled citizens for whom the real issues may become
obscured or distorted in the fire of political controversy.

However, it seems to me that the true value of Mr. Poats'
work goes well beyond the confines of the Korean problem
as such. The real question which he asks us to face is not
"was Korea worth the cost?" but "what is the objective of
American foreign and military policy today?" Are we concerned only with "stopping Communist aggression" on this
or that troubled frontier or are we really interested in trying to create conditions under which the average free man
and woman—and family—can enjoy some dependable
measure of security from the constant threat of war and of
atomic destruction? Have we tried to formulate this aim in
definite terms, and are we directing our policies from day
to day and from year to year toward its accomplishment?

Such an objective, of course, goes far beyond the mere
preservation of the independence of the Korean Republic,
although a rescued Korea may have been a necessary step
toward its attainment. For the moment, the essence of our
purpose seems to be to deter the Soviet leaders from resort-
ing to war by making it clear that they have nothing to
gain by engaging in it. Korea was an object lesson, and a
necessary one. So, for that matter, was our support of the
Greek government and the Berlin airlift. But the end result at which we aim is surely what Harold Nicolson, in his
book, *The Congress of Vienna,* calls "civic repose": we are
in desperate need of a respite from the pressures and threats

of atomic war and Communist conquest, just as Europe in 1814 was in desperate need of repose from the pressures and threats of Napoleon's armies and his determination to rule the world. Furthermore, we are in need of obtaining this tranquility without actually having to fight a war with nuclear weapons, for that would in all likelihood destroy the foundations of our civilization.

It is in the light of this over-all objective that we must assess what Mr. Poats refers to as "the Allied decision to seek peace rather than total victory, to fight a limited, defensive war rather than risk the consequences of touching off a global atomic carnage." For, as his book makes clear step by step, our purpose in fighting at all in Korea was not to overthrow the Chinese Communist government, or that of the Soviet Union, but to demonstrate in unmistakable terms the determination that these states are not to be permitted to extend the area of their respective tyrannies by armed might. This is what Clausewitz calls a "war of limited aim," and that was the kind of war we were fighting in Korea: the aim could not have gone beyond that limit, because the governments associated with us in the effort would not have acquiesced.

"War being a political act," observes Sir Frederick Maurice, "the political object must govern the other objects of war. The political object may be such as to require the complete overthrow of the enemy . . . or it may be to cause the enemy to abandon the purpose for which he went to war. Each of these objects influences variously the amount of force required to gain the object and the method of employing that force. To achieve the first of these objects, it may be necessary to employ forces which are greatly superior to those of the enemy, and to occupy his country, or at least the most important centers in it. The latter of these objects may be obtained by forces which are inferior to the enemy's whole armed power."

The use of the strategic mobility of sea power to produce a concentration of force at a particular point on the perimeter of the huge Russian empire, a concentration sufficient to accomplish a specific object against the fragment of its total force which the Russians were able to deploy against it, is no new thing in Russian history. It was such a sea-supported concentration in the Crimea in 1854–56 which convinced the Russian leaders of that day that they had no hope of continuing their cherished conquest of the Ottoman dominions and compelled them to abandon that enterprise. It was such a sea-supported concentration in 1904–05 which wrested from the Russians their hoped-for dominance of Korea and Manchuria. Neither the Anglo-French armies in the one case, nor those of Japan in the other, were in any way equal to the *total* fighting power of Russia. They were, however, sufficient "to cause the enemy to abandon the purpose for which he went to war" and so were sufficient to accomplish the limited objective, which in neither case extended to the total overthrow of the Russian state, of those who sent them forth.

Regarding the Communist aggression in Korea as what it surely was, a Soviet-inspired and Soviet-supported attempt not only to conquer South Korea but, as Mr. Poats points out, to acquire a springboard for the ultimate Communist dominance of Japan, the United Nations forces were likewise successful in causing the enemy to abandon his purpose. They enjoyed the same logistic advantages that were possessed by the Allies in the Crimea or by Japan in Manchuria. The effect produced on the minds of the Soviet leaders remains to be assessed, but it can hardly be one of encouragement to attempt other military breakouts where the dice will again be loaded against the Soviet armies.

Beyond these immediate strategic and logistic considerations, however, we must also consider the psychological effect of the Korean resistance on the Soviet mind. The Kremlin was put on notice that there will be no more easy and riskless conquests: that the people of the United States and of other free nations are prepared to fight rather than to allow the free world to be overrun piecemeal. Every decision in war, hot or cold, is based on the weighing of risk against advantage: our sacrifices in Korea have added weight, perhaps decisive weight, to the scale of risk in future Soviet calculations.

And that is perhaps the most important accomplishment of the Korean war. For if our immediate objective in Korea was to preserve the integrity of the Korean Republic against Communist assault, our long-term objective in the global struggle with Soviet Communism is still the distant but golden goal of civic repose from the threat of war, of atomic war. To achieve this without actually accomplishing the overthrow of the Soviet state, we must surely find some other means to cause the enemy to abandon the purpose for which he entered upon the cold war in the first place—that purpose being the overthrow of our way of life and the establishment of a Soviet world.

We may be—almost surely are—a long way from reaching that goal as yet. Despite the fact that there have been a few indications that the new Soviet government is not unmindful of the yearning of its own people for civic repose, there is no suggestion in their current attitude that this ultimate purpose of Soviet world domination has as yet been abandoned. The greatest gain for "our side" is perhaps that all of us are seeing a little more clearly, day by day, the nature of the terrible problem which still confronts us, that Mr. Average Citizen is a little less likely as time goes on to be misled by wishful thinking or deceived by the raucous outbursts of ignorant self-seekers. The free nations are acquiring a steadiness of purpose, an understanding of the true nature of the ultimate objective toward which they strive, as well as of the means necessary to that end and of the sacrifices which they must yet offer on the altar of freedom.

To this clearing vision, the outcome of the Korean war may well make a considerable contribution. For when the tumult and the shouting has had a chance to die away a little, when the light of thoughtful consideration—such as that of Mr. Poats—has had a chance to illumine our soberer reflections, we may come to agree with him that in rejecting the idea of seeking "total victory" over the Red Chinese—and thereby risking World War III—the United States has in fact gained a moral triumph of even greater importance. In Mr. Poats' words, "we have shown that we meant it when we said we sought peace and opposed the use of war to settle international disputes. We have strengthened our claims to moral leadership in the eyes of millions of Europeans and Asians who had viewed the United States with distrust. In this frequently damned policy of limited war, we may have done more to achieve our ultimate objectives of free-world solidarity and peace than we could have accomplished in a successful offensive to the Yalu River."

GEORGE FIELDING ELIOT

New York
February 24th, 1954

# Prologue

THEY CALLED IT "Truman's Folly" and "the war we didn't fight to win." They hailed it as the salvation of the United Nations and the turning point in the struggle against Communist expansion, damned it as "the mess in Korea," and made it the most overworked and unsettled issue in the repertoire of parlor orators. It was the most disheartening and frustrating, the coldest and dreariest, the least inspiring and least popular war in American history. Yet it was, for the United States and its United Nations allies, an effort of high purpose and the most selfless idealism, earnestly dedicated to the preservation of peace and freedom.

It was some of these things to all men because it was and will remain an episode of endless controversy.

At the heart of the controversy, widely misunderstood and clouded by serious doubts even in the minds of its authors, was the basic decision in Korea. This was the Allied decision to seek peace rather than total victory, to fight a limited, defensive war rather than risk the consequences of touching off global atomic carnage. Underlying this decision was a lack of faith in war as a means of untangling the world's problems. Whether finally judged to be wise or shortsighted, it was, nevertheless, a new departure in the search for a way out of the pattern of ever more destructive world wars. It was a product of deliberate and even courageous leadership and worthy of the name "decision." But it was also called indecision, appeasement, and cowardice.

To prove the case of one side in the many controversies

which often overshadowed the fighting and the truce negotiations is not the purpose of this book. This is a reporter's survey of the Korean War through the first half-year of armistice, a brief narrative of review for those who seek a firmer basis on which to form their own opinions. Nor is this presented as a definitive and thoroughly documented history. The professional historians must await release of many of the key official documents and the reports of the men who made the vital decisions. They must learn much more than we now know about the motives and objectives of the North Korean, Chinese Communist, and Soviet governments. But because it was an intensely controversial war, debated regularly in the halls of the United Nations, subjected to repeated public criticism and dissection, we do have now nearly all the facts required for popular appraisal.

Although painstaking efforts have been made to achieve objectivity, some personal opinion inevitably weights and colors this writer's report. Interpretation cannot always steer clear of prejudice. Readers may find an offensive tendency here to support implicitly the Korean policies generally followed by the administrations of both President Truman and President Eisenhower. Some may detect a nationalistic American prejudice in treating the stormy old patriarch of South Korea, Syngman Rhee. All such unavoidable compromises with clinical objectivity are admitted in advance. In no way are any opinions expressed or implied here the responsibility of the United Press.

Rutherford W. Poats

Tokyo
February, 1954

# I

## Storm Warning

Dawn came slowly through rain-filled clouds shrouding the 38th parallel. In Korea it was Sunday, June 25th, 1950, another day in the nearly five-year-old armed truce along the border separating Communist North Korea and the American-sponsored republic in the south. In Washington, where a new stack of intelligence reports on North Korean invasion threats had been received, discounted, and filed away, it was a quiet Saturday afternoon. President Truman was visiting his Missouri home. In Tokyo, General Douglas MacArthur was asleep, apparently undisturbed by the hissing fuse of the Korean powder keg. His staff shared the belief of American officials in Seoul and Washington that the Soviet satellite state north of the 38th parallel was not ready to strike. "Exaggerated" intelligence reports on Korean Communist strength and troop movements had been received many times before.

In Moscow, Peiping, and Pyongyang the leaders of world Communism knew that Sunday was not just another day in the cold war. This was the day set for the great gamble. Infiltration and subversion by armed Communist guerrillas had failed to overthrow the Seoul government, created by the United Nations supervised elections of 1948 and now recognized by most of the democracies as the only

1

legitimate government of Korea. The Republican army was growing stronger, the southern economy more stable. If this toehold of the western powers on the rim of Red Asia was to be eliminated, and a southern springboard for eventual Russian conquest or domination of Japan assured, the gamble of military invasion of South Korea must be attempted, and soon. Now the Kremlin was ready to change its tactics and directly challenge the West with an armed attack on a sovereign republic.

It looked like the safest bet an aggressor had made since Hitler's march into Czechoslovakia. The obliging Americans had widely publicized the United States Joint Chiefs of Staff decision not to fight on the Korean peninsula. Congressional testimony and news reports from Seoul, Tokyo, and Washington had catalogued the exact strength and weaknesses of the South Korean armed forces. The United States government, fearful that belligerent old President Syngman Rhee would precipitate World War III by carrying out his often-voiced threat to invade North Korea, had armed Rhee's forces with only a minimum of defensive weapons. Under the American military-aid program, the southerners were not allowed to have tanks, heavy artillery, combat airplanes, or even a large supply of ammunition.

An extensive network of espionage agents in South Korea and Japan undoubtedly filled in all the missing details, including the fact that the American occupation forces in Japan were under strength, poorly equipped, and poorly trained—in no sense "combat ready," as American military leaders had wishfully proclaimed. If the spies operating in the guise of advisers to the Soviet member of the Allied Council in Japan had been earning their pay, they had reported that MacArthur's headquarters did not even have a tentative plan for United States intervention in Korea in the event of Communist invasion.

If further evidence were needed of America's disposition not to become involved deeply in Korea, Congress provided it during the Spring by initially voting down the Truman administration's economic-aid program for South Korea and threatening to cast this problem child of American postwar diplomacy to the wolves. Only an eleventh-hour reversal of the original vote saved the republic's economic lifeline and kept ECA in business in Korea.

Moscow and Pyongyang thus knew precisely their military advantage in Korea. They knew that the "exaggerated" reports by South Korean, Nationalist Chinese, and American agents of a heavy buildup of North Korean armed strength were true. Thousands of battlewise Korean veterans of the Chinese Communist armies had been repatriated from North China and injected into the already well-trained but green "Korean People's Army." Russian T-34 medium tanks and Yak fighter planes had been brought across Manchuria and down from Vladivostok to give the Soviet satellite army the extra muscle it needed to win a quick, knockout victory.

Instead of the ninety-six thousand troops, sixty to one hundred tanks, one hundred obsolete airplanes, and inadequate supplies which American intelligence credited to the North Koreans, they had one hundred and fifty thousand to two hundred thousand troops, more than two hundred tanks, and at least two hundred propeller-driven Yak fighters. This fighting machine had numerical superiority, but it had something more important. It had two to four years of intensive training for war under Soviet supervision, plus thorough indoctrination and iron discipline enforced by Communist "political officers" with full authority to execute slackers on the spot. During the early part of 1950, it acquired the junior leadership it needed with the arrival of Korean veterans of the Chinese civil war,

South of the Thirty-eighth parallel, the Republic of Korea army was improving every month. In two years a hardworking staff of five hundred American military advisers, comparable to the Soviet military mission in the north, had organized a one hundred thousand-man force along United States army lines. The ROK army and the fifty thousand-man national police force had wiped out all major Communist guerrilla bands and removed the once-serious threat of conquest from within by an armed minority. The army could draw for conscripts upon a population of twenty-one million, as against North Korea's nine million.

Brigadier General William L. Roberts, chief of the United States military mission (called Korean Military Advisory Group, or KMAG), considered the ROK army "the best doggoned shooting army outside the United States." But he and MacArthur* and all visiting American officials knew that, despite its progress, it was still essentially an oversized, motorized police force with only the trappings of an army.

It had virtually no experienced military leadership. Its colonels and generals were twenty-five to thirty-five-year-old Koreans who had served in the Japanese forces and had escaped the postwar purge of important pro-Japanese. Its battalion and company commanders were former policemen and young men barely out of their teens. Its non-com-

---

* MacArthur had no direct military responsibility for Korea in 1950. As United States Far East Theatre Commander, however, he was concerned with the situation there and received intelligence reports from representatives of his command operating in Korea.

missioned officers were picked from the ranks during training after a few months of military service. In the professional arms—signal communications, engineering, motor maintenance, and medical services—the ROK army was even more primitive and poorly led.

Despite these obvious weaknesses, the KMAG officers and men were intensely enthusiastic about the ROK army's progress during the final months before invasion. They believed that a strong force, capable of defending South Korea and thus reducing the chances of war, was in the making.

This cautious optimism among the military was matched among American political and economic experts in Seoul. South Korea was moving toward political and economic stability. It was becoming, if not "an outpost of democracy," at least a good friend of the West and a bulwark against further Communist expansion toward Japan. With the slackening of Communist guerrilla activity in the south, there was a chance for democratic elements to curb the police-state tendencies and absolute authority of President Rhee and win stronger popular support for the government. At the outbreak of war, the National Assembly seemed well on the way toward stripping the presidency of its broad powers and strengthening the rôle of a premier responsible to the legislature. Even to Americans who sympathized with Rhee's policy of fighting fire with fire and compromising on the ideals of democracy, this looked like a healthy step toward real representative government and a stronger republic.

Coupled with slow gains in the Economic Cooperation Administration's fight against inflation and the reviving export trade, the Korean picture in June of 1950 seemed bright enough to cause official Washington to begin revising its opinion that the Korean Republic, like Formosa, was doomed to eventual Communist conquest.

Optimism bred wishful thinking. State Department officials in Seoul privately theorized that Indo-China, Tibet, and Formosa were next on the Red timetables in Asia and would absorb all Communist military and diplomatic energies for some time to come. South Korea was described as a poor prize, not justifying a sudden switch by world Communism to direct military invasion and the consequent risk of world war. Military men added the wishful argument that Communist tanks would be worthless on Korea's primitive roads and would bog down in its rice paddies and mountains. Economists pointed out that North Korea was no drain on the Russian economy, whereas South Korea, in spite of its economic gains, would be a serious burden after conquest.

In this atmosphere, the storm signals went unheeded. Full North Korean divisions were shifted from their northern training camps toward the Thirty-eighth parallel during May and June. Tanks, guns, and ammunition poured into North Korea across the Yalu and Tumen rivers. Reserve units were called up. The strength of Communist forces along the Thirty-eighth parallel was noticeably increased in some sectors. Most of this ominous activity was reported to Tokyo and Washington, but discounting interpretations were added along the way.

In June North Korean propaganda adopted a soothing tone. At the same time Pyongyang offered what proved to be its final proposal for unification of the country. It called for merger of the two national assemblies—without regard for the south's more than two-to-one population advantage

—immediate withdrawal of the United Nations Commission from South Korea, and punishment of "enemies of peaceful unification" and of "traitors." The offer was immediately rejected, but behind this smokescreen North Korea made final invasion preparations. A two-mile-wide belt north of the Thirty-eighth parallel was cleared of civilians, as intelligence investigations later disclosed. Captured documents* have proved that orders for the attack went out while the unification offer was being made.

Syngman Rhee's sabre-rattling speeches threatening invasion of the north—he once declared that if America would release its restraining hand and give him some combat planes and gasoline he could conquer North Korea in two weeks—gave the Communists a ready-made propaganda theme to justify the attack. The almost constant border clashes which ranged back and forth across the ill-defined boundary provided the final stage-setting for a "defensive" war against the southern republic.

* Two of these documents were made public by President Truman April 11, 1951.

# II

## Challenge Accepted

A<small>T ABOUT</small> 4 A.M. on June 25th, sleepy South Korean sentries heard the muffled rumble of what seemed to be a thunderstorm across the mountains. At Kaesong and near Korangpo in the west, the ROK garrisons soon knew the sounds came from Communist artillery, not thunderclouds. But along most of the two hundred miles of lonely border outposts there was only the rustle of a light rain to disturb the morning calm.

By 5 A.M. the invasion was on. North Korean tanks and seventy-five thousand infantrymen, concentrated astride six invasion routes, struck across the Thirty-eighth parallel in a carefully co-ordinated offensive. The thunder of mortars and artillery, the clank and roar of Russian tanks, and the staccato voices of Russian sub-machineguns were the Communists' only declaration of war.

By mid-morning the North Korean propaganda radio at Pyongyang, the northern capital, was beaming out an explanation: the "people's forces" had repelled a sneak offensive launched by the South Korean "puppets of American imperialism" and now had counterattacked; the northern forces would not stop until they had crushed the régime of Syngman Rhee and unified the country as a "people's democracy."

The Communists charged that John Foster Dulles, Republican party adviser to the United States State Department, had given the order to attack when he visited South Korean troops along the border on June 18th. (Dulles ridiculed the allegation, saying he had been impressed by the unpreparedness of the South Korean forces and had planned to recommend more United States arms aid.)

The attack overran the South Korean border outposts without losing momentum and rammed into the main ROK defense forces. Roaring, rough-skinned tanks and artillery and mortar barrages threw terror into some South Korean troops. Others fought valiantly with grenades, rifles, anti-tank guns, and dynamite charges to stop the armored drive, but the tanks came on. The few available American anti-tank guns—firing mostly high-explosive, rather than armor-piercing, shells—lasted only a few hours in the uneven duel before they were overrun and abandoned.

The confusion was greater than the most pessimistic American adviser had feared. Units failed to report their positions to higher commands, and when they did report they often claimed face-saving victories. Officers led many a panicky retreat. Equipment which could not be replaced for months was abandoned to the Reds.

Kaesong, headquarters of an ROK division and only a mile inside South Korea, fell within four hours. Another Communist column took Korangpo and crossed the Imjin River on a bridge which somehow was not destroyed. Another column swept down the center of the peninsula and knifed behind Chunchon, major city and military base northeast of Seoul.

In a few moments the Thirty-eighth parallel ceased to exist as a political boundary in the eyes of officials on both sides. By word and deed the North Koreans proclaimed a fight to the finish, an all-or-nothing battle to unify Korea. By violating this temporary boundary, they forfeited all claim to protection behind this mapmaker's line when the Allied forces later were to march northward and when the armistice negotiators sought a cease-fire line.

No one before the war had recognized the Thirty-eighth parallel as a permanent dividing line between the two Koreas. At the moment of invasion, Syngman Rhee's government welcomed the challenge to settle the issue on the battlefield. The border had not been made in Korea, however, and it could not so easily be erased from the minds of world political leaders.

Korea had been arbitrarily divided at the Thirty-eighth parallel to facilitate the entry of Russian troops from the north and American forces from the south at the end of the war against Japan. The decision was made one hot night in Potsdam, Germany by the military staffs advising President Truman, Premier Stalin, and Prime Minister Attlee at the Big Three Conference in August of 1945. After the two occupation forces had accepted the surrender of Japanese troops in Korea, arrangements were to be made for reunifying Korea under a single trusteeship régime and a subsequent independent government.

Once in control of North Korea, the Russians lost interest in restoring Korean unity. The impoverished agricultural south was cut off by an iron curtain of Soviet guns from the Japanese-developed industrial north. Without interchange of southern food for northern electric power and manufactured goods, Korea was sick and helpless. Russia brought in a thirty-three-year-old expatriate Communist, who adopted the legendary name of Kim Il Sung, and made him puppet leader of a North Korean régime modeled in the Soviet image. The Russians blocked repeated American efforts in the Joint United States–Soviet Commission and later by the United Nations General Assembly to unify Korea under a single, freely elected government.

After the Russian and American occupation forces withdrew, "Russian" Koreans and "American" Koreans faced each other across the Thirty-eighth parallel. Leaders on both sides hurled militant threats and destroyed all hope of peacefully putting broken Korea back together again. Here United States and Russian prestige and interests met, and here a warlike move by an impetuous Korean general could mushroom into World War III. Korea had become the powder keg of Asia.

It blew up in a series of muffled explosions which took many hours to register fully in the minds of men far from the scene. Instinctively, people in New York, Tokyo, London, and Washington looked to the skies. Were the Russian atomic bombers coming? Was this the way another great slaughter was to begin? Had the Communists chosen remote Korea as the starting point of World War III, or was this just another phase of piecemeal aggression in a corner of the earth not quite worth fighting for? It was too portentous an event for the mind to grasp in the first flash of news from Seoul.

The first word of the attack reached Washington and Tokyo over the wires of the United Press. Forty-five minutes after UP correspondent Jack James filed his first bulletin from Seoul, United States Ambassador John J. Muccio notified Washington. It was early Sunday morning in Tokyo. The duty officer who received the official message at General MacArthur's headquarters did not disturb the sleeping general. MacArthur arrived at his office at mid-morning, as usual. In Washington, Secretary of State Dean Acheson read the reports and telephoned President Truman at Independence, Missouri. Truman decided to continue his visit, keeping in touch with Acheson during the night.

Within twenty-four hours there was no longer any room for hope that this was another minor incursion across the border. The United Nations Korea Commission in Seoul, acting on the reports of its military observers, notified Lake Success that a full-scale war which "may endanger maintenance of international peace and security" had broken out in Korea. Both the United Nations observers and American military advisers with the ROK divisions testified that Pyongyang's pretense of "defensive" action was totally false. The United Nations Commission urged swift Security Council action to halt the Communist aggression.

Acting on Acheson's instructions, the United States delegate to the Security Council, Ernest A. Gross, already had telephoned Secretary General Trygve Lie and convinced him that the situation required an emergency meeting of the Council.

The Council met Sunday afternoon. Russia, which had been boycotting the United Nations in protest against Chinese Nationalist membership, failed to appear. It was a grave blunder by the Kremlin. Unobstructed by the Soviet veto, the Council was free to take forceful action.

Gross declared that the North Korean Communists had committed "armed aggression against a government elected under United Nations supervision." Such an attack, he said, "openly defies the interest and authority of the United Nations" and required immediate action. Three hours and forty-five minutes after Chairman Sir Benegal Rau of India had opened the session, the Council voted nine to zero, Yugoslavia abstaining, to:

1. Order a cease-fire in Korea and withdrawal of the northern forces to the Thirty-eighth parallel.

2. Instruct the United Nations Commission in Korea to supervise compliance with the order and make recommendations for further steps which the parent organization should take to restore peace.

3. Call upon all members of the United Nations to "render every assistance to the United Nations in the execution of this resolution and to refrain from giving assistance" to the North Koreans.

The vote in effect branded the Communists as aggressors. It set in motion the chain of events which threw the moral force and untested military strength of the United Nations into action against a Soviet satellite. Russia, by failing to attend and use its veto, had lost the first round.

While the Council was acting, President Truman flew back to Washington and went into an all-night conference with Acheson, Secretary of Defense Louis Johnson, and other government officials. By early Monday morning a second momentous decision had been reached. Secretary of the Army Frank Pace, Jr. notified General MacArthur in a radio-teletype exchange of the President's dual decision—to support the South Koreans with United States air and naval action and to use the United States Seventh Fleet to "neutralize" Formosa. In a stroke he scrapped the controversial "hands-off Formosa" policy, ordering the Seventh Fleet to prevent either Communist attacks on the Nationalist-held island or Nationalist raids on the Chinese mainland.

At noon Monday, Truman issued a public statement disclosing the decision and announcing plans to speed the flow of military aid to Communist-threatened French Indo-China and the Philippines. He declared:

"The attack upon Korea makes it plain beyond all doubt that Communism has passed beyond the use of subversion to conquer independent nations and will now use armed invasion and war. . . . I know that all members of the United Nations will consider carefully the consequences of this latest aggression in Korea in defiance of the Charter of the United Nations. A return to the rule of force in international affairs would have far-reaching effects. The United States will continue to uphold the rule of law."

MacArthur's air force already was going into action. Ambassador Muccio set in motion a pre-arranged plan for evacuating two thousand Americans and other foreigners from South Korea to safety in Japan. Transport planes for the evacuation airlift were ordered concentrated at Itazuke Air Base, Kyushu, across the one hundred-mile-wide Tsushima Straits from southern Korea. Fighter squadrons based in Okinawa and the Philippines were alerted to move to southern Japan and provide air defense and aerial cover for the airlift of Americans out of Korea.

Tuesday morning the North Koreans were within ten miles of Seoul. Rumor had them on the outskirts; the flight of Americans before the invaders began. Carrying only a suitcase apiece and abandoning automobiles, furniture, homes, and other possessions, they boarded United States Air Force planes at Seoul's Kimpo Airport and at Suwon, twenty miles to the south, or sailed in ships from Inchon. Overhead, American F-82 Twin Mustang fighters and F-80 jets watched for Communist planes. Kimpo already had been strafed and a grounded United States transport plane burned.

The Yaks came and, while transports loaded and took off, a dogfighting American pilot drew the Air Force's first blood of the war. By the end of the day, six Yaks were shot down and two American escort fighter planes damaged. All airlift transports got through safely.

Members of the United Nations Commission and some American military advisers attached to the rear head-quarters of the South Korean army joined the flight to Japan. The British and French diplomatic staffs and several religious missions elected to remain in Seoul and paid heavily for their faith in North Korean scruples.

Before abandoning its Seoul headquarters, the United Nations commission radioed a warning to Lake Success: Communist invaders had ignored the United Nations cease-fire order. Pleas by the Security Council were not likely to halt the war, the message said. The Communists were carrying out a "well-planned, concerted, and full-scale invasion of South Korea" and "in a matter of days" the Republic's army might be destroyed and the entire peninsula lost. The commission furnished additional evidence that the South Koreans were not responsible for the outbreak of war and had been taken by surprise while holding defensive positions.

Radio Moscow and the North Korean Pyongyang radio confirmed the commission's fears that the cease-fire order would be ignored. The Communist propaganda voices declared that the Security Council's resolution was illegal because neither Russia nor Communist China was represented at the emergency meeting.

The Council reconvened Tuesday afternoon; Russia once more boycotted the session. Before the Council was an issue much larger than the fate of South Korea: the life of the United Nations was at stake. The civilized world's waning hopes that collective security through the United Nations could insure peace and prevent a third and more terrible global war hung in the balance. Never had the Security Council used its ultimate power to order military sanctions against an aggressor. How military sanctions could be enforced without a United Nations police force was still a matter of theoretical dispute.

The United States proposed, with strong British support, that the Security Council call on all United Nations members to come to the aid of the South Koreans with military force and repel the aggressors. Yugoslavia cast the only opposing vote. India and Egypt postponed their votes; later India approved and Egypt abstained. By a final vote of eight to one the Council committed the United Nations to battle. It was probably the gravest decision an international organization had ever made, but events were moving so fast that to some it seemed an empty gesture.

The news did not reach Seoul in time to cheer the defenders. In Korea it was early Wednesday morning. Communist shells were falling on the outskirts of the capital, and tanks were waddling down darkened streets. A nervous ROK army engineer officer ordered the main Han River highway bridge below Seoul dynamited while most of the South Korean forces were still on the north side. The bridge was jammed with bumper-to-bumper traffic when the explosion shattered the first span.

The last members of the government and the ROK army headquarters fled southward before dawn. Colonel W. H.

Sterling Wright, acting chief of the American military advisory group, led a motley company of American officers and soldiers on the first stage of what was to become a nightmare of humiliating retreats before a third-rate army of Oriental Communists.

The tragedy of Korea was enacted on the roads leading south that day. Nearly a million Koreans, from Seoul and towns to the north, streamed southward in the first great exodus of the war. The human flood trickled along railroad embankments and tributary trails, and swelled to a torrent on the main highway from Seoul and Inchon to Suwon and the south. It was a scene to be repeated all over Korea until it became a persistent nightmare.

In the ragged column of refugees were farmers and merchants, the poor, and a few of the rich. Some had escaped the trek by paying their life savings to owners of rickety busses and trucks who capitalized on national misery. Trudging down the dusty roads into the unknown, bowed under the weight of a pitiful collection of possessions hurriedly assembled, were bearded old men, mothers, round-faced children, and more children. Some led oxen drawing two-wheeled carts piled high with clothing, rice, earthenware urns, and occasionally, in sharp contrast, an American sewing machine or a radio. Most of the refugees escaped with only what they could carry—and it was an unbelievable load—on wooden "A-frame" back-packs.

Seoul fell Wednesday morning as fast as disorganized South Korean troops could escape across the Han River.

It was a dark day, unrelieved by the hopeful decision at Lake Success. Russia's puppet army seemed victory-bound, with nothing but rugged terrain and the shattered remnants of the ROK army standing between Seoul and Pusan. Those ROK units still in fighting formation had only a few days' ammunition supply left. Most of the South Koreans' artillery and anti-tank guns were lost. Seven of the ROK "air force's" ten light trainer planes had been shot down, and General MacArthur's emergency donation of ten American Mustang fighter planes meant little, since there were no South Korean pilots trained to fly them.

Syngman Rhee declared bitterly through a spokesman that his warnings of Communist strength and pleas for more arms aid now were being borne out. "We have nothing to stop those tanks," he said. "Our soldiers are very brave. They sacrifice themselves against the tanks. Korea is very hard-pressed, because aid was so slow. It is too little and too late."

From high in the cloudy sky that Wednesday morning came a silvery flicker of hope, but few of the plodding refugees from Seoul saw it. A flight of United States Air Force jet fighters streaked across the Han River and dived with rockets and machine guns blazing at the vanguard of the Communist army. General MacArthur, acting on Washington's decision to support the South Koreans with air and naval action, had sent the Japan-based Fifth Air Force to war.

*Standing in front of a fighter squadron's operations shack at Itazuke Air Base in Japan that morning, I watched the F-80 pilots take off. No one grasped the full significance of the moment; there was too much confusion. Were we at war? How would an American pilot distinguish a North Korean soldier on the ground from a South Korean? Where were the front lines?*

*I was no less confused. There was no censorship, only a*

*vague sheet of mimeographed instructions from MacArthur's Public Information Office. Correspondents were not to disclose troop movements, planned or incomplete military operations, and a number of other broad subjects. Not knowing whether competing reporters would follow a similar interpretation of the rules, I decided against filing a dispatch on the departure of the first Air Force combat mission flown in this war.*

*This struggle between conscience and the competitive demands of modern news coverage was to torment the press and strain its relations with the military for six months. Without censorship, the correspondent often felt—as I felt that Wednesday morning—like a suspected spy. Often he was treated as one, particularly in rear areas. At times it seemed that MacArthur's experiment in fighting an uncensored war was near success. Then some reporter, completely loyal to the United Nations cause, would give the entire press corps a black eye by indulging in what a fellow-correspondent called "competitive irresponsibility."*

In the ancient walled town of Suwon, twenty miles south of Seoul, there was another faintly hopeful scene that morning. Brigadier General John H. Church, an almost emaciated little man whose unpretentious appearance concealed great capacity for combat leadership, was establishing an advance American headquarters in Korea. He and a staff of officers and signal communications men had flown from Tokyo late Tuesday. His job was to find out what could be done to save the Korean republic and to attempt to reorganize the ROK army.

What he found Wednesday was not encouraging. It was impossible to establish contact with most ROK units. No one knew where the enemy was, except that he had entered Seoul. There was an ominous blackout of information from the east, where two Communist amphibious landings far down the coast had been reported. Reports of valiant South Korean stands before tens of thousands of enemy troops and of the capture of Russian tank crews were trickling in, but experience already had indicated that their accuracy could not be trusted.

Yet, here at Suwon was a feeble, tentative move toward real American intervention. Confusion was to be expected at first. For the more farsighted observer, who knew what was then unknown at Suwon—that the Security Council had ordered military intervention in support of the South Koreans—there was room for hope that the Soviets' boldest bid for conquest would not succeed.

# III

## *Lives for Time*

THE FINAL DECISIONS sending America to war came in the next thirty-six hours.

Hardly had General Church's first discouraging report been received in Tokyo when General MacArthur decided to go to Korea for a first-hand examination. He and his immediate staff and four allied newsmen flew to Suwon Thursday morning with plans to spend two days in Korea. His big four-engined transport bore a name appropriate to the desperate peninsular battle ahead: *Bataan*.

The big silver plane landed on Suwon's concrete airstrip between attacks on the field by red-starred Yak fighters. President Rhee and Ambassador Muccio joined MacArthur there after dodging pursuing Yaks in a hedge-hopping flight from Taejon, now the Korean government's refugee capital.

A few hours of conferences and a jeep trip to the "front" overlooking the Han River were enough to convince MacArthur that American air and naval support and advice to the ROK Army could not save South Korea. He saw ROK soldiers streaming southward, apparently without leadership or thought of fighting. He found the main railway bridges across the Han River still undestroyed. He saw for himself that reports of utter confusion and disorganization had not been exaggerated.

21

MacArthur returned immediately to Tokyo to recommend that American army divisions in Japan be thrown into the battle. He decided that President Truman's original order on air support, plus the Security Council's military sanctions decision, could be interpreted to permit him to bomb the sources of the Communist offensive in North Korea. However, thinking in terms of his prewar intelligence reports and still hopeful that the South Korean forces could be rallied, he seriously underestimated the extent of American army intervention which would be needed. He told correspondents on the way back to Tokyo that only two American divisions should be sufficient to form a rallying force for the ROK Army and permit him to "hold South Korea."

MacArthur was asking Washington to gamble that the Korean action was an isolated Soviet move. Not many months earlier he had appealed for more troops to defend unarmed Japan against a possible Soviet attack from the north. Russian infantry and airborne divisions were known to be based in the Kurile Islands and Sakhalin, less than an hour's flight from Japan's northern island. Russia's air force in Siberia and its submarine fleet in the Far East were stronger than defensive intentions would justify. Japan was still nominally an enemy nation under occupation rule, and no one could be sure that anti-American elements would not make trouble if the islands were stripped of one or more of the four occupation divisions.

President Truman accepted MacArthur's assurance that the risk was worth taking. Associates said later that the President already had decided independently that American troops would have to fight in Korea before peace could be restored. He reasoned that the American people were ready to call a halt to Communist aggression and would support strong leadership. He assumed correctly that the public recognized the dangers of failing to meet a direct challenge. On Friday, June 30th, he authorized MacArthur to send American divisions in Japan to Korea. At the same time he put the official stamp of approval on MacArthur's decision to attack military targets in North Korea. He ordered the Air Force and Navy to extend their action to the entire Korean peninsula, bounded on the north by the borders of Communist China and Russia.

Within minutes after the President's order had been received, the United States Twenty-fourth Infantry Division, based in Kyushu, was alerted for movement. Early Saturday morning two battalions of the Twenty-first Infantry Regiment were loaded aboard waiting transport planes at Itazuke Air Base and flown to Pusan, on the southeast tip of the Korean peninsula.

It all happened too fast for this chosen handful of Americans to realize what lay ahead. Perhaps it was just as well. They were routed out of their comfortable occupation barracks during the night, told to make up their combat packs, collect ammunition for their weapons at the supply rooms, and "fall in" for a truck movement. GIs grumbled that it was another of the army's fiendish schemes for making a peacetime soldier miserable. Some officers tried to brief their men on what it was all about, but no one could really know.

*On the loading ramp at Itazuke I talked to some of the men that dawn. They sprawled on the grass and the asphalt beneath the transport planes, wearing green fatigue uniforms and field packs which had never been exposed to the sweat and filth of war. There was no excitement on their faces, and few of them bothered to ask each other the question that fiction writers find in soldiers' minds.*

*A lieutenant asked me, "What's the score," and I told him what little I had heard from Tokyo.*

*"Do you think you'll have to fight after you get there?" I asked.*

*"I dunno—hope not," he replied.*

*A major who had joined the group added, "I figure that once the Reds hear Americans are up against them they'll stop and think this thing over a while."*

*On a latrine wall was better evidence that Americans knew they were at war. Kilroy had returned! A jingle, scrawled in pencil, read:*

> *"Clap your hands and jump for joy,*
> *You were here before Kilroy."*

*Below, signed by the legendary, omnipresent GI of World War II, was:*

> *"Sorry to spoil your little joke,*
> *I was here, but my pencil broke—"*
> *Kilroy*

Saturday morning, six days after the North Koreans launched the invasion, these one thousand-odd American soldiers were transplanted from a world of peacetime pleasures and occupation comforts to the unreality of war and sudden death. They had been given little military or psychological preparation for the shock or for the job ahead. Many of them had entered or stayed in the army to see the world, earn credits toward a "GI Bill of Rights" education, or find the advertised "security" of a "peacetime army career."

They had no medium or heavy tanks, no effective weapons for stopping tanks, limited artillery, and no immediate source of replacements for lost men or heavy equipment. Only recently had they begun to get realistic unit training in field exercises, and even this was carried out without mental conditioning for war.

Again America, despite common knowledge of the dangers all about and the imminent threat of war, despite its ambitious global commitments to defend freedom, was caught unprepared. These men of the Twenty-fourth Division were to suffer the full penalty of unpreparedness. The blame could be assessed not only on General MacArthur and his army commander, Lt. Gen. Walton H. Walker, but also on the United States government, which had failed to give MacArthur the troops and equipment he needed, and on the American people, who never in time of relative peace have been willing to pay in taxes and conscription the price which preparedness demands.

However, Americans had not forgotten so quickly all the skills they had learned in World War II. Except for the crowding of aircraft on the southern Japan airstrips, vulnerable to Communist air attack, the air bases were beginning to look like well-oiled war machines. Low-slung, silver F-80 jets, their wings weighted down with racks of five-inch rockets, roared and whined on the warm-up ramps, raced down the runways with the noise of a dozen typhoons, and disappeared into the clouds to the northwest. F-51 Mustangs, workhorses of the World War II propeller-driven era, and tired-looking old B-26 light bombers joined the air war in daily increasing numbers. Returning fighters streaked low over the fields and sometimes turned victory rolls to boast of a "kill" against a North Korean Yak.

A few planes—but only a very few—failed to return. In a matter of days the bulk of the North Korean Air Force was knocked out of the sky. Ground fire, engine failures, and weather soon became the American airman's only enemies in this peculiar war that still was not called a war.

There was one striking contrast with the remembered picture of an air force at war. Here fighter pilots and bomber crews left wives and children after early morning breakfasts, went off to war like commuters in any big city back home, and returned to waiting families at the end of the day's work over Korea. Only when the Fifth Air Force established its major bases in Korea did the "commuters' war" generally end. It remained the daily pattern of life for B-29 bomber crews based in Japan and Okinawa.

If the Air Force had a soft rôle in the beginning, the Navy's was even easier. There was no naval opposition other than mines. Lurking submarines, presumably Russian, occasionally were reported, but they never challenged the Seventh Fleet's absolute control of the seas around Korea.

The day that first handful of American ground troops landed in Pusan, British naval vessels went into action on a shore-bombardment mission with the United States Navy. Two days later a squadron of Royal Australian Air Force Mustangs based in southern Japan escorted a B-29 bombing raid against North Korea. By the Fourth of July, forty-four member governments of the United Nations had announced support of United Nations intervention in Korea. It was becoming a United Nations operation, although only the United States was moving quickly to put strong forces in the field.

No government formally declared war. President Truman described American action in Korea as support of United Nations "police action," and the unfortunate term stuck—later to become the subject of much acid humor.

Nationalist China, a member of the United Nations, offered thirty-three thousand troops to General MacArthur, and the United States government politely rejected the offer. The Chinese troops would require arms and complete logistical support—critically short supplies which Washington believed could best be used by South Koreans defending their homeland. In addition, Formosa's defense might require all the strength Chiang Kai-shek could muster. Washington was uneasy about the possibility of Chinese Communist intervention in Korea. The use of Chiang's troops in Korea might falsely imply an American plot to take the war back across Korea's northern border and help the Chinese Nationalists carry out their threatened invasion of China. This was Washington's decision, but it had the support of most allied nations.

Some Republican congressmen denounced the administration's decision, and it became the first break in the almost solid front of bipartisan support for President Truman's Korea policy. Never since the close of World War II had the United States been so unified for action. When Truman, acting on his own authority as commander-in-chief, ordered American forces into action in Korea, the only important voice raised in opposition was that of Republican Senator Robert Taft. His challenge of the President's authority to commit the United States to war was coupled with an attack on Secretary of State Acheson, whom he blamed for the failure to arm the South Koreans adequately.

# IV

## *To the Brink of Defeat*

GREAT DECISIONS CAME with breathless rapidity, but events dictated by swarms of brown-uniformed Communist soldiers in Korea were moving faster. After pausing only three days to regroup and resupply, the Communist army plunged across the Han River and drove on Suwon on July 2nd. The American advance headquarters had fled the night before, when wildly exaggerated reports of Communist troops on all sides sent a wave of hysteria through the headquarters staff. Suwon was occupied by the enemy on July 4th. To the east, South Korean troops were falling back even more hastily, and there was no trace of a battleline on the war maps.

Major Gen. William F. Dean, commander of the United States Twenty-fourth Division, was named commander of United States Forces in Korea on July 2nd. He set up his headquarters in Taejon, sixty-five miles down the western Korean rice lowlands below Suwon. Dean, a modest, soft-spoken veteran of World War II, did not share the cocky attitude of some Tokyo strategists that the sight of American troops would throw fear into the Communists' hearts. When he ordered two green, under-strength battalions northward to meet the main force of the Communist drive, he knew they were in for a bloody beating.

The first battalion of the Twenty-first Infantry Regi-

28

ment moved into defensive position near Osan, seven miles south of Suwon. The Communists were somewhere to the north; it was easy to imagine that every distant rumble was the sound of their Russian tanks. At any moment these five hundred nervous Americans would be killing other men and facing instant death. The unreality of the moment was heightened by the quiet and by someone's reminder that it was the Fourth of July.

There was an attack, but it came through a hole in the clouds. Australian Mustang fighters, attacking what they presumed to be enemy troops in an area designated by Fifth Air Force, strafed part of the American truck convoy as it moved up to the front south of Osan. No one was killed.

Early the next morning the North Koreans came, and the first American battle of the war began. It was over quickly.

Four thousand Communist troops led by forty medium tanks moved down the narrow dirt road—Korea's main north-south highway—between hills held by five hundred Americans. Clouds again shut out the American Air Force. The lightly armed battalion commanded by Lieutenant Col. Charles B. Smith, thirty-four-year-old West Point graduate from Lambertville, New Jersey was on its own.

Long before the tanks were within effective range, American bazooka and recoilless rifle crews opened fire. Their shots bounded harmlessly off the low, thick hulls of the Russian tanks. Light artillery bracketed the tank column and began scoring hits, but the Communists came on. In a few minutes they were within the American lines. The Yanks' ammunition was running out. Communications broke down. Colonel Smith ordered a retreat, but many survivors never heard the order and were isolated. Wounded men were necessarily abandoned on their litters.

This was the United States Army's baptism of fire. It was only the first of a series of defeats suffered by a few men whom fate had selected to pay the ultimate price for time. Facing odds seldom better than eight to one, the Twenty-fourth Division gave ground slowly before the main weight of the Communist army until help could arrive.

The Osan story was repeated three days later at Chonan, and again at Chochiwon. Each defeat was an affront to American pride. Fighting and watching their comrades die only to fall back again, winning no victories, embittered soldiers cursed "Truman's police action" and the United Nations.

Piecemeal the available American strength from Japan was committed, and piecemeal it was sacrificed in the name of "delaying action." For MacArthur there was no other way. He needed time to ship from Japan two more American divisions—the Twenty-fifth Infantry and the First Cavalry (Infantry)—land them in Korea, and move them to the front. With this force, some luck in reorganizing the South Korean army, and effective use of his growing air and naval forces, MacArthur believed he had a good chance of stalling the Communists short of Pusan and then destroying them at the end of their overtaxed supply lines.

Just as the United States was receiving the shocking, uncensored story of the first battle at Osan, MacArthur notified Washington that the situation "is not considered serious in any way." His eye was on the bigger picture. The United States First Marine Division had been alerted for transport to Korea; more B-29s were on the way. Carrier-based navy fighters and dive bombers from the U.S.S. *Valley Forge* and H.M.S. *Triumph* were bolstering the United Nations air counter-offensive. Three more American aircraft carriers—the *Philippine Sea,* the *Bataan* and the *Sicily* —were either en route to Korea or preparing to sail. More British and Australian warships had joined the United States Seventh Fleet, and three Canadian destroyers had sailed for Korea on July 5th.

If MacArthur's self-confidence needed further reinforcement, he received it on July 3rd when President Truman named him Commander-in-Chief of the United Nations Forces. The United Nations had formally authorized the United States Government to co-ordinate military action in Korea and name the commander. Thus another historic "first" went to the seventy-year-old, five-star general.

That same day, Chonan fell in the west and Chechon, near the center of the peninsula, was abandoned by South Korean forces. At Fort Lewis, Washington, the United States Second Infantry Division was alerted for Korea.

Hope-stirring plans and long-range strategy did little to ease the burden on the only Americans fighting on the ground in Korea. For them the broad, muddy water of the Kum River meant more than all the promises of distant aid. Two regiments of American infantrymen—the Twenty-first and the Thirty-fourth—each with only two battalions instead of the standard three—fell back on the Kum River on July 11th, 12th, and 13th and formed what was hopefully called a "defense line." (The newly arrived Nineteenth Regiment replaced the Twenty-first on the Kum River during the lull.) To the north, moving down two roads below Chonan, were at least three North Korean divisions. To the south were Taejon and a network of roads branching out over all southern Korea. To the east, a Communist drive through central mountain passes held by regrouped

South Korean units threatened to sever the American supply and escape route to Taegu and Pusan.

In less than three weeks the North Koreans had advanced one hundred miles and occupied nearly half of South Korea. They had chewed up the ROK army, brushed aside small American units, and looked like a well-oiled fighting machine in the process. Their mortars and artillery were on the target with hardly a wasted round. They were masters at infiltration, unscrupulous with deception. They wore American uniforms or white civilian pantaloons and blouses as often as their own uniforms. There were many of them, and they knew what they were doing.

A close-up view was less impressive.

*A sergeant herded five filthy, underfed North Korean soldiers into a G-2 interrogation station at Taejon. They joined fifteen others squatting on the wood floor. They wore flimsy rubber-and-canvas shoes, ill-fitting mustard brown cotton jackets and trousers. Some clutched visored cotton caps, removed on order from their close-cropped, bullet-shaped heads. They apparently had not washed their bodies or their clothes for nineteen days, since the invasion. Some nursed old wounds.*

*There was no flicker of emotion or intelligence in their yellowed, dirt-encrusted eyes. Like sick animals they stared into space while waiting their turn at the interrogation desks. Before the intelligence questioners, they revealed everything they knew without hesitation or pressure. This was the enemy.*

The Communist attack on the Kum River line did not come until July 15th. It is not likely that the delay was caused by concern over the strength of what news dispatches called "the first American defense line in Korea." There was no secrecy about the Twenty-fourth Division's lone stand. The North Koreans were being held back by the problem which later was to be the chief source of their defeat—logistics. Gasoline for the tanks and ammunition for the troops were slow in arriving. Allied air strikes raked daytime rail and highway movements behind Communist lines. The Red Army began to face the alternative that it could never escape: bring up supplies during the short nights or pay a prohibitive price in destroyed trains and trucks.

While the Twenty-fourth Division waited for the attack, General MacArthur took the occasion in Tokyo to spank the Allied press for "exaggerating" American army losses. He praised the Twenty-fourth Division's performance as "one of the most skillful and heroic holding actions in history." MacArthur disclosed that up to July 13th only forty-two American soldiers had been killed, one hundred and ninety wounded, and two hundred and fifty-six missing. This total of nearly five hundred casualties presumably would appear small and encouraging to the American public and would prove the assertion that losses had been greatly exaggerated. Actually, the official casualty figure represented more than one-fourth of the American troops directly engaged in combat to that date—very heavy losses, indeed.

The Twenty-fifth Division began landing at Pusan on July 12th, and the next day MacArthur named his Eighth Army Commander, sixty-year-old Lieutenant General Walton H. Walker, to the command of United Nations ground forces in Korea. Forty-seven United Nations members had announced support of intervention in Korea, but only token military contributions from a dozen countries were in prospect. Nevertheless, MacArthur raised the blue-and-white flag of the United Nations in the place of honor to the right of the United States flag over his Tokyo headquarters on July 14th. At Lake Success the United Nations secretariat renewed the call for more combat forces from member countries.

The news from Korea quickly underlined the need for more men and guns. The North Koreans infiltrated across the Kum River during the night of July 14th. At dawn they swarmed through and over the thin American line where two thousand men were attempting to hold twenty miles of riverfront. At one point they attacked an American artillery battery, wearing captured United States field uniforms and shouting, "Don't shoot! We are friends." Others changed into peasant whites and drifted across the hills toward Taejon, linked up with other "refugees" behind the United States lines, and set up roadblocks. The biggest of these roadblocks forced the Nineteenth Regiment to abandon its river line and fight southward toward Taejon on July 16th. A series of river crossings and infiltration maneuvers drove the Thirty-fourth Regiment back on the western flank.

The battle of Taejon opened haltingly. The airport, north of town on the road to the Kum River, was abandoned on July 17th, then re-occupied when the Communist attack slackened. Twenty-fourth Division staff officers predicted that the Communists would be in Taejon within hours.

The North Koreans had a more elaborate plan. One of their divisions by-passed Taejon and raced southward

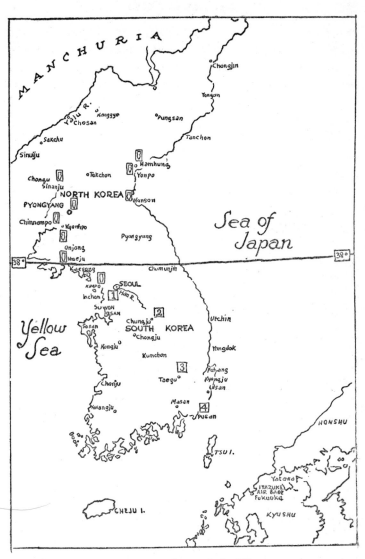

1. Opening Phase of the War

around the Americans' open western flank. Only a few hundred South Korean policemen stood between the Communists and the southern tip of the peninsula.

Two other divisions moved into position for an enveloping attack on Taejon. On July 19th Communist artillery shells began falling on Taejon's clusters of tile-roofed mud huts and shaking its Japanese-constructed public buildings. Fires spread rapidly. Tanks led the assault early the next day, Americans armed with the new 3.5-inch bazookas knocked out seven of them. North Korean infantry and more tanks attacked from the west. General Dean was everywhere at once, firing rocket-launchers, dueling with Communists at pistol range, shifting and encouraging his men. The battle rolled through the smoke-filled streets, now mysteriously stripped of their "Welcome U.N. Forces" banners.

By nightfall Taejon was encircled and much of it was in enemy hands. Retreat meant running a mile-long gantlet of fire. Thirty-fourth Regiment jeeps and trucks loaded with men, many of them wounded, raced down the dusty, poplar-lined road toward Yongdong. General Dean assembled the last Americans in a makeshift motor column and paced the final dash to freedom on July 21st. Roadblocks and a stalled truck blocked their escape road, and they took to the rice paddies.

(This was the last that was publicly known of Dean's fate until eighteen months later, when he told the story of his wanderings and capture to Communist newsman Wilfred Burchett, who gave it to the Allied press. The small band Dean led had disintegrated within five days. Dean wandered on alone, slowly making his way southward toward American positions or the sea. Dysentery and starvation sapped his strength and slowed his pace. In five weeks of hiding by day and creeping through the hills and fields by night he traveled only thirty-five miles, moving generally due south of Taejon. He needed a guide and finally decided to gamble his life on the loyalty of two South Korean civilians he met near Chinan. They almost immediately betrayed him to a platoon of Red troops who overwhelmed the enfeebled general before he could carry out his resolve to kill himself with the last silver bullet in his pearl-handled .45-caliber automatic. So began the three-year ordeal of America's most famous war prisoner.)

The Twenty-fourth Division was shattered; its Thirty-fourth Regiment was never to be rebuilt. The division pulled back to the Naktong River, halfway between Taejon and Pusan, to rest and patch up its casualty-ridden ranks.

But the Communists paid heavily both in men and time. They had spent sixteen days and more than one thousand lives in the uneven battle against the Twenty-fourth's delaying action. The timing of their blitz conquest was upset, possibly wrecked. The Twenty-fifth and First Cavalry Divisions had arrived at the front and were waiting for the North Koreans astride the main roads north and northwest of Taegu.*

The North Korean Army, General Douglas MacArthur declared on the day of Taejon's fall, had "lost its chance for victory."

Was MacArthur whistling in the dark? At the front in Korea it was impossible to share his optimism. Tragedy was everywhere, unrelieved. Darker days were still ahead.

---

* The First Cavalry Division, an infantry outfit which retained its old name, landed at the South Korean-held port of Pohang, east of Taegu on July 18th, without wetting feet. It moved by truck convoy westward along the Taegu-Taejon highway to meet the North Koreans.

# V

## Pusan Beachhead

THE COMMUNIST STRATEGY was simple: take all roads to Pusan, striking at so many points that the outnumbered South Koreans and Americans could not muster adequate strength to meet all attacks; occupy Taegu and Pohang, depriving the American Air Force of advance bases in Korea; seize Pusan, the only major port in southern Korea, or drive General Walker's forces into the sea there. Russian advisers, remaining far to the rear, called the tune, but North Korean generals executed the tactics.

Communist propaganda voices boasted that "the American aggressors and the Syngman Rhee puppet troops" would be destroyed or swept from Korea by early August. They ridiculed MacArthur's confident statements. The hard facts posted in red on the Eighth Army's situation maps during the first six weeks after Taejon made their boasts sound reasonable.

Eight North Korean divisions attacked in four main drives: down the east coast toward Pohang, through the central mountain passes toward Taegu, down the main Seoul-Taejon-Taegu highway from the northwest, and around the western flank in a sweeping movement toward the south coast and Pusan. Seven additional North Korean divisions were reported either in reserve or en route to the front from northern training centers.

Against this force of a potential one hundred and fifty thousand combat troops, the United Nations in late July had two green American divisions, one exhausted American division, and five partially reorganized South Korean divisions—hardly sixty thousand effective troops. The South Koreans had virtually no artillery left; riflemen often had no rifles or no ammunition; they had nothing to protect them against tanks except the mountains, which fortunately kept most Communist armor out of central Korea. The Americans had only a few companies of World War II Sherman tanks and no heavy artillery. They had tried to match light tanks against the Communist T-34's and learned a bitter lesson in the action along and north of the Kum River.

Reinforcements were on the way and, during the last days of July and the first week of August, they landed at Pusan: Five thousand marines of the United States First Marine Brigade, two regiments of the Second Infantry Division, the Fifth Regimental Combat Team from Hawaii, the Twenty-ninth Regimental Combat Team from Okinawa, and a marine air wing. This was about all Walker was to get, and his army still was less than a hundred thousand strong, counting cooks, truck drivers, and mechanics. Five more nations—Britain, Australia, Turkey, Canada, and the Philippines—promised troops, and the United States Navy started bringing forty-eight more ships out of mothballs. But time and space were running short.

Two North Korean divisions, described in GHQ communiqués as "roving bands" of Communists, swept across the undefended southwest quarter of the Korean Republic, pivoted near the southern coast, and drove toward Pusan. One week after the fall of Taejon they were fifty miles west of the allies' lifeline port. The exhausted and dispirited Twenty-fourth Division, now commanded by General Church of the Suwon headquarters days, was ordered back into action after only four days' rest and sent to meet again the most critical threat on the front. The newly arrived Twenty-ninth Regiment joined it on what was to become the southern front.

In the northwest, the Communist drive down the Taejon-Taegu axis gained twenty-five miles in four days, rolling over and around the Twenty-fifth Division. Yongdong fell, and the attack swept on toward Kumchon, where the First Cavalry Division moved in while the Twenty-fifth shifted to new positions.

South Koreans, fighting furiously with what they had to regain lost face, slowed the Communist advance across the mountains thirty miles north of Taegu. American staff officers were fearful that the North Koreans had not yet attacked in strength on this front, however, and they still had no confidence in the ROK Army's ability to hold.

When General MacArthur flew to Taegu on July 27th, Pusan was threatened in the south, and nothing seemed capable of stopping the Communist drive on Taegu from the northwest. A fifty-mile-wide gap of undefended territory along the Naktong River invited the Reds to strike eastward below Taegu and cut off the bulk of the Allied forces from escape to the only possible evacuation port—Pusan.

Against this background of approaching disaster, MacArthur met the press at Taegu's red-clay airstrip. With incredible assurance he declared: "There will be new heartaches and new setbacks," but "I was never more confident of victory—ultimate victory—in my life." Few knew then the real extent of his confidence: he was already planning the amphibious landing and counteroffensive which would destroy the North Korean Army.

Two days later General Walker made an unfortunate attempt to emulate his chief's performance. On a flying visit to the First Cavalry and Twenty-fifth Divisions on the northwest front, he issued public orders to "stand and fight." There would be "no more withdrawals," he told the hollow-eyed, openly dubious division officers and assembled news correspondents. He warned his command to abandon any hopes of a token fight and evacuation by sea to Japan.

More withdrawals followed immediately, as Walker must have known they would. The incident marred an otherwise brilliant performance by the real hero of the Pusan beachhead. "Bulldog" Walker was not an eloquent man nor a deep thinker. He was a believer in "spit 'n polish," even in Korea. But he knew his old infantry tactics, and he knew the importance of calculated risks. He had learned modern, offensive warfare from the old master, General George Patton, when he was a corps commander in Patton's Third Army during World War II. He had never fought the shoestring defensive war with a handful of men at the end of the supply line that was the lot of commanders in Pacific operations against Japan. In August he proved that he could learn fast.

Walker took the first of many long-shot gambles that saved the Pusan beachhead during the first week of August. He pulled the Twenty-fifth Division out of the path of what was assumed to be the heaviest Communist drive and shifted it to the southern front west of Pusan. The Twenty-fourth Division had been unable to hold before Chinju and had fallen back to within thirty-five miles west of Pusan. Another Communist advance twenty miles north-east of Chinju threatened to spill across the lower Naktong River before it could be exploited as a natural defense line. A more cautious, unimaginative commander with such limited forces would have ordered retreat to a tight beach-head line around Pusan. Walker ordered attack in the south.

Task Force Kean, commanded by the Twenty-fifth's Major General William B. Kean, and composed of the Thirty-fifth Regiment of the Twenty-fifth Division, the Fifth Regimental Combat Team, and the Marine Brigade, launched the first important American counterattack of the war west of Pusan on August 7th. Communist intelligence learned every detail of the attack preparations. When the task force jumped off, it ran into a paralyzing North Korean artillery barrage and counterattack. Green American marines and infantrymen wilted in the heat, one army regimental commander lost control of his men, and the ambitious operation seemed doomed to failure. The marines and the Thirty-fifth Regiment rallied, however, and slowly drove the Reds back ten miles, relieving the threat to Pusan.

There was no time for victory celebrations. The Communist assault across the Naktong River had carved out a deep bridgehead. Two regiments of the Twenty-fourth Division and a battalion of the Second Division were fighting a losing battle to prevent a complete breakthrough which would cut the Pusan-Taegu road. To the north were thirty miles of virtually undefended river line southwest of Taegu, site of Eighth Army and Fifth Air Force headquarters and the refugee capital of South Korea. The First Cavalry Division had abandoned Kumchon and dropped back to the Naktong northwest and west of Taegu on August 2nd, facing elements of four enemy divisions.

On the northeast corner of the beachhead the Communists opened a simultaneous attack down the east coast road toward Pohang and its fighter airstrip.

Walker gambled again. He gave up all the ground gained in the southern front counterattack, rushed the Marines into action to block the Naktong River breakthrough, split the Second Division into small combat teams and sent one of them, a predominantly Negro task force, to Pohang to defend the airstrip. At the same time he ordered the South Korean army to withdraw to a northern line linking the defense of Pohang on the east and Taegu on the west. The Pusan beachhead now was fifty miles wide and eighty to ninety miles long—about half the size of the state of Connecticut.

Every move worked, and the North Koreans failed to exploit the new weaknesses created by Walker's shifting of forces.

The Marines, in their first major action, won the "Battle of No-Name Ridge" and sparked the counterattack which within a week wiped out the menacing Naktong River bulge. After a slow start in the Chinju advance, these new Marines demonstrated on the Naktong that they had the same extra drive, discipline, and fanatical devotion to their traditions that have always characterized the corps.

Pohang airstrip was saved, although the Fifth Air Force evacuated planes from the strip after the town fell on August 10th. By August 17th Pohang was recaptured, and South Korean troops supported by United States naval vessels working as artillery pushed back up the coast.

*An American warship stood offshore near Pohang, its gunnery officer eager to show what the Navy could do to support the Army. It was a dark night. Finally the ship's radio made contact with a field radio ashore and offered fire support to the outnumbered Negro infantrymen of Task Force Bradley.*

*"Fihya one round, eee-lumination," came the deep, drawled reply.*

*The ship's guns obliged, sending a brilliant illuminating flare over Communist lines.*

*"Fihya one round, eee-lumination," the voice on the radio again requested.*

*Another flare turned night into day. "Now give us a target," the naval officer barked.*

*"Fihya fo' effect, eee-lumination," the voice commanded, with more enthusiasm.*

*The naval officer's voice crackled back over the radio, "We've lit up half of South Korea for you. If you can't give us a target, put an officer on that radio."*

*Back came the surprised answer, "Officer? Ain't no officers up here. This-here's the front line."*

Before the threats at Pohang and the southern Naktong had been eased, the North Koreans opened a determined drive to take Taegu from the north. New fires also broke out along the Naktong line west and southwest of the headquarters city.

A lone Communist artillery piece on the west bank of the Naktong seven miles away began lobbing shells into Taegu every night, apparently aiming at the railway station. The refugee capital, its population swollen from a normal three hundred thousand to an estimated eight hundred thousand, was ordered cleared of civilians. The South Korean government fled again, this time to Pusan. A skeleton Eighth Army headquarters remained. Military police were alerted against a possible uprising by Communists lurking in this onetime hotbed of guerrilla activity.

At least a full American division appeared to be needed to check the northern threat; the Eighth Army had less than a regiment of uncommitted reserves. Walker turned to his most dependable army regiment Lieutenant Colonel John H. Michaelis' Twenty-seventh Regiment of the Twenty-fifth Division, pulled it out of the already under-manned southern front west of Pusan, and gave it a divi-sion's job in the north. Michaelis and his "Wolfhounds" traveled more than one hundred backbreaking miles by truck and went into action fourteen miles north of Taegu almost as soon as they set foot on the ground. For three days this single army regiment stood its ground and turned back frontal and flanking attacks, while the ROK First Division and the United States Cavalry Division stamped out lighter attacks around the northwest corner of the perimeter.

The First Cavalry expected heavier blows. Three to four North Korean divisions were reported massing northwest of Taegu, near the west bank of the Naktong, well-camou-flaged in the hills and narrow valleys. Big bombers had been used against such a concentration of enemy troops near friendly lines with only partial success during the Nor-mandy beachhead battle of World War II. An error in lo-cating the bomb zone had caused heavy infantry losses. Now the Air Force wanted to try again, this time with B-29 Su-perforts. MacArthur had approved the plan, and on the morning of August 16th a mass flight of ninety-eight Super-forts dropped eight hundred and eighty tons of high-explosive bombs on a twenty-six-square-mile carpet within two miles of the First Cavalry Division's lines near Waegwan. The bombing was accurate, but the results were disappointing. Low-flying fighters and spotter planes which searched the area immediately after the attack found no evidence that large Communist forces had been caught by the raid. Later it was learned that the North Koreans had shifted eastward from the Waegwan area in preparation for a new assault against ROK troops.

"Firechief" Walker had but a moment to catch his breath. He used it to proclaim that "Taegu is certainly saved." In almost the next breath he was forced to order a new reshuffling of his forces to meet the next Communist assault—this time aimed at South Korean army lines across the northern arc of the beachhead.

On August 25th the Reds attacked, carving a ten-mile hole in the United Nations' northern line between Taegu and Pohang. But they were slow to exploit the penetration. The Communist commanders either failed to discover that they had scored a clean breakthrough, or they lacked the strength and supplies to sustain the drive. A Twenty-fourth Division task force arrived in time to plug the gap.

*Two lumbering "six-by-six" army trucks churned the pulverized dirt of the narrow road and powdered the low poplar trees and rice paddies lining the route with another coat of dust. As we gained on the trucks, our jeep came into their dusty wake and kept on the road more by feel than by sight. Each particle of dust stank from its own little quota of the filth which reeks from the pores of Korea—a filth compounded of "night soil," preserved by all and used liberally to fertilize the fields, the decay and squalor of cen-*

turies-old poverty, and the common recognition of the streets and the great outdoors as the best of all possible toilets. We swallowed this dust—the basic diet of American GI's throughout the war—until a light rain began falling.

The trucks, each loaded with twenty replacement infantrymen just in from the United States, were heading for a First Cavalry Division battalion on the Naktong River front west of Taegu. They stopped at regimental headquarters, a couple of open-front tents and a spider-web of telephone wires and radio jeeps set off from the road in a nearly dry stream bed. The young soldiers in the trucks looked at the elderly colonel who was to be their "old man," then stared apprehensively down the stream bed toward the white sands of the Naktong bank, two miles away. They looked to the craggy, eroded mountains which rose to the left of the road, while a truck driver with studied casualness told his passengers, "A couple of gooks took a few shots at me from up there when I come along here last night." He added, after seeing how successful he'd been, "They say there's a thousand of 'em that sneaked across the river and collected up in those mountains the last two nights."

Even now along the river valley, the mountains, low but steep and long ago sheared of their trees and their beauty, did not allow the farmer or the road-bound infantryman of this American army much flat land for operations. They rose five hundred to two thousand feet from narrow rice-valley floors and tumbled into each other without pattern or clearly defined ranges. They were everywhere. In the twilight they looked like sleeping dinosaurs against the sky. In the darkness, here and all around the beachhead, they were the hiding place of the enemy and thus to be *feared. In the military jargon they were known as "commanding high ground" or, more familiarly, as "hills." If these terribly fresh young replacements were to live and come out of Korea with a winning army, I said to myself in an entirely unoriginal reflection, they would have to conquer these mountains and make them the Communists' enemy.*

*The trucks were directed on to the battalion command post—two miles of nearly straight road paralleling a bend in the Naktong. The little convoy passed through the smoldering remains of a Korean farm village destroyed the day before by order of the division commander. It had been cleared of all residents shortly after this became the battle zone. Now its thatch-roofed mud huts, unless destroyed, would be a convenient hiding place for Communist infiltrators. Another village off to the right of the road near the river bank was still burning. North Korean troops who crossed by night had been flushed out of it earlier that morning.*

*A Japanese-American sergeant boarded one of the trucks near a small schoolhouse that was battalion headquarters. He directed them on down the road to the front. Three rifle companies there would be glad to see these forty replacements.*

*If there were sounds to warn these young men that they were about to end the harsh transition from civilization to war, they were drowned by the high whine and metallic rattle of the six-by-sixes as they topped a low hill and raced across an open area toward the ridge that was the battlefront. Then a sharp crack in the air overhead—not to the front—and a mushroom of dust and smoke from the mountain to the left rear announced that the journey was ended.*

*To the right front, across the river, white puffs and the hollow coughs of Communist mortars defined the battle arena. The sharp crack and almost simultaneous explosion of a North Korean seventy-six-millimeter, high-velocity gun, this time striking closer, came again. Then "wham" went an incoming mortar shell, thirty feet from the road and the racing truck. "Wham—zee-ow" went another that hit in the limbs of an apple tree and sprayed jagged shrapnel against the second truck. "Wham-wham" went two more almost astride the road, and the trucks stopped. Three young privates already were wounded before they could fire their first shots.*

*No one needed to tell the replacements to hit the dirt. But if the sergeant hadn't stopped them, they would have taken a shot at the first thing that moved, and it would have been at their future foxhole mates dug in along the ridge and sweating out the mortar barrage.*

*I joined the second truckload in a ditch beside their pock-marked truck, no happier about the situation than the greenest recruit among them. I wore no insignia, and tried to act like an old soldier.*

*"How long you been here?" the nineteen-year-old boy beside me asked, groping for assurance that a man can live through days or even weeks of this.*

*Grenades that bounced out of their pockets and clips of rifle ammunition from their belts lay on the ground about the truck wherever a man had jumped. The sergeant ordered them picked up while sprays of mortar fragments slapped at the top of the truck and the road. Then there was a moment of silence. The sergeant herded his men back on to the trucks and started them off on the last few hundred yards. A rifle was discharged accidentally aboard the*

*second truck and another man was wounded. Before the
delivery mission was completed, one replacement was killed
when a mortar round fell beside one of the trucks. Four
wounded, one killed, out of forty—a sobering introduction to a new world for the rest.*

Like a piston, the Reds struck again in the west on September 1st, then to the east near Pohang on September
2nd, then north, east, and west of Taegu. Walker prophetically called the attacks the North Koreans' "last-gasp offensive." In the next twelve days it often seemed that Walker
would be forced to eat his words.

The attack along the Naktong line was the Reds' biggest single effort since the invasion of South Korea. Nearly
forty thousand troops were thrown into the drive to destroy
the American river defense line, cut the Taegu-Pusan
highway, and capture Pusan. Within twenty-four hours
they had seized more than a dozen bridgeheads on the east
bank of the Naktong. The main thrust, through the "bulge"
battleground past "No-Name Ridge," penetrated twelve
miles against the Second Division before collapsing under
combined marine-army counterattacks. Another thrust
along the southern highway pushed the Twenty-fifth Division back to within thirty miles of Pusan. A weaker attack
was launched on September 7th between these two actions,
but it also faltered when it met serious resistance.

In the north the Communists struck with all the force
they could muster and failed only because they could not
sustain the attack. They recaptured Pohang, broke through
South Korean lines west of the port, and carved a deep
bulge in the front east of Taegu. Another assault across
the Naktong River established a menacing bridgehead

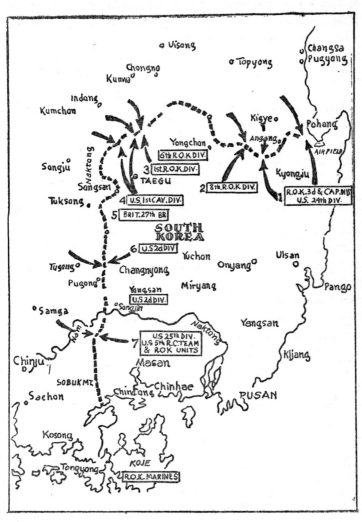

2. The Pusan Beachhead

51

southwest of Taegu. The first non-American United Nations troops to reach Korea, a battalion of the Scottish Argyll and Sutherland Highlanders and a battalion of the English Middlesex Regiment, were thrown into the thinly held Naktong front to check this threat. With Taegu menaced from west and east, the Reds attacked from the north, down the same mountain passes where they had been stopped thirteen miles from Taegu two weeks earlier. This time they rolled the defending First Cavalry Division and First ROK Division back to within seven miles of Taegu and lobbed shells into the outskirts before the offensive collapsed.

This was the turning point, but it took a trained eye to call it.

The North Korean Army had thrown its entire strength into this supreme bid for victory. MacArthur's headquarters estimated that the Reds had suffered twenty-five thousand casualties, including 11,142 men killed, in the unavailing September offensive. In six weeks of poorly conceived assaults on the beachhead line, the Communist army sacrificed its great numerical superiority. Allied guns had whittled away the ranks of trained Communist units and forced the North Korean high command to replace soldiers with youngsters and middle-aged men just off the farms. Desperately the Communists poured untrained boys into the line, forced South Koreans from occupied areas to carry their supplies, and even pressed some southerners into front-line military service. Their firepower declined faster than their manpower. The blackened hulls of Communist tanks, riddled and blasted locomotives, charred remains of trucks, and the daytime emptiness of the roads and railways behind the Communist front testified to the success of the allied air and naval blockade of enemy supply lines. Reflecting the failure of Communist leadership, increasing numbers of North Korean troops surrendered during late August and early September, many of them bearing "safe-conduct" passes dropped by psychological warfare planes.

Many factors contributed to the North Koreans' failure, but poor generalship must be placed high on the list. The Communist army repeatedly failed to exploit opportunities. Early in July Communist generals overestimated the strength of American intervention and underestimated their success in shattering the ROK Army. They paused to fight with small groups of American and ROK troops instead of racing to Pusan for a quick, knockout victory. They failed to anticipate supply problems and solve them in advance. Their plans were bound to the timetable of human pack trains from the beginning. Later, when General Walker held a thin patchwork defense line along the beachhead perimeter and juggled and shifted to meet each attack, the Communist commanders again failed to see the obvious. One concentrated, sustained attack accompanied by feints elsewhere around the perimeter would have ripped so deep a hole in the Eighth Army line that it could not have been repaired without a major retreat. More than once, when Walker had no reserves left to commit, only a few hundred American troops stood between a Communist division and Pusan. But the attack had been launched with insufficient supplies and without means of troop replacement or continuing logistical support. For six weeks the North Koreans frittered away their superiority with half-measures, while the American and South Korean forces grew stronger and wiser.

All this is obvious in retrospect, but that week in dust-coated, sweltering Taegu victory seemed a long way off. Every last infantryman and artilleryman of the Eighth Army had been needed to stop the Communist offensive. The Reds had taken a beating, but American and South Korean losses had not been negligible, either. There were reports of feverish recruiting in North Korea to raise two hundred thousand more troops. Only a trickle of replacements for American losses was reaching the front, and except for the fifteen hundred excellent British troops which arrived on August 29th, there was only distant promise of further reinforcement on the ground.

The men who had fought through one crisis after another for six beachhead weeks were tougher and wiser now, but they also were tired and uninspired. If this was a United Nations war, where were the other United Nations troops? Uncle Sam again was Uncle Sucker, according to the guy in the next foxhole or the orator in the latrine. Men fought on, not for "the cause" or the defense of South Korea, but for survival and self-respect. Loyalty meant not letting your buddy down, or, positively, showing the rest of the team that the first squad, or Baker company, or the First Regiment, or the Fifth Marines were the best damn outfit in Korea. This was progress, and something like this mixed with skill and justified self-confidence is the definition of morale among professional soldiers. But neither high morale nor the superior strength required to turn the tide against the Communists was evident that final week of the defensive war.

Consequently, "realists" among the military men and correspondents on hand were not convinced when Walker predicted that the North Korean army would "fold" under a United Nations offensive soon to begin. The South Korean National Assembly reached what many Americans considered the height of naïveté when it appealed to General MacArthur on September 8th to drive the Communists out of the Republic before the fall rice harvest, three to four weeks away.

Momentous events which were to deliver the Republic out of Communist hands on just this schedule and produce the near-miracle of lightning allied victory over the North Koreans already were in motion. Hints of impending action came in late August, when South Korean marines landed on two tiny islands, Tokchok and Soijak, astride the main channels leading from the Yellow Sea into Inchon, the port for Seoul. The United States Navy disclosed that its fleet in the Far East had grown from fourteen combat ships at the outbreak of war to one hundred and fifty on September 3rd. From the Soviet mission in Tokyo and the amateurish spy ring of Korean and Japanese Communists around Japanese ports, the North Koreans must have learned that a major amphibious operation involving United States Marines was imminent. There was little they could do with the knowledge.

# VI

## *Hammer and Anvil*

COMMANDERS EITHER GAMBLE with the lives of their men or they lose wars. They may reduce the risks of a daring action by meticulous planning, the collection of reliable intelligence information, and precision timing and execution, but in the end they must gamble—with lives and with their own place in history.

Twice in Korea MacArthur resorted to the bold stroke in defiance of dangers. The first, at Inchon, turned near defeat into brilliant victory and assured him a permanent rank of greatness. The second, in far northern Korea, backfired in near disaster and qualified history's judgment of a military genius.

The Inchon gamble was about to begin. It was the second week of September. The Eighth Army was holding on in southeast Korea with a bare minimum of men and guns against the Communists' most determined assaults on the beachhead. Intelligence reports said that the North Koreans had thrown every effective division into a supreme bid for a breakthrough to Pusan, leaving Seoul, its port city of Inchon, and all northern Korea lightly garrisoned. The Red army was at the end of a long supply line, fed and armed by night-moving ox-carts, human pack trains, and a few trucks and trains which had escaped daily attacks by the United Nations air and naval forces.

This was the moment for the United Nations to take the offensive. MacArthur had been planning for this moment since the second week of American intervention in Korea, when it became apparent that all the strength the United States and its allies could commit immediately would be needed to save South Korea. Since late July, navy and army planning staffs in Tokyo had been laboring over the complex details of carrying out his strategy.

There were two roads back to victory. One followed the course of throwing all available United Nations strength, including the full United States First Marine Division (three-fourths of the division had not yet been sent to Korea) and the United States Seventh Infantry Division (still in Japan) into the Pusan beachhead. The Eighth Army then might hope to take the offensive and slowly roll the Communists back, in a mountain-by-mountain battle across one hundred and fifty to two hundred bloody miles. Even if successful, such an operation would give the North Korean army a chance to retreat intact and escape, improving its supply problem as it back-pedalled.

The other road back was a three-lane highway over water, land, and airways. It offered a chance to exploit fully for the first time the Allies' absolute control of the sea and air and thus end the costly matching of man for man with the Communists on the ground. In exchange for great risks it offered quick and complete victory.

MacArthur's conception of the strategy was simple, but its execution was highly complicated. An amphibious force would land two reinforced divisions at Inchon on the west coast, where they would establish a second front one hundred and fifty miles northwest of the present battle zone, behind Communist lines. This force would drive inland the twenty miles to Seoul, cutting the main highway and rail supply lines behind the North Korean army, liberating Seoul, and threatening the Communists with envelopment from the rear. Almost simultaneously the Eighth Army would attack, forcing the Communists to stay in place and fight until the Inchon landing was secure, then drive for a breakout from the southern beachhead. Caught between the southern hammer and the northern anvil, already low on supplies and trained manpower, threatened with the loss of his chief supply and escape routes, the enemy commander could be expected to order a hasty retreat. Then, out on the roads where mobile American forces could run them down and air power could pound them, the Communist troops would be forced to abandon heavy equipment and flee in disorganized retreat. Motorized task forces would race ahead of these retreating bands and block their escape, while mop-up forces moved northward and destroyed them.

It was a hope-stirring, ambitious scheme for a command which at the moment was only narrowly escaping defeat in southeast Korea. Everything had to go according to plan and expectation or all chance of early victory would be lost. Failure would weaken General Walker's chance of holding the Pusan beachhead and might lead to twin disasters at both Pusan and Inchon.

There were numerous chances for failure.

Inchon was probably the worst place ever selected for an amphibious invasion. Its "harbor" was a shallow channel dredged through gently sloping mudbanks. Its twenty-eight- to thirty-two-foot tides were among the world's most extreme, permitting shallow-draft vessels to approach shore during mid-September for only a few hours of high tide in the early morning and late afternoon. A small assault force landed in the morning could not be reinforced for eight to ten hours. The landing of a single division might take three days, and supplying a sizable invasion force by sea in the face of such natural obstacles could prove impossible after it was too late to turn back.

Hopeful intelligence estimates had been very misleading in the past. There was no absolute assurance that the North Koreans were fully committed in the south. There could be unreported divisions holding permanent fortifications at Inchon and defending Seoul. Reinforcements from North Korea could reach the area within a week after the landing. There was every reason to assume that the Communists knew an amphibious operation was likely and that Seoul would be its objective.

If the North Koreans had saved their limited air power for use at a critical moment, or if Russia had furnished a new air fleet to its satellite, the allied flotilla confined in the waters off Inchon by the slow debarkation process would be a vulnerable target.

The landing was to be a navy show, and the navy approached the task with many reservations. At one point in the planning, the United States Chief of Naval Operations, Admiral Forrest Sherman, and the Army Chief of Staff, General J. Lawton Collins, flew to Tokyo to discuss with MacArthur the uneasiness which Washington felt about the undertaking. The eloquent five-star general won his case during a meeting in late August, and orders to begin setting the plan in motion went out almost immediately.

The greatest allied naval armada assembled since World

War II rode at anchor in three Japanese harbors and at
Pusan. Docks were jammed with trucks and tanks and
mountains of crated supplies and gasoline drums.

The United States Seventh Infantry Division, stripped of
most of its manpower and equipment when the other three
occupation divisions sailed for Korea, completed training
and moved to its port of embarkation. It had been rebuilt
with American replacements from the United States and
more than eight thousand Korean draftees secretly brought
to Japan in early August. Fifteen thousand United States
Marines, many of them reserves called back to service for
the Korean War, staged in southern Honshu and boarded
transports. At Inchon they would join the First Marine
Brigade to reform the First Marine Division. The Marines,
the dependable Seventeenth ROK Regiment, and two battalions of ROK marines were taken away from the Eighth
Army and moved to Pusan.

In Tokyo Major General Edward M. Almond, MacArthur's chief of staff, who was to lead the forty-thousand-man
invasion force, completed formation of his new command,
the United States Tenth Corps. Planning staffs under Vice-
Admiral Arthur Dewey Struble, Seventh Fleet commander
and over-all boss of the operation, worked day and night until the final hour on the intricate details of supply and
troop movements, convoy schedules, air and naval support,
command arrangements, communications, medical evacuation, and a hundred other problems of amphibious warfare.

Admiral Struble's flagship, the heavy cruiser U.S.S. *Rochester*, slipped out of Sasebo Naval Base in southwest Japan
the afternoon of September 12th and proceeded full speed
toward Inchon. Command, supply, and troop ships already
were sailing down Japan's east coast from Yokohama.

Almost immediately it seemed that the pessimists were right. A Pacific typhoon swept out of the south and headed for the Korean Straits. If it turned to the northeast it would rake the invasion fleet just as it was setting out from Japanese ports. If it shifted to the northwest, a course that the weathermen said was very unlikely, it could strike Inchon on D-day. The weather experts were right, but this was small comfort to the men who rode out the storm while sailing toward Korea on September 12th and 13th.

Six American destroyers and one American and two British cruisers joined the *Rochester,* and at dawn of D-minus-2 the squadron sailed up "flying Fish Channel" into the mined waters of Inchon anchorage. For two days the squadron and supporting naval planes bombarded the beaches where the Marine assault waves were to land. Before they had finished, they must have removed all doubts in the enemy generals' minds about when and where the amphibious attack would strike. But they silenced Inchon's shore defenses and insured the landing's success.

*The* Rochester *dropped anchor and turned its eight-inch and five-inch batteries toward the tiny island of Wolmi-do, connected by a thousand-foot-long causeway with Inchon proper. The scrappy little destroyers moved in to within rifle range of Wolmi and challenged the Communists to come out and fight.*

*I climbed to the flag bridge and joined Admiral Struble to watch the show. In a moment the Communist shore guns flashed and the destroyers answered. Geysers of water spouted near the American ships, but they moved in closer. The long-range guns of the cruisers rifled whispering shells across the bright autumn sky, blasting Wolmi's deeply en-*

trenched defenders and the entire Inchon shoreline. The destroyers and shore positions dueled beneath the cruisers' barrage of steel. Then long-range fire ceased and carrier-based Navy dive bombers went to work with bombs, jellied gasoline, and rockets. Black smoke billowed from the Inchon dock area, and red dust mingled with the smoke of exploding shells and bombs on Wolmi.

Two destroyers were hit and limped out with wounded aboard. The men in these little fighting ships had seen war at close range.

Aboard the Rochester we were in another world. Everything was calm, gentlemanly efficiency. There was no dirt, no blood, and no fear. At lunchtime a white liveried Negro steward served dainty sandwiches from a silver tray and coffee from a handsome silver service to the officers and correspondents on the bridge. Men from each station on the ship went to the galleys and wardrooms and brought picnic lunches back to their posts. The worst inconvenience was the ear-shattering din of the eight-inch guns during the morning and afternoon "gunnery practice" against the Communist shore positions.

Recalling the filth, stench and blood of the Army's war ashore, I was tempted to ridicule the comfortable gentlemen of the navy. Yet, there was no reason here to abandon the small decencies of living. For most of them it was a strange half-war, without opposition worthy of the name. Many a civilization-hating army or Marine commander in the same situation would have manufactured discomfort "just to keep the men toughened up and ready for anything." Maybe the gentlemen of the navy have a saner sense of values.

D-Day, September 15th, began with a good omen. As the destroyers, transports, LST's, and LSD's of the initial Marine assault force snaked in column up the channel, they were greeted by the friendly glow of lighthouses along the route. South Korean navy landing parties had turned on the lights for the first time since Inchon fell to the invaders.

"All the comforts of home," said a less nervous Marine.

Thus it went all day, according to plan. Cruisers rifled glowing shells into the gray dawn against the Inchon coastline. Navy planes dived through the clouds and smoke hovering over Wolmi-do to give its surviving defenders a final pummelling. Destroyers and rocket-firing LSM's moved in close to cover the Marine assault waves. Just as the sun began tinting the still bay waters, the first six landing craft shoved off from their mother ships and plunged through the eternity of agonizing seconds to the island's western shore.

Within less than thirty minutes the Stars and Stripes was flying from Wolmi's peak, and Marine guns were trained on the concrete causeway leading across the mud flats to Inchon. Casualties were extremely light.

Now the tide was running out, however, and there was no chance of reinforcing the single battalion of Marines holding Wolmi. A strong Communist counterattack could wipe them out before the late afternoon high tide permitted the second phase of the operation to begin. Planes and ships continued pounding Inchon to guarantee that this would not happen.

MacArthur and his staff watched the landing from the deck of the command ship, the *Mt. McKinley*.

At 5:30 P.M. the main assault began. The remainder of

the Fifth Marines and the newly arrived First Marines hit
the western and southern sea walls of Inchon proper. Marine artillery batteries landed on Wolmi. By midnight it
was all over. Inchon was secured. Despite the warning of
pre-attack bombardments and delays dictated by the tides,
the North Koreans failed to bring in sizable reinforcements.

Two feints were attempted to throw the North Korean
high command into confusion and delay a decision to reinforce Inchon. On the way to Inchon, a light force of
American rangers and South Koreans landed at Kunsan,
100 miles south of Inchon, on a hit-and-run raid. On D-Day,
the navy gave the Communists a bigger scare in the east.
The mighty battleship U.S.S. *Missouri* arrived off the port
of Samchok, directly opposite Inchon on the peninsula, and
opened up with its sixteen-inch guns. After a tremendous
barrage by the Big Mo's two-thousand-pound shells, South
Korean marines landed in a mock amphibious operation.

It later became evident, however, that the only persons
fooled by the east coast feint were some American news-
papermen in Tokyo who reported a "two-pronged amphibious envelopment" operation. Their blunder, however, could hardly match the performance in Tokyo the following day by a venerable news agency and a well-known
newspaper. In the most imaginative reportorial job of the
war, they described a lightning marine drive which carried
twenty miles from Inchon to Seoul and planted the American flag in the capital—all this within twenty-four hours
after the landing. A week later they were still waiting for
the story to come true.

The Seventh Infantry Division landed behind the Marines and fanned out to the south. One marine column

drove on Kimpo airfield, Korea's finest, and another (the First Regiment) pressed on against stiffening resistance toward Yongdungpo, industrial suburb of Seoul on the south bank of the Han River. Kimpo fell Sunday, and by Monday afternoon United States Air Force "flying boxcars" were landing with supplies. The airlift relieved the pressure on Inchon's port facilities and removed the last doubts about the success of the landing. The beachhead was secure, and the anvil was taking shape. The time had come for the Eighth Army's hammer to strike.

The breakout did not begin dramatically. The day after the Inchon landing General Walker's army pressed forward slightly all around the Pusan perimeter to hold the North Koreans in place. On the third day, the United States Second Division carried out a bridgehead across the Naktong River southwest of Taegu. The First Cavalry Division rammed into an unyielding wall of Communists along the northwest corner of the beachhead. The South Koreans did a more spectacular job on the east coast. By September 19th, the breakout drive was underway, but it was slow going. The Communists seemed to be determined to stand and fight in the south, ignoring the threat to their rear. On the twenty-second the picture changed suddenly. Just as Walker had predicted, the Communist army "folded," taking to the hills and racing northward, sometimes leaving rear guards to delay the Allied advance, sometimes disappearing entirely.

In the north on the same day, a reconnaissance company of the Seventh Division occupied Suwon and its airstrip. We were back where we had started.

The First Cavalry Division broke loose and began the most spectacular armored dash since Patton's race through

France. In three days the Cav's tank-infantry task forces knifed a hundred and five miles across central and western Korea and linked up with the Seventh Division on September 16th near the scene of the first American battle of the war. The Twenty-fourth Division and the British Commonwealth Twenty-seventh Brigade* took the old retreat road back through Yongdong, where they released two American prisoners of war—the first liberation of Americans—and then battered their way into the rubble of Taejon. To the south, the Twenty-fifth and Second Divisions raced toward the west coast. Each drive cut off a pocket of Communist troops. The Fifth Air Force had a continuous field day against those who attempted to escape along the roads to the north.

But the honeymoon was over in the Seoul campaign. The Marines cut the highway south and northwest of Seoul before the end of the first week, and the city was no longer militarily useful to the North Koreans. The garrison commander, however, called on his men to emulate the heroic defenders of Stalingrad and fight to the death. The division-size defense garrison barricaded the streets and turned every sturdy building into a fortress.

General Almond's decisions in the face of this resistance have not yet been fully explained. He ordered the Marines to fight their way into this hornet's nest, using whatever aerial bombardment they needed to win the city. In the next eight days sixty-five per cent. of the city was destroyed. Thousands of South Korean civilians who had remained in Seoul and hundreds of Marines were killed in this furious battle. The Seventh Division was hurriedly thrown into

* The British suffered about 50 casualties under an accidental strafing attack by American fighter planes during the breakout.

the attack. One regiment crossed the Han and seized the southeastern section of Seoul on September 27th. The ROK Seventeenth Regiment swung around the eastern outskirts the same day.

The slower and less costly course would have been to surround Seoul, cutting all roads to the north, northeast, and northwest. The Communists then might have been forced to surrender, sparing the city the holocaust which engulfed it in "liberation." Alternately, General Almond might have left only one escape route open and allowed the Communists to escape when it became apparent that the entire North Korean army was in retreat and that no help was coming. He chose to attack vigorously, rooting the Communists out of their barricades and destroying them, leaving the back door open if they should decide to escape. He seemed to want complete and dramatic victory, to establish a date which history could remember. His course might have been best in terms of the larger strategy, but to those who did not have to make the decisions and had the advantage of hindsight, the terrible loss of life and destruction in Seoul were the only blots on a brilliant operation.

The bloodiest battle was still ahead in the center of Seoul when Almond declared on the night of September 25th, three months to the day after the Communist invasion, that Seoul had been liberated. For the next two days, while the Marines fought from house to house and the army joined them on the eastern side of the city, the general hopefully predicted that the "crust" of Communist resistance was about to crumble, or had crumbled.

*I followed the First Marines through the smoldering rubble of central Seoul the day after its premature "libera-*

tion." *The last, desperate Communist counterattack had been hurled back during an eerie 2 A.M. battle of tanks firing at pointblank range, American artillery crashing less than a city block ahead of Marine lines, the echoed and re-echoed rattle of machine guns—all against the background of flaming buildings and darting shadows.*

*Now it was almost quiet. The angry chatter of a machine gun up ahead now and then punctuated the long pauses between mortar and artillery strikes. But on this street corner was condensed the full horror of war, stripped of the vital challenge and excitement which make it bearable to the men who must fight wars.*

*Telephone and power lines festooned the streets or hung from shattered poles which resembled grotesque Christmas trees. Bluish smoke curled from the corner of a clapboard shack—the only building even partially spared destruction along the left side of the street. A young woman poked among a pile of roof tiles and charred timbers for her possessions, or perhaps for her child. A lump of flesh and bones in a mustard-colored Communist uniform sprawled across the curb up ahead, and the white-robed body of an old man lay on a rice-straw mat nearer the street corner. Marine ammunition and mess trucks churned the plaster and adobe rubble into dust as they shuttled back and forth from the front, six blocks north. Southbound ambulance jeeps, almost always fully loaded with four stretcher cases on their racks, told the story of the pre-dawn battle.*

*A tiny figure wrapped in a Marine's wool shirt stumbled down the street. Her face, arms, and legs were burned and almost eaten away by the fragments of an American white phosphorous artillery shell. She was blind, but somehow alive. She was about the size of my little girl. Three other*

*Korean children, luckier than she, watched as the child*
*reached the curbing, stumbled, and twice failed to climb up*
*on the sidewalk. The kids laughed.*

Liberation and relative peace finally came to Seoul on
September 28th, three months to the day after it had fallen.
The following morning General MacArthur and President
Rhee made a triumphal entry and drove at the head of
motorcades to the American-style capitol building. The
interior had been largely gutted by fire, but the legislative
chamber had escaped with only a shattered glass skylight.
In a simple ceremony before an audience of United Nations Commission members, Republic of Korea Government officials, and high American officers and correspondents, General MacArthur symbolically returned the capital
to the Republic and declared that the complete liberation
of South Korea from the Communist invaders was near.
Glass splinters rained from the skylight during the ceremony.

Was this the end of the war? Was this victory, or was the
liberation of South Korea only a milepost on the road?

South Korean divisions of the Eighth Army were marching through eastern Seoul that night. Their destination
was not the Thirty-eighth parallel, but the Yalu River.
Other ROK divisions raced up the east coast toward the
boundary which both sides had wiped off the maps on
June 25th. President Rhee and every important South Korean leader had proclaimed even in the darkest days that
they would not stop fighting until the Red northern régime was crushed and all Korea, from Pusan to the borders of Russia and Communist China, was united under
the Republic.

If the South Korean army were allowed to "invade" North Korea, would that now be aggression? Even if such a course were justified, and unification the only hope for preserving the peace bought by allied soldiers' lives, could the ROK army do the job alone? Should the United Nations take on the job of solving the problem of Korea by force, or was this implied in the decision already made in June to "repel the armed attack and restore international peace and security?"

The questions spun around, and no answers were forthcoming from Lake Success. The rush of events demanded a decision, but action on the ground in Korea again rushed ahead of the diplomats.

# VII

## *On to the Yalu*

OCTOBER WAS A month of great decisions on both sides of the Yalu. The groundwork had been laid long before, but October forced the issues irrevocably into the open.

The South Korean army took the fateful step across the Thirty-eighth parallel.

The United Nations majority, belatedly determining their war aims, decided to support a campaign by MacArthur to destroy the northern Communist régime and army, then step in and direct the creation of a unified nation, democratically governed.

The Chinese Communists decided to intervene and do what their Korean allies had failed to do.

The North Koreans, thus encouraged, decided to fight on until help arrived. For them, October was a sort of Communist July.

Cautious men in Washington and London politely suggested that the United Nations forces stop and look for storm warnings along the "waist" of the peninsula, north of Pyongyang. MacArthur decided to plunge on to the Yalu and Tumen River borders.

Giddy with victory, the Allied army marched almost blindly toward disaster. The two worlds, acting on decisions taken in the name of peace, rushed toward a collision which might destroy them all.

The crisis for Allied arms and the confusion and controversy in the Allied ranks which followed did not, however, spring primarily from rash military actions. They grew out of basic conflicts in American and United Nations objectives which never were fully resolved in Washington and Lake Success until MacArthur dramatized them in Korea.

Almost from the beginning, the United States and most of its allies under the United Nations flag had three basic objectives in Korea:

1. To draw a line against further Communist aggression and demonstrate that, wherever aggression was attempted, it would be met by the arms of the free world.

2. To reduce the likelihood of World War III by discouraging aggression and by confining the fighting to the area of Korea.

3. To take the fuse out of the Korean powder-keg so that, after finishing the job of stamping out aggression in Korea, the United Nations army would not be compelled to return and fight the same battle a year or two later.

The potential conflicts between these objectives were immediately apparent. If stamping out aggression in Korea required action which might spread the war, which objective was paramount? If United Nations intervention was to achieve permanent stability and peace in Korea, could the arbitrary, foreign-imposed division of the country into violently opposed camps be allowed to continue? And if the United Nations majority assumed for itself the authority to dictate a settlement unifying Korea by force, would that not provoke China and Russia to counteraction threatening World War III?

The questions could not be answered flatly in advance. Without answers and without knowledge of Chinese and Russian reactions, Washington, London, and Lake Success followed uneasily along behind MacArthur's confident leadership. They could not escape responsibility, however, and when the crisis came the blame could not honestly be passed to the commander in the field.

The United States Government began groping toward a clear-cut set of war aims before the first American troops landed at Pusan. In committing the youth of America to what he called the "police action" in Korea, President Truman said: "We hope we have acted in the cause of peace. There is no other reason for the action we have taken."

On July 11th, President Truman predicted that the Allies would regain all South Korea, right up to the Thirty-eighth parallel, but he refused to say publicly whether that would be the stopping place for the United Nations forces. Mere restoration of the status quo was not an inspiring goal for fighting men or for the people on the homefront.

In late July, according to State Department officers then in Korea, the United States Government decided that the United Nations could not call the job finished when it had driven the Communist army out of South Korea. A quiet campaign of private persuasion was said to be planned to sell Korean unification—by peaceful means if possible, by force if necessary—as the goal of United Nations intervention.

Warren Austin, chief United States delegate to the United Nations, openly declared on August 17th that the United Nations' obligation was to enforce the General Assembly decision of 1947–1949 to unify Korea under a single, freely elected government. He warned against leaving Korea "half slave, half free," but he stopped short of defining publicly the means of applying his admonition.

President Truman remained noncommittal during August, saying only that the aggressor "will be expelled." There were persistent reports, however, that he was considering proposals for a military campaign in North Korea. A congressman reported to the press after a talk with the President on August 23rd that Truman had not yet made up his mind about pursuing the Communists across the parallel.

Secretary of State Acheson said on August 30th that the decision rested with the United Nations, but he broadly hinted what was coming. The United States, he said, was doing everything possible to assure the Chinese Communists that neither America nor its United Nations allies had any designs on Chinese territory. If the Chinese Communists entered the war, he said, it would be totally without justification and a clear case of aggression.

MacArthur's blitz counter-offensive caught Lake Success far short of agreement on the next step. The non-Communist majority began serious debate on whether to authorize crossing of the Thirty-eighth parallel just as South Korean divisions neared the old border and Syngman Rhee exhorted them to "unify Korea . . . for all time." Russia had returned to the Security Council, preventing a veto-free review and current interpretation by the Council of its June 27th resolution recommending military sanctions.

The United States State Department held that this resolution, calling for restoration of "peace and security," gave MacArthur all the authority he needed to pursue the Communist aggressors back into North Korea, eliminate the causes of conflict, and clear the way for the United Nations to carry out its long-standing desire to unify Korea.

The West took the issue before the General Assembly. The United Nations had gone to war in Korea on the basis of a Security Council recommendation—not an order. The Assembly also had power to recommend. Canadian External Affairs Minister Lester B. Pearson told the Assembly on September 27th that the United Nations must "do whatever is practicable to make certain that the Communist aggressors . . . are not permitted to re-establish some new base in the peninsula from which they could sally forth again."

While the diplomats debated, Syngman Rhee's troops acted. The ROK Third and Capitol Divisions crossed the parallel near the east coast on October 1st. Washington had left MacArthur free to take what action he considered best, and he had given the ROK's free rein.

MacArthur, like the State Department, regarded the Thirty-eighth parallel as having lost all significance as a political boundary when the North Koreans first trampled it under their marching feet on June 25th. Thereafter, he accepted the fight on the original Communist terms—all or nothing. An aggressor had no claim to protection behind boundaries he ignored.

At noon on October 1st MacArthur called on the North Korean Communist government and armed forces to surrender. Radio stations in Seoul and Tokyo beamed his message to Communist Premier Kim Il Sung. The demand clearly implied determination to seize control of all Korea in the name of the United Nations. MacArthur ordered Communist forces "in whatever part of Korea situated" to "lay down your arms and cease hostilities under such military supervision as I may direct."

No answer came immediately from Pyongyang, the North Korean capital. The reply that counted came in a thinly veiled warning from Peiping. Chinese Communist Premier and Foreign Minister Chou En-lai declared that "the Chinese people will not stand idly by" while "imperialists wantonly invade the territory of their neighbor." He set the pattern for an increasingly vitriolic propaganda campaign by calling the United States "the most dangerous enemy of the Chinese People's Republic."

Peiping's warning won more serious attention in Europe and India than it did in the United States. It was more by coincidence than designed appeasement that the Defense Department chose this moment to order MacArthur's Far East Air Force to stay well away from the Chinese and Soviet frontiers of North Korea except under controlled conditions which would guarantee against chance flights over non-Korean territory. For some time the United States Government had been mildly concerned about the possibility of Chinese intervention in Korea and twice had admitted that American planes accidentally had attacked Chinese territory just across the Yalu River.

Chou's speech was not the first threat of a new and terrible war with Red China's millions. Peiping propaganda broadcasts had taken on a shrill and progressively more belligerent tone against the United States after the Inchon landing. Chinese Nationalist intelligence had reported large-scale Communist troop movements from southern and central China toward Manchuria and North Korea since mid-July. In August the Nationalists reported that four Chinese Communist army corps of three divisions each had entered North Korea; two other Chinese corps had been reported massed along the Yalu River inside Manchuria. On August 16th, the Peiping Radio disclosed that a twenty-three-man Chinese Communist delegation had departed for North Korea to "convey thanks to the Korean people for their aid to the Chinese people" during the Chinese civil war.

The cry of "Wolf" had been uttered too often; one more Communist propaganda broadcast could hardly be expected to influence American policy.

Chou En-lai's statement had a marked effect on the men at Lake Success, however. Twenty-four members agreed to the proposal advanced by India's Sir Benegal Rau on October 3rd before the United Nations Political and Security Committee that Allied forces be ordered to stay south of the Thirty-eighth parallel while a sub-committee attempted to settle the Korean issue by negotiation. The United States won a narrow victory in the vote by persuading the majority that there was no chance for compromise, and that delay would only give the Communists the opportunity to reorganize their forces.

When the committee met at Lake Success on October 4th for a final decision, ROK troops were already fifty miles inside North Korea on the east coast and advancing almost without opposition. MacArthur was holding American and other United Nations forces south of the Thirty-eighth parallel, but apparently only because Communist resistance north of Seoul had slowed the advance on that part of the front occupied by foreign troops. The United States insisted that, until MacArthur received orders to the contrary, he was free to cross the parallel. For the uncertain committee members and their governments it was now a case of taking the plunge after someone had already jumped in and tested the water.

Only the Soviet bloc and India cast negative votes when the committee adopted the resolution which set the pattern of United Nations policy in Korea throughout the later phases of the war. Quieting their fears of inciting a war with Red China, the majority:

1. Declared that MacArthur was operating within the terms of the Security Council's original instructions (implying that he was free to pursue the North Korean army across the Thirty-eighth parallel).

2. Accepted United Nations responsibility for insuring "conditions of stability throughout Korea."

3. Proposed United-Nations-sponsored elections in which all Koreans, north and south, would take part as soon as possible to create a single "unified, independent and democratic" government.

4. Agreed that United Nations armed forces should withdraw from Korea when these aims had been achieved.

5. Accepted United Nations responsibility for rehabilitation and relief of war suffering in Korea.

6. Proposed the creation of a new United Nations Commission for the Unification and Rehabilitation of Korea to replace the present commission.

The General Assembly, by a vote of 47 to 5, approved the committee resolution on October 7th, a few hours after the first United Nations troops—those of the First Cavalry Division—crossed the parallel near Kaesong and opened the drive on the Communist capital. In debating the policy statement, spokesmen for both the United States and Britain sought to allay Chinese and Russian fears by promising immediate withdrawal of foreign troops after a unified Korean government was established in free elections.

The Chinese Communist radio retorted prophetically that the war "in its real sense has just begun" and predicted a "drawn-out war of attrition perilous for foreign aggressors."

North Korean capitulation now became most unlikely. Mighty assistance to Kim Il Sung was on the way. But for the record and "for the last time," MacArthur demanded on October 9th that the Communist army surrender immediately or face "such military action as may be necessary" to destroy it.

Kim defiantly replied the next day with orders to the North Korean Army and people to "fight to the last" against United Nations "aggression."

Allied headquarters in Tokyo believed that Kim's army was on its last legs and could not offer serious resistance. It was estimated that since June 25th the North Koreans had lost two hundred thousand men in killed, wounded, isolated, and captured; POW compounds held forty thousand North Korean prisoners. Even by scraping the barrel at training camps, Kim probably could not put in the field more than one hundred thousand men, and he could not arm half of these effectively. However, unless destroyed and its manpower sources removed from Communist control, this beaten army could become the nucleus of a revived Soviet-satellite force in a matter of months.

A lightning campaign employing all the forces of the United Nations command probably could have destroyed the North Korean Army and driven out the Communist rulers within two months. If the Red Army of China were to enter the war in force, which official Tokyo still con-

sidered unlikely, a blitz Allied drive to the Yalu River offered a chance of settling the issue and presenting Peiping
with a *fait accompli* before it could intervene effectively.
What China would do after the United Nations Allies withdrew their troops was a matter for diplomats and generals
of the distant future to decide. Hours and days were as far
ahead as American generals, close to the scene and caught
in the rapids of October's events, could look.

However, the perspective improved at a greater distance
from the battlefront. It was difficult, moreover, for the
cautious Washingtonian to challenge MacArthur's confident assurances after he had proved to the skeptics his bril-
liance at Inchon. President Truman and the Pentagon felt
some concern about the headlong race toward a possible
collision with China, but their thoughts already had leaped
ahead to victory and the problems to follow. Truman and
Acheson were concerned primarily to insure that out of the
Korean War the United States would gain prestige among
all Asiatics as an altruistic defender of freedom. To prevent
a repetition of the past "MacArthur incidents" which in
the administration's view might jeopardize this policy, a
face-to-face meeting with MacArthur apparently appealed
to the President as the best approach. Such a meeting probably seemed doubly timely in view of the approaching congressional elections. MacArthur's popularity with the
American public was at its zenith. As a good political
strategist, Mr. Truman could hardly have failed to realize
that close association with MacArthur would help to iden-
tify the Democratic administration with success in the Korean War. Furthermore, it seemed wise to establish a personal, handshaking relationship between the chief executive and his balky, independent proconsul in Asia. After

publicly reprimanding MacArthur in late August for declaring his anti-administration views on Formosa to the
Veterans of Foreign Wars, the President presumably felt
he could afford to be friendly. He offered MacArthur a
choice of the meeting place—either in Honolulu or on
Wake Island. The general chose Wake, eight air hours
from Tokyo, thirty flying hours west of Washington.

President Truman left for Wake in an outwardly mellow
mood toward the general and optimistic about the future.
He announced that they would discuss the "final phase of
U.N. action in Korea." He praised MacArthur for "carrying out his mission with the imagination, courage and effectiveness which have marked his entire service as one of
our greatest military leaders."

MacArthur and Truman met for the first time on Wake's
airfield as the President stepped from the *Independence*.
They conferred privately in a quonset hut for one hour,
then called a full-dress meeting of their staffs for one hour
in the Civil Aeronautics Administration building. Five
hours after landing, the President was on his way back to
Washington, after issuing a communiqué the generalities
of which suggested only vaguely the optimistic tone of the
meeting. Six months later the administration released its
record of the conference and gave history proof of Mac-
Arthur's fallibility. Having announced "complete unan-
imity" of views with MacArthur in the conference communiqué, however, the administration, in publishing the
record, revealed how heavily it had relied for semi-political
judgments on a general whom it subsequently dismissed
for encroaching on the political sphere.

Two Chinese Communist divisions crossed the lower
Yalu River into northwest Korea on October fourteenth,

fifteenth, and sixteenth. They were on the march, and other divisions were preparing to join them when MacArthur, an acknowledged military genius and regarded by some as an expert on Asia, declared at Wake Island that there was "very little" chance of Chinese or Soviet intervention in Korea. "We are no longer fearful of their intervention," he is quoted as saying in the administration's record of the conference.

Despite growing evidence that trouble was brewing, MacArthur told the President: "I believe that formal resistance will end throughout North Korea by Thanksgiving" and "It is my hope to be able to withdraw the Eighth Army to Japan by Christmas."

The record quoted him as asserting that the Chinese, lacking protection from American air power, could not get large forces across the Yalu and into action against the United Nations: "Now that we have bases for our air force in Korea, if the Chinese tried to get down to Pyongyang there would be the greatest slaughter."

There was nothing in the immediate dispatches from Korea to challenge MacArthur's predictions. After breaking through a crust of North Korean resistance above the Thirty-eighth parallel in the west, the Eighth Army rolled unobstructed toward Pyongyang and the Yalu. A mighty armada of thirty-six warships led by the "Big Mo" bombarded Chongjin, fifty miles from the Siberian border, then ranged up and down the coast destroying bridges and rail and road facilities along the supply line from Vladivostok.

The rampaging ROK Capitol and Third Divisions captured the east coast port city of Wonsan to climax a ten-day, one hundred-mile drive up the east coast. A week later they were in Hamhung and Hungham, twin industrial and port cities of northeast Korea and heart of the former Japanese industrialization program on the peninsula.

The American First Cavalry and Twenty-fourth Divisions, the British Commonwealth Twenty-seventh Brigade (now including an Australian battalion) and four ROK divisions closed on Pyongyang from the south and east. Exactly one month after they had sparked the breakout from the Pusan beachhead, the First Cavalry and the First ROK divisions raced into the enemy capital. A die-hard garrison of about fifteen thousand Communist troops fought on the southeastern outskirts, then fell back across the Taedong River which bisects Pyongyang.

The next morning the Eighth Army released a surprise in what looked like the closing moments of the game. Four thousand paratroopers of the United States 187th Airborne Regiment* dropped astride two roads thirty miles north of Pyongyang. Their mission was to block the Reds' escape route, liberate American prisoners of war believed to be moving north from Pyongyang under guard, and capture Communist governmental leaders. They arrived too late. The bag of Communist prisoners taken was small. They failed to prevent the massacre of sixty-eight American soldiers who had been taken off a prison train near the parachute drop zone and shot the previous afternoon.

This atrocity added to the record of North Korean brutality written by the Seoul-Pyongyang "Death March," which cost the lives of nearly all the 283 captured Americans involved. In both Pyongyang and along the east coast, Allied troops had uncovered the mass graves of thousands

---

* The regiment, an element of the Eleventh Airborne Division, first saw action in Korea as regular infantry in late September when it joined the Tenth Corps on the Inchon-Seoul beachhead.

of Koreans executed by the Communist régime. Five hundred bodies were found at Yonghung, more than a hundred near Pyongyang, five hundred and thirty at Wonsan, and seven hundred at Hamhung. MacArthur's headquarters estimated that twenty thousand Koreans and more than three hundred Americans had been executed by the Communists. Plans for war crimes trials were announced, but no important suspects were in custody, and the key figures seemed to be escaping.

Kim Il Sung's government departed only hours ahead of the Allied vanguard. The Soviet military advisory staff departed early in the month, almost as soon as United Nations troops crossed the parallel. They left a city thoroughly Russianized during five years of Soviet "tutelage." The Taedong River was "Lenin" River. A main thoroughfare had been renamed "Stalin Street." Portraits of Lenin and Stalin were plastered on walls and billboards and hung in all public buildings. The best hotel was called the "Russian Hotel." Some reports said the Korean Communist rulers had gone to Kanggye, in far north-central Korea; other reports placed the refugee capital in Sinuiju, border city across the Yalu from Antung, Manchuria. Communist town and village bosses joined the Red leaders and the army in the flight. They left behind anarchy and confusion. Where there had been rigid governmental control for five years of Communist rule, there now was disorder and a political vacuum.

Before Syngman Rhee could move into this void with his own governors (many of whom he had appointed before the war as part of the republic's claim to authority over all Korea), the new United Nations Commission ruled at Lake Success that Rhee's government had no civil authority north of the Thirty-eighth parallel. The General Assembly had decided that the future government of all Korea, north and south, would be determined by national vote, supervised by the United Nations, without discrimination against North Koreans. Rhee protested violently against the suggestion that a new election was required in South Korea, but he bowed to the "hands-off-North-Korea" judgment. The American Army brought in civil affairs officers who attempted to choose non-Communist North Koreans to run temporary local governments until election day.

The political disputes, harbingers of the harsher postwar problems which would have followed, could be dismissed for the moment as annoying noises from offstage. The victory-flushed army held the spotlight, and it was still possible to cling to the happy illusion that military action could settle everything.

The Tenth Corps, pulled out of action after the liberation of Seoul, re-entered the war on the northeast Korean coast, joining the Eighth Army in the race for the Manchurian border. After losing six days while the navy cleared channels through a dense field of three thousand Russian mines, the Marines landed at Wonsan on October 25th; the war had passed on to the north fifteen days earlier. Bob Hope, the Air Force, the Marine Air Wing, the ROK's, KMAG, correspondents, and Hope's blonde songstress, Marilyn Maxwell, were on hand to cheer and good-naturedly jeer as the Marines hit the beach.

The United States Seventh Division stayed aboard ships and caught up with the ROK Third and Capitol Divisions one hundred miles north of Wonsan. The division landed at Iwon on October 29th and struck inland across the mountains toward Manchuria.

General Almond's Tenth Corps was assigned the cleanup of northeastern Korea, General Walker's Eighth Army the northwest. Each command answered separately to MacArthur, who in effect became the overall ground force commander as well as United Nations supreme commander. The two forces had separate supply channels, separate responsibilities, and areas clearly delineated by the great range of mountains which splits central North Korea. The battlefront was growing longer by the day, as Allied columns fanned out into the broad northern base of the peninsula. Under the circumstances, there was no immediate criticism of the split command arrangement; later, however, it was to become the subject of sober attacks on MacArthur's war leadership.

# VIII

## *New War*

PYONGYANG WAS THE climax, and now the glow of victory
chilled as winter came on night winds out of the north.
Four of MacArthur's six American divisions were out of
the race for the border, fighting a nasty, unsung "mop-up"
campaign against bypassed North Koreans. Sick of war and
of Korea, GIs counted the days and circulated rumors
about sailing dates for Japan. The First Cavalry Division
started making plans for a victory parade through Tokyo
on Armistice Day.

South Korean generals trumpeted, "We will not stop until we bathe our swords in the waters of the Yalu," and
drove their summer-uniformed soldiers northward in a race
for the final great distinction of the war. The United States
Twenty-fourth Division and the British Twenty-seventh
Brigade took the west coast highway toward Sinuiju and
the mouth of the Yalu. Four ROK divisions—the First,
Sixth, Seventh, and Eighth—rolled uncontested miles of
northwest Korea under their marching feet, outrunning
supplies and communications. In the northeast, men of the
ROK Capitol and Third divisions and the United States
Seventh Division fanned out across the white-etched mountains and up the coastal road toward the Siberian and Manchurian borders.

There was no front. Isolated fingers of advancing groups spread farther and farther apart. Few bothered to look to right or left. The enemy was beaten, and there was no need for caution. In one period of a little more than twenty-four hours, twenty-six thousand Communist troops had surrendered; MacArthur's headquarters estimated that only forty thousand remained to be captured or destroyed.

On the afternoon of October 26th a battalion of the Seventh South Korean Regiment, Sixth Division, won the race. Six weeks and five hundred marching miles north of the Pusan beachhead, this wiry band of footsore men entered the frontier village of Chosan and looked across the Yalu River into the Communist world.

That night they were trapped, cut off from the rest of the division, still far to the south. Two days passed before survivors escaped with a story of Chinese Communist troops in brown quilted uniforms, of roadblocks, and Russian weapons. By then it was becoming a familiar tale, but still the Eighth Army and GHQ tried hard not to believe it.

Chosan is one hundred miles upstream from the mouth of the Yalu, just above the great, Japanese-built Suiho hydroelectric basin. The Yalu dams produce the electric power which drives Manchurian industry. On the approaches to the Suiho basin a new war began.

The beaten enemy struck back against the Eighth Army's four ROK divisions twenty to thirty-five miles southeast of the dams on October 27th and 28th. First there was stiffening resistance, then assaults against the exposed flanks of the ROK columns.

South Korean spearhead units were ambushed on narrow mountain roads, surrounded, and massacred.

A few Communist prisoners were taken. They were Chinese, and they glibly told of crossing the Yalu during the second and third weeks of October. At least four divisions of General Lin Piao's Fourth Field Army had entered the war, and many more were on the way.

South Korean commanders rushed the electrifying news to American First Corps Headquarters. American KMAG advisers with ROK divisions sent supporting reports. At First Corps, Eighth Army, and General Headquarters, the reports were treated with supreme disdain. Intelligence officers questioned the ability of South Korean generals to distinguish Chinese soldiers from Chinese-speaking Korean émigrés, many of whom already had been released from Peiping's army to fight in Korea. It was suggested that South Korean officers had seized upon flimsy evidence of Chinese intervention to excuse their unwary blunder into enemy ambush. The reports had noted that North Koreans and Chinese were fighting side by side, and this was cited as further soothing proof that the Chinese Communist Army had not entered the war.

Furious night attacks hit the South Korean divisions as they attempted to reorganize. The Sixth ROK Division and parts of the Seventh and Eighth were nearly surrounded. Fighting to the rear was heavier than on the north. Elements of the First ROK Division fell back to Unsan, forty-five miles from the border, but the Communists already were south of the town in strength. The revived enemy, reports from the South Koreans said, were armed with Russian artillery and multiple-rocket launchers resembling the Russian "Katushka's" of World War II. Mongolian cavalrymen led some of the assaults.

The First Cavalry Division was jerked out of its homecoming plans and rushed forward to bolster the South Koreans. The Eighth Cavalry Regiment dug in on snow-flecked hills near Unsan. It was Hallowe'en, and a full moon flooded the snow-flecked ridges. Sometime after midnight, a private reported from an outpost that he had heard a bugle in the distance, "faint-like." From another direction came the unmistakable sounds of horses' hooves striking the cold ground. Then the bugles blared again and closer, this time in what sounded like "Taps." Chinese firing Russian "burp-guns" charged up the hills, howling and seemingly laughing. Sleepy GI's awoke in their foxholes for a split second to see a flash of fire and feel whatever a man feels when a bullet crashes into his brain.

One battalion fought its way southward, leaving heavy equipment and its light observation planes behind. The Chinese swept around the forward battalion as had the Indian raiders of the Eighth Cav's earlier war in the American West. At daybreak, eight hundred men were surrounded, many of them dead or wounded. A relief column ran into withering fire and abandoned an attempt to break through from the south. The men were given up for lost. Then the Chinese staged a baffling maneuver; they pulled back and virtually ceased firing. Small groups of men from the surrounded battalion made their way southward and rejoined the division; others followed. One group of wounded reported that the Chinese watched its escape without firing a shot.

The disastrous first meeting of American and Chinese Communist forces touched off a general Eighth Army withdrawal. The Twenty-fourth Division, the advance task force of which had reached to within fifteen miles of the Yalu, retreated fifty miles down the west coast road to avoid a tank attack from the north. The remnants of four ROK divisions made their way southward to the Chongchon River, which flows into the Yellow Sea forty-five miles north of Pyongyang. There General Walker collected his forces and went on the defensive.

In the Tenth Corps zone, the Chinese appeared in the same rôle—as defenders of the two important hydroelectric systems built around the Chosin (Changjin) and Fusen (Pujon) reservoirs. South Korean reconnaissance units encountered Chinese troops between Hamhung and the mountain lakes. The United States First Division called off its mop-up campaign around Wonsan, loaded on trucks, and went to meet the new enemy. For the Marines and the army, this "anticlimax war" was to bring as severe a trial as American fighting men ever faced.

General MacArthur broke his silence on the Chinese intervention on November 6th in a special communiqué which realistically defined the challenge to the United Nations hurled by an unnamed Communist power across the Yalu. He charged that in the face of complete United Nations victory and approaching peace in Korea,

> *"the Communists* * committed one of the most offensive acts of international lawlessness of historic record by moving without any notice of belligerency elements of *alien Communist forces* across the Yalu River into North Korea and massing a great concentration of possible reinforcing divisions with adequate supply behind *the privileged sanctuary of the adjacent Manchurian border.*
>
> *"A possible trap* was thereby surreptitiously laid, calculated to encompass the destruction of the United Nations Forces engaged in restoring order and the processes of civil government in the North Korean border area.

* Author's italics throughout.

"This potential danger was avoided with minimum losses only by the timely detection and skillful maneuvering of the United Nations commander responsible for that sector who, with great perspicacity and skill, completely revised the movement of his forces in order to achieve the greater integration of tactical power necessitated by the new situation and avert any possibility of a great military reverse.

"The present situation, therefore, is this:

"While the North Korean forces with which we were initially engaged have been destroyed or rendered impotent for military action, *a new and fresh army now faces us,* backed up by a possibility of large alien reserves and adequate supply within easy reach to the enemy but *beyond the limits of our present sphere of military action.*

"Whether and to what extent these reserves will be moved forward to reinforce units now committed remains to be seen and is *a matter of the gravest international significance.*

"Our present mission is limited to the destruction of those forces now arrayed against us in North Korea, with a view to achieving the United Nations' objective to bring unity and peace to the Korean nation and people."

In a special report to Lake Success later the same day he was more specific. He named the "new foe" as "Chinese Communist military units" and recited the details of their identification.

Three days later MacArthur's headquarters estimated that sixty thousand organized Chinese Communist troops had gone into action against the United Nations in Korea, and that sixty thousand more were on the way. Four CCF (Chinese Communist Forces) divisions were named. Headquarters intelligence estimated that the Chinese had expanded their army in Manchuria by from three to five hundred thousand and that this massive force was available for rapid deployment against the United Nations army in North Korea.

There was no longer room for doubt that Chinese troops, operating in regular CCF units under orders from Peiping and with Moscow's knowledge, had entered the war. Prisoners named the units, and their stories confirmed each other. There was still room, however, for the hopeful theory that these were only token forces, sent to fulfill Peiping's promise of aid to a defeated ally but not to reopen a full-scale war against the United Nations. Intelligence officers in Tokyo repeated the argument General MacArthur had used at Wake Island: if the Chinese Communists intended to intervene effectively in Korea, they would have done so during the Summer when one strong offensive would have driven the Eighth Army into the sea at Pusan.

The Chinese took pains to encourage such wishful thinking. As suddenly as they had struck and snatched victory from our grasp, they retreated. Marines pursuing them below the Chosin reservoir found recently dismantled power-plant equipment near small hydroelectric dams. The North Korean refugee radio at Sinuiju claimed that the main Chosin dam equipment had been dismantled to keep it out of enemy hands. Speculation that the Chinese troops were screening a gigantic theft of entire power plants prior to abandoning North Korea received serious consideration. The Peiping Radio offered for the gullible the fiction that the only Chinese fighting in Korea were "volunteers" who had gone to help the "Korean people" resist "western imperialism" and to protect China from American "invasion."

Hindsight is easy, but in early November of 1950, no one in the western world could claim to know the Communist masters' intentions.

In Washington, Secretary Acheson and General Omar Bradley, chairman of the United States Joint Chiefs of Staff, admitted publicly that they were completely in the dark. Acheson suggested that the United States and the United Nations should reserve judgment until they could find out whether a "sincere but needless fear" that the Manchurian border or the Yalu power facilities were threatened had caused the Chinese to intervene. "Everything possible must be done to disabuse them of such an illusion," he said. He warned, however, that if the Chinese had deliberately precipitated a major war, it would be "a tragedy of colossal nature" and that the United Nations must then take firm action against such "aggression."

President Truman offered Peiping assurance that "we support and are acting within the limits of U.N. policy in Korea." (The Chinese Communists and Russia throughout the Korean War had attacked United Nations policy as "aggression" and treated the United Nations majority as enemies of China.) Truman declared that "never at any time has the United States entertained any intention to carry hostilities into China" and "will take every honorable step to prevent extension of hostilities in the Far East."

The new United Nations Commission on Korea assured China that its frontier would be respected and that all frontier questions, including access to the Yalu power sources, would be mediated.

The Security Council voted to "invite" the Chinese Communists to explain their action during a forthcoming hearing, already scheduled, on Red China's charge of "U.S. aggression" in the Far East.

British and other European political figures informally pressed for outright appeasement. They suggested, according to press reports from European capitals quoting "informed sources," that the United Nations buy off the Chinese with the grant of a large belt of Korea's border territory, including the Yalu River basin. A group of Labor members of the British Parliament proposed in the House of Commons that the United Nations forces halt their advance and not attempt to occupy the remaining section of North Korea. The Marquis of Salisbury, Conservative leader in the House of Lords, suggested that the United Nations announce a line short of the border beyond which MacArthur's forces would not advance.

Even where cold realism might be expected, in the minds of military men close to the battlefront hope still held sway over reason. General MacArthur allowed the Tenth Corps to race on up into the northeast corner of Korea, spreading its forces thinner and thinner. The Eighth Army's demand that General Almond pull back and help form a solid line across the narrow waist of North Korea, between the Chongchon River and Hamhung, went unheeded. The United States Third Infantry Division, commanded by an "old China hand," Major General Robert Soule, landed at Wonsan after staging in southern Japan, and made a token effort to link up with Eighth Army. But the rest of the Tenth Corps continued the race for the border seemingly as if it had not been informed of the Chinese intervention.

Prisoners captured by the Eighth Army had described the fear which United States Air Force attacks sent through the ranks of the first Chinese troops to come under the terrible punishment of modern airpower. From these reports some officers, including those in MacArthur's headquarters, gained confidence that the United Nations forces could handle the Chinese with dispatch. They gave the Air Force great credit for forcing the Chinese to fall back after their initial attacks. (A more realistic appreciation of aerial capacities and limitations and of Chinese tactics came later in the war.) Maximum air attacks were ordered.

Sinuiju, the northwest Korean city just across the Yalu from Antung, Manchuria, was believed to be the main funnel through which Chinese troops and equipment were entering northwest Korea. The United States Air Force attacked it with a tremendous display of aerial might calculated to impress the Chinese still on the safe side of the river. Seventy-nine B-29 Superforts and three hundred fighter-bombers virtually wiped the city off the map on November 8th with more than six hundred tons of demolition bombs and eighty-five thousand incendiaries. Four F-80 Shooting Star jets flying near Sinuiju that day engaged eight to twelve swept-wing Russian MIG-15 jets, presumably of the Chinese Air Force, in the first all-jet dogfight in history. One MIG was shot down, another damaged, against no American losses.

The most important target of the mass raid on Sinuiju was the concrete-and-steel railway bridge spanning the Yalu. B-29 crews, operating under rigid instructions to remain on the Korean side of the center of the Yalu and flying high to avoid anti-aircraft fire from both sides of the river, failed to score a clean hit on the bridge. Navy dive-bombers took over the job the next day and scored direct hits, but did not destroy the bridge. A carrier-based Pantherjet covering the dive-bombers shot down the navy's first MIG of the war.

From Sinuiju the air force and navy turned to Hyesanjin, crossing point for Chinese forces entering northeast Korea, and a half-dozen smaller bridgesites along the Yalu. B-29 saturation raids hit Hoeryong, northernmost Korean town on the Manchurian border; Kanggye, railway junction in north central Korea; and other important communications centers. Air force fighters raked the narrow belt of Korean territory still in enemy hands. But the supply lines they sought to cut were short and secure. The Manchurian storehouse of Communist manpower and firepower was only a night's truck ride or two nights' march from the battlefront.

# IX

## *Home by Christmas*

MACARTHUR'S SECOND MAJOR gamble actually began early
in November with the decision to send the Tenth Corps
charging on across northeast Korea toward the Manchurian
and Siberian borders. He elected to remain on the offensive, despite a Chinese threat of catastrophic dimensions
which he had clearly defined in his public statements and
reports to Lake Success. He pursued the strategy of blitz
victory, well aware of the risks, but hopeful of completing
the occupation of all Korea before the bulk of Red China's
massive army could cross the Yalu from Manchuria. He
gambled on the last remaining hope—that the Chinese
Communist divisions already opposing him were token
forces sent as symbolic fulfillment of Peiping's promises to
Kim Il Sung.

He launched the ill-fated "end-the-war" offensive in the
northwest as the second, and decisive, play of the gamble.
As completely and dramatically as he had won at Inchon,
he lost in North Korea. On November 6th he had described
the "surreptitiously laid" Chinese trap his forces had narrowly escaped; less than three weeks later, he seemingly
walked back into a trap three times as deadly. His intelligence reports, the accuracy of which had produced victory
in September, now misled him disastrously.

This is the hindsight view of what happened. At the moment, there was great concern among capable military men and civilian observers in Korea, Tokyo, and Washington over the increasingly vulnerable disposition of the Allied forces, but no responsible voice was raised in opposition to the course MacArthur was taking. If victory was to be won and a long and costly war with China carrying the explosive potential of a third world war was to be avoided, bold and immediate action was necessary. If MacArthur abandoned the last fleeting chance of a knockout victory and withdrew his scattered forces to a defense line, he might give the Chinese time to bring invincible strength into Korea. Which course was he to take? He was "damned if he did and damned if he didn't."

Critics since have argued that no time would have been lost to the Chinese, and no important territorial gains forfeited, if MacArthur had used the first three weeks of November to withdraw the hundred thousand troops of the Tenth Corps from the northeast and integrate them with the Eighth Army in a solid defense line across the Korean "waist." From this line he could have conducted more extensive reconnaissance, made greater use of Korean intelligence agents behind the Chinese lines, and continued air attacks on the enemy buildup areas.

In defense of his strategy, MacArthur repeatedly has asserted that the offensive actually was a large-scale reconnaissance which succeeded brilliantly in determining the Chinese strength and aggressive intentions and forcing the Communists to fight before they were fully prepared to strike in sufficient force to destroy the United Nations armies. He denied that he had walked into a trap, asserting rather that he had exposed the intended trap and thereby saved his forces from annihilation.

MacArthur's communiqués and public statements during the first two days of the Eighth Army offensive do not support his contention that he was acting with caution while probing the enemy's intentions. His words radiated confidence in early victory. (Of course, it would be utterly contradictory to MacArthur's personality or to his concept of a commander's rôle for him to issue any but the most confident statements.) In personally launching the offensive from the Chongchon River line on November 24th, he described it as a "general attack" and said: "If successful, this should for all practical purposes end the war." In a joking, casual remark to one of his field commanders, he said he hoped this operation would make it possible for him to keep his promise (presumably made at Wake Island) to get the American soldiers "home by Christmas." His headquarters in Tokyo began issuing frequent communiqués during the day and night to report in eloquent terms the great "pincers movement" against the enemy.

Whatever the final verdict of history—and a unanimous finding is not likely—this much is certain:

1. The Allied public and the men of the Eighth Army, from high staff officers down, were led to believe that this was, as proclaimed, an all-out offensive which carried the hope of quick and final victory.

2. Unwarranted optimism and underestimation of the enemy were factors in the command decision. This was evidenced by the dispersion of the Tenth Corps on a relatively unprofitable advance into northeast Korea, away from known concentrations of enemy forces. Some alarming intelligence reports were collected on the Eighth Army front during the final days before the November 24th offensive, but GHQ's published estimates of enemy strength on the day of the attack indicated that the reports were dis-

counted. The question whether any other commander could have made a better decision under the circumstances will be a subject for professional military debate for many years.

3. MacArthur's strategy did not cause Communist intervention in Korea. State Department reports and the record and nature of Chinese Communist military movements furnished conclusive support for MacArthur's assertion, made in a statement to the New York *Times* on December 1st to defend his actions that: "It is historically inaccurate to attribute any degree of responsibility for the onslaught of the Chinese Communist armies to the strategic course of the campaign itself. The decision by the Chinese Communist leaders to wage war against the United Nations could only have been a basic one, long premeditated and carried into execution as a direct result of the defeat of their satellite North Korean armies."

The prelude to disaster was appropriately deceptive. Allied morale climbed back toward the heights when the Chinese abandoned their initial counterattacks and virtually disappeared from all fronts. United Nations patrols ranged a thousand yards, then two miles, and finally eight to ten miles out in front of the Chongchon River line in the northwest without encountering large Communist forces. Most of the small troop units encountered were North Korean. The Eighth Army established bridgeheads north of the Chongchon. The United States Second and Twenty-fifth Divisions, relieved of their rear-area mop-up assignments, moved up to the front and bolstered the Eighth Army line. When the Third Division landed on the east coast, there was promise of a solid integration of the two virtually competing United Nations ground commands.

In the northeast, the Marines reached the frozen Chosin

reservoir after overcoming initially stiff resistance from Chinese delaying forces along the mountain road north of Hamhung. They drove up both sides of the lake, and there was talk of a great Marine flank attack across Korea's highest mountains against the Chinese facing the Eighth Army. The Marines also captured Chinese who paid tribute to fearful Allied air and ground firepower.

On November 21st, the Seventh Division's Seventeenth Regiment planted the American flag on the bank of the frozen Yalu River at Hyesanjin. This was supposedly a major crossing point for Chinese troops entering northeast Korea, but there was no sign of Chinese as the men of the Seventeenth dug into the snow-covered ridges overlooking Hyesanjin and peered through field glasses at the towering "Blue Haze" mountains of Manchuria.

The illusion of imminent victory returned. It was strengthened on November 22nd when a flurry of peace rumors spread in Seoul, Pyongyang, and Tokyo. Twenty-seven wounded American prisoners of war were returned to Eighth Army lines with a message from their former captors: "The Chinese do not want to fight Americans." The attempt to determine whether this was a serious peace bid started the rumor mill.

One sobering note came from Peiping. The official radio voice of Communist China rejected as "worthless" American and British assurances that MacArthur's forces would respect China's borders and withdraw quickly from Korea after a national government was elected. The radio spokesman declared that China had learned not to trust the western powers since they had violated earlier "promises" to stop at the Thirty-eighth parallel, or at the "MacArthur line" across the narrow waist of North Korea. Furthermore,

he said, the United States had, when convenient, reversed
its decision to keep hands off Formosa and Indo-China. The
Chinese people, he said, were "volunteering" to fight in
Korea because they knew that MacArthur already had
drafted his plans for invading China through North Korea.

During the lull before the storm, America's miracle-
working supply machinery was building great piles of ammunition and equipment behind the Chongchon line and
at the Tenth Corps' Hamhung-Hungnam base in the east.
Winter clothing arrived, and the few minor cases of poor
distribution of cold-weather equipment were corrected.

Replacement troops and the bountifully equipped British Twenty-ninth Brigade arrived in Korea to strengthen
General Walker's hand.

In the endless supply line of trucks, trains, and transport
planes came the Quartermaster Corps' annual proof of genius—Thanksgiving turkeys and all the trimmings. The
feast was served on schedule on Thursday, November 23rd,
but it was eaten to the accompaniment of humorless jokes
about the "fattening for the slaughter." Most of the men
of the Eighth Army knew what the next morning would
bring.

The offensive opened with about as much surprise and
secrecy as the rising of the sun. For three days the uncensored Allied press had been predicting a renewed Eighth
Army attack, describing the buildup of Allied men and ma-
terial, and naming the divisions on the line. GHQ in Tokyo
had published its estimates of the strength of the enemy,
and press reports quoting frontline intelligence sources had
filled in estimates of the enemy's disposition. Finally, at
H-hour General MacArthur landed at an airstrip near the
front and released a statement explaining his strategy, al-

though the advancing United Nations troops were not expected to make contact with the main forces of the withdrawn enemy for nearly two days.

The heaviest Allied artillery barrage to date roared and flashed from dusk to dawn. At 8 A.M. on Friday, the "end-the-war" offensive jumped off into biting north winds. Three American divisions—the Twenty-fourth, Twenty-fifth, and Second—and the First, Seventh, and Eighth South Korean divisions opened the attack. The First Cavalry Division, the British Twenty-seventh and Twenty-ninth Brigades, the recently arrived Turkish Brigade, and the Sixth ROK Division were in reserve, ready to move into the attack line as the front fanned out into northwest Korea. General Walker went forth to knock the Communists out of the war with an army of one hundred and twenty-five thousand men.

The enemy was officially credited with about the same numerical strength on the northwest front—sixty to a hundred thousand Chinese and thirty to forty thousand North Koreans.

The first day went smoothly. When American tanks cut their engines and infantrymen of lead battalions dug in that night, they had advanced five to twelve miles and nearly closed no-man's land before the waiting Communist army. The ROK Second Corps—Seventh and Eighth Divisions—on the right of the attack lines, made less progress in their push up the central mountains, due to stiff resistance from unidentified Communist troops.

Before dawn on Saturday, Chinese horse cavalry and infantry hit the First ROK Division near the left flank of the front. The ROK's fell back nearly two miles, then held. More cautiously now, the offensive jumped off for the second and critical day. Again the Americans advanced, but more slowly. The ROK's bogged down, and soon it became apparent that the main Communist strength had been shifted in front of the South Korean sectors. Counterattacks hit the entire line, except in the extreme west. By nightfall the Eighth Army had waded into a buzz-saw.

The Chinese deftly singled out the South Koreans. During the moonlit night they swarmed across the hills, infiltrated behind ROK lines, and massed for attack. North Koreans moving through the still unclosed gap between the Eighth Army and the Tenth Corps knifed behind the ROK right flank. On Sunday morning the Communists attacked across nearly the entire front, concentrating on the ROK Seventh and Eighth Divisions, battered survivors of the first round with the Chinese exactly one month earlier.

The South Koreans broke under the attack. An avalanche of Chinese infantrymen poured through a breakthrough in ROK lines near Tokchon, sixty miles northeast of Pyongyang. The Red attack swelled like a tidal wave and crashed against the United States Second Division, on the South Koreans' western flank. Chinese striking southward from Unsan and southeastward along the main road to the Yalu power dams hit the Twenty-fifth Division and the ROK First Division. The Americans fell back, but kept their lines intact.

The Allied offensive collapsed; it became a fight for survival. The ROK Second Corps disintegrated under the attack; the Chinese streamed southward through a gaping hole where the South Koreans had been, then wheeled westward against the rear of the United States Second Division.

Fighting along a broken arc near the village of Kunu, south and east of the river, some units of the division were inundated by the Red wave, surrounded, or cut off from retreat by roadblocks set by infiltrating Chinese. The yet untested Turkish Brigade joined the division in the desperate battle to hold the sagging right flank. There was no front; the Chinese seemed to be everywhere.

If the Communist drive swept around the American-Turkish force and cut the roads south to Pyongyang, the bulk of the Eighth Army would be trapped and pinned against the Yellow Sea. The First Cavalry Division moved into position, south of Kunu and near the scene of October's paratroop landing, to block this threat. The Twenty-fifth Division, heavily engaged along the north side of the river, fell back in a professionally executed withdrawal. The Twenty-fourth and ROK First Divisions withdrew to the river under lighter pressure.

The Eighth Army was in full retreat forty-eight hours after the Chinese opened their counteroffensive. Reports reaching army headquarters painted a darkening picture of disaster; casualties suffered by the Second Division and the Turks alone made it the worst Allied defeat of the war. The ROK Second Corps was officially described as "disintegrated."

In Tokyo, General MacArthur declared in a bluntly worded communiqué issued on November 28th that the United Nations now were fighting "an entirely new war" with Red China. He doubled his pre-offensive estimate of Chinese strength. In a closing paragraph he called for new political decisions to deal with this new situation. In later statements he made it clear that he wanted authority to carry the war back to Red China with all the air and naval force at his command.

In the United Nations Security Council, the United

States demanded that the Council order the Chinese to evacuate Korea. Russia cast three vetoes to block action on the resolution.

The spectre of World War III returned. Had Russia, the real enemy, maneuvered Communist China and the United States into a terrible, exhausting war which would drain off American strength and slow the rearmament of western Europe? Mighty but unprepared America had scraped the barrel to muster enough strength to defeat the North Koreans. Had we now been tricked into war with China's millions? Americans were dismayed, frustrated, and angry. Western Europe, looking eastward toward Moscow for the final stroke, was haunted by a fear that, in retaliating against China, the impetuous Americans would plunge the world into atomic war.

The hour demanded a scapegoat, and the imperious five-star general in Tokyo fitted the specifications. Europeans charged that MacArthur had virtually declared war on Communist China in his November 28th statement, far exceeding his military prerogatives. Still hoping against hope that the Chinese could be cajoled into a bargain on Korea, some European diplomats and newspapers attacked both MacArthur's military judgment and his alleged political indiscretions. British Foreign Secretary Ernest Bevin came to MacArthur's defense, however, declaring that the General was abiding by United Nations directives.

President Truman injected another explosive note into the near-hysteria of the moment. In response to press-conference questions as to whether the United States would use atomic bombs to meet the Chinese threat in Korea, he said their use always was under active consideration. The implications of the essentially routine statement were not lost on the jittery world public.

Now a second crisis arose in the northeast. For two critical days after the Chinese smashed the Eighth Army's offensive in the west, the probing fingers of the Tenth Corps continued to push deeper into the winter-locked mountains and up the coastal highway. Despite misgivings, the Marines advanced farther up the western shores of the Chosin reservoir, fifty tortuous mountain miles north of their supply base. Seventh Division regiments moved westward toward the Marine line of advance. Howling Siberian winds brought sub-zero temperatures. Weather, the coldest an American fighting man had ever endured, was the only enemy they encountered; the Chinese had slipped away in the night.

By night, to the haunting sound of bugles and whistles, they returned. They knifed behind the overextended Marines, cut the road along the western shore of the Chosin reservoir, then swept down out of the mountains east of the lake to overwhelm isolated Seventh Division battalions. Full Chinese divisions struck eastward across the single supply and escape route between the reservoir and the sea. They surrounded Marine units at Koto, ten miles south of the reservoir, and Hagaru, at its southern tip. General Almond estimated that ten Chinese divisions, consisting of about a hundred thousand troops, had surrounded Tenth Corps forces in the reservoir area.

The Seventeenth Army regiment belatedly abandoned its lone stand on the Yalu and headed for Hamhung. The ROK Capitol Division turned back after advancing to within less than thirty miles of the Russian border. Scattered units of the Third ROK Division joined the retreat.

On both fronts now, the free world was in retreat. High hopes were shattered and replaced by fear.

General MacArthur again increased his estimate of Chinese strength in Korea to three hundred thousand; on December 2nd, for the fourth time in ten days, he once more raised the figure, this time to five hundred thousand troops, half of whom were supposedly in reserve or on the way to Korea. The North Koreans, he said, had been reinforced by Korean troops trained in Manchuria, and now a Communist army of six hundred thousand men "overwhelmingly outnumbered" his United Nations force of two hundred and fifty thousand. The two United Nations armies were split and threatened with separate encirclement and destruction against the shore. For days it was uncertain whether the Eighth Army could break contact and withdraw fast enough to escape envelopment. The Tenth Corps had no alternative but to withdraw into a beachhead at Hungnam and attempt to escape by sea.

The Eighth Army was saved by raw courage, American firepower, Turkish bayonets, and deft use of reserves to meet the flanking threat from the central breakthrough corridor. Salvation also came through Chinese weakness; the Red Army could not sustain its offensive long enough to exploit the breakthrough. Supplies did not keep pace with its ridge-running, lightly armed swarms of infantrymen. This short-windedness of Chinese offensives—each one expiring after five days almost to the hour—later was to become the key to Allied success against the enemy's numbers.

When the Second Division and the Turkish Brigade, their ranks thinned by terrible casualties, fought through the last Chinese roadblocks to safety on November 30th, the Communist attack was already slackening. No one could be sure that the crisis had passed, however, until December 2nd, when the bulk of the Eighth Army broke contact and withdrew in road-clogging, leapfrog stages toward Pyongyang.

Terror-stricken Koreans who had co-operated with the United Nations lined the roads and watched the tide of men and machines roll southward. Thousands of them chose to join the swelling ranks of refugees streaming south, leaving their homes to escape Communist reprisal or the return to totalitarian rule. In Pyongyang, "Welcome United Nations" banners and United Nations flags disappeared from the streets and shop windows. Houses were shuttered; normal life stopped; South Korean currency became worthless. The Allies were abandoning all North Korea to the Communists, and the most illiterate peasant soon knew it.

Pyongyang had just become the site of Eighth Army advance headquarters; now it was once more about to become the capital of Communist Korea. General Walker ordered a "scorched earth" evacuation. Demolition crews set dynamite and torch to the water works, power plants, bridges, railways, airport facilities—all utilities which had been repaired and restored to use by the American army. In its haste, the army and air force also burned millions of dollars' worth of bulky supplies which could not be salvaged quickly. A mile-high pall of red-tinged smoke hung over the city as rear-guard British tankers crossed the main Taedong River bridge and American engineers blew the last span during the first hour of December 5th. Next stop: the Thirty-eighth parallel.

Retreat for the Marines in the northeast meant fighting

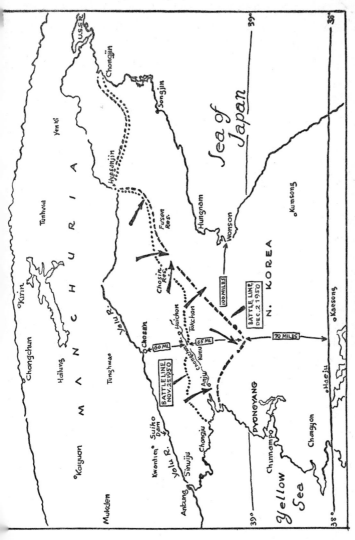

3. Winter Defeat, December, 1950

down an icy canyon of death and running a gantlet of fire from Chinese, outnumbering them perhaps five to one, who waited in ambush and gnawed at the column like jackals. Down the west side of the reservoir they came, fighting toward Hagaru where other Marines held off a tightening noose of encircling Chinese. They stuck together and fought as a unit, bringing out wounded and equipment; there was no reckless dash down a road lined with Chinese. Marine companies knocked the Chinese off flanking hills and out of roadblocks and ambushes as the column advanced.

At Hagaru the force swelled to fifteen thousand men, including survivors of the Seventh Division units hit near the east shore of the reservoir and a small detachment of Royal British Marine Commandos.

There, under almost constant fire from all sides, they held while Marine and air force transport planes dropped down through Chinese-infested hills, landed on a crude dirt runway, loaded wounded men aboard, and flew them to safety. More than twenty-five hundred wounded and frostbitten Marines and soldiers were evacuated in this heroic airlift.

The airlift was the only supply line. Everything which the division required to fight and survive came by air, in evacuation planes or by parachute drop. An umbrella of navy, Marine and air force fighter planes covered the surrounded men and with rockets and machine guns partially evened the odds. Without this air support, thankful Marine commanders said, the division might never have survived the ordeal.

The epic withdrawal to the sea resumed on December 6th; no Marine was ready to call it retreat. Major General

Oliver P. Smith, scholarly, white-haired "old man" of the division, eloquently expressed the Marines' unbroken esprit: "Retreat, hell!" he said. "We're just attacking in a different direction."

December 6th and 7th were the worst days. Crossfire ripped the Marine-infantry column; snow clouds protected the Chinese from air attack much of the time. When the tanks and trucks in the rear of the convoy pulled into Koto, ten miles south of Hagaru, they carried a tragic cargo of lifeless, frozen bodies and wounded and frostbitten men. (In the Chosin action alone, the Marines suffered thirty-five hundred casualties, about half of them due to frostbite.)

At Koto part of the First Marine Regiment was waiting. Nearly twenty thousand men were in the column when it set out through the final series of Chinese roadblocks along the narrow mountain trail leading down to the Hamhung-Hungnam coastal plain. The ten-mile-long bumper-to-bumper convoy met a Third Division relief force on the road northwest of Hamhung on December 10th, and the fight out of "frozen hell" was over.

Off Hungnam an Allied evacuation fleet was forming. Nearly a hundred thousand American and South Korean troops were funneling into a semi-circular beachhead, pursued by an estimated eighty thousand to one hundred thousand Chinese. All land routes to South Korea were blocked; an amphibious "landing in reverse" was the only way out. If the Chinese loosed their airpower on the beachhead it could become another bloody Dunkerque battle on Hungnam's beaches.*

* At the beginning of what the military termed the "redeployment" from northeast Korea, small groups of ROK Marines and soldiers and some Americans were evacuated from the extreme northern coast and from Wonsan.

Rear Admiral James H. Doyle, amphibious veteran of World War II and chief technical planner of the Inchon landing, took command of the delicate operation. His assignment was to withdraw into a shrinking beachhead, loading men, supplies, and equipment aboard ships and leaving a progressively smaller force ashore to hold off an enemy of constant or increasing strength. The last troops on the beach, like the assault waves of an amphibious landing, might face suicidal odds. Maximum use of American ground, naval, and air firepower was the key to the plan Doyle worked out with General Almond.

Dunkerque was not repeated. The Communist army of the northeast watched the Tenth Corps escape and, as Admiral Doyle said later, "never laid a glove on us." Small North Korean and Chinese probing forces braved the ceaseless rain of steel death around the perimeter to assault American outposts, but mounted no major attack. Again here, as on the Eighth Army front, the Chinese Communists' inability to sustain an offensive gave American fighting men a heaven-sent respite.

For ten beachhead days, however, no one could be sure what the next night would bring. Hungnam was unflagging drama, played by professionals. It was a near-miracle of planning, organization, and teamwork.

The Marines were first aboard the waiting transports; the two ROK divisions followed. Elements of the Third and Seventh divisions held the perimeter, twelve miles north, west, and south of Hungnam. Every day it shrank a little, while men and supplies left the beach. First, the industrial city of Hamhung, then the Russian-built airport at Yonpo, slipped outside the perimeter. Fires and demolitions ringed the beachhead; only scorched earth was left to the Communists.

Now only the Third Division remained ashore to hold the shortened line. The perimeter fell back to the outskirts of Hungnam, and with it came a teeming multitude of terrified North Koreans, many of whom had worked for the Americans, all of whom sought refuge from the returning Communists.

Howitzers, practically on the front lines, fired from city streets. The sharp crack of their muzzle blasts was answered almost instantly by a crescendo of explosions where their curtain of shells descended. Cruisers, joined by the battleship *Missouri,* laid down the outer curtain of fire. Carrier planes searched the enemy out and blasted him before he could launch an attack.

Black coal dust and soot from fires and destroyed factories mingled with the half-frozen slush and mud churned by trucks and tanks. Piles of supplies and fields of gasoline drums disappeared from the dock area into the bowels of LSTs and freighters.

Finally only a regiment remained ashore, then a battalion, then a handful of demolition men. A series of mighty explosions along the dockside signalled the end.

It was Christmas Eve, and more than a hundred thousand men of the Tenth Corps were on the way south to Pusan and Pohang—to live and fight again. The 193-ship evacuation task force also brought out ninety-one thousand Korean civilians, seventeen thousand five hundred vehicles, and three hundred and fifty thousand tons of matériel.

President Truman called it "the best Christmas present I've ever had."

# X

## Black Christmas

THE CRITICAL BATTLES of late December were fought in the minds of men and on the diplomatic front far from this bleeding peninsula. Again the hour of decision had arrived. Was it to be Munich, or Dunkerque, or something new under the sun—a war of attrition fought almost without hope of military victory?

Fifty-five per cent. of the American public, according to a Gallup poll of December 7th, believed that World War III had started. Much of the Allied world believed Korea was irretrievably lost. Influential American and European voices spoke out for conceding defeat and abandoning the United Nations venture in Korea before another life was lost in a "hopeless" battle.

No assurance of ultimate victory came from American military leaders. The United States Army Chief of Staff, General Collins, flew to Korea to obtain for Washington a first-hand estimate of the defeat and of prospects for future resistance. His most encouraging conclusion was that the Eighth Army could "take care of itself." General MacArthur offered hope of victory only through expanding the war in a campaign of retaliation against the cities, industries, and military bases of Communist China. The Korean victory he offered was priced at the risk of even greater war, possibly World War III.

116

At the height of the controversy over what the Allies' policy should be, two apparently conflicting official voices spoke for America:

From Tokyo, General MacArthur issued a series of statements to prominent newsmen and publications between November 30th and December 5th which, in effect, told the American public that Washington's policy of confining the war to Korea was an important cause of the defeat and possibly a critical obstacle to United Nations victory. The restriction against air retaliation on Chinese Communist cities and bases, he told *U.S. News and World Report,* was "an enormous handicap, without precedent in military history." The restriction, he announced in a general press statement, to a large extent nullified American air supremacy in Korea. The situation facing the United Nations in December, he stated to United Press President Hugh Baillie, "results largely from the acceptance of military odds without precedent in history—the odds of permitting offensive action without defensive retaliation." He added that "these odds have been and are being cheerfully accepted . . . to further the universal desire that the war be localized." But in privately and publicly expressed opinions during the next three months he increasingly sought recognition of the fact that a state of war existed between the United Nations forces and Communist China which required maximum retaliation.

From Washington, President Truman declared that the United States would continue to do everything possible to confine the war to Korea and reduce the threat of expanded war. Truman and British Prime Minister Clement Attlee, in a policy statement ending their four-day Washington conference of December 4th to 8th, proposed:

1. Continued resistance to aggression.

2. Continued efforts to confine the war to the Korean peninsula (no bombing of Manchuria or blockading of China ports).

3. Support of the United Nations majority's decisions on Korea policy.

4. No "appeasement" of Red China, but an offer to negotiate peace with the Chinese Communist government if it would agree in advance to creation by the United Nations of a "free and independent Korea."

This statement became the foundation of American and United Nations policy in Korea. MacArthur's openly expressed dissatisfaction with it ultimately led to his relief from command.

At this critical moment there was agreement within the American government and among the major allies on one minimum point: the Republic of Korea, in defense of which the United Nations went to war against Communist aggression, would not be surrendered to Communism without a fight. The Eighth Army rapidly withdrew to the Thirty-eighth parallel and dug in against a second invasion of South Korea.

General Walker was reported to have promised President Rhee on December 11th that Seoul would be defended, but he did not guarantee a battle to the finish for the city. If the Chinese launched a full-scale offensive across the old border, fixed resistance might be suicidal.

Nevertheless, Rhee assured the people of Seoul on December 20th that the capital's defenses were "impregnable" and tried to discourage the civilian exodus already under way. An American embassy officer predicted publicly that the Eighth Army would "not yield one more inch." For tunately few war-wise South Koreans heeded the soothing words.

MacArthur was already mapping a strategy of withdrawal, patterned after the July retreat before the North Koreans. He privately outlined to visitors his scheme for salvaging something out of defeat: fight and withdraw, sucking the Chinese southward at the end of increasingly vulnerable and overtaxed supply lines until their numerical superiority would be balanced by Allied firepower and control of the air and sea. The balance might come near the old Pusan perimeter; after a slow process of attrition against the Chinese, the battle line might move northward. This was not a blueprint for victory, but it was the best that could be conceived within the terms of Washington's decision to limit the war to Koreea.

The prospect was another miserable Winter campaign, another retreat, another bloodbath for South Korea and for Allied fighting men—all leading at best to a stalemate. The Eighth Army had no stomach for this; its morale had climbed to the heights with October's victory march, dipped dangerously with the Chinese intervention, then soared with false hopes of "home by Christmas" in the November 24th offensive. It fell to the depths in Black December; among officers and GI's alike, only a faint flicker of fighting spirit survived. Morale in the Tenth Corps was sustained only by the prospect of escape from war; the let-down following Hungnam was complete.

The fighting man's despair was shared at home and in the chancelleries of the democratic world. December brought more than twelve thousand war casualty notices to American homes.

Against this background, the United Nations allies

sought an honorable way out, and Communism trumpeted demands and threatened annihilation to the United Nations army.

Acting within the framework of the Truman-Attlee declaration, the United Nations General Assembly voted on December 14th to seek an armistice in Korea and set up a three-man Cease-Fire Committee to lay the offer before Peiping and Pyongyang. The attempt was doomed from the outset when Russia voted against it.

Before the committee could go to work, Communist China destroyed all hopes of a compromise settlement. The Peiping radio announced the Communist terms for agreeing even to discuss Korean peace: United Nations withdrawal from the peninsula, American withdrawal from the defense of Formosa, and cessation of all western rearmament plans.

Kim Il Sung served notice in a belligerent speech quoted by Peiping radio that the "People's Army," supported by the "Chinese volunteers," intended to "annihilate the enemy" throughout Korea and drive the United Nations forces into the sea.

Semi-official rejection of the first cease-fire appeal came on December 16th when Peiping's General Wu Hsiu-chuan, departing for home after appearing before the Security Council, called the United Nations plan an American "plot" to gain time and rally from its Korean losses. Twice the committee renewed its appeals to Peiping before it received the official reply.

On December 22nd, Premier and Foreign Minister Chou En-lai slammed the door on the West's last hopes. In a lengthy statement bristling with Communist propaganda, he named China's price for sitting down at peace talks:

1. Recognition of the Peiping régime as the representative of China in the United Nations.

2. United States withdrawal from the defense of Formosa.

3. Withdrawal of all foreign (presumably United Nations) troops from Korea.

He rejected completely the American proposal of ceasefire first, followed by discussion of peace terms. Under his proposition, the United Nations would withdraw from Korea, the Chinese Communist "volunteers" might or might not go back to China, the United Nations majority would give Red China everything it demanded at the point of a gun. The Communists would then oblige by attending a peace conference. Interesting in terms of the Communists' later attempts during the Kaesong Conference to resurrect the Thirty-eighth parallel as the truce line was Chou's declaration that the parallel had been "obliterated forever" as a "demarcation line of political geography."

Chou's terms obviously were unacceptable to the United States, and the Peiping government must have known this. They offered no prospect of security for the Korean Republic, no chance of establishing a free and united Korea. They would award two prizes for aggression; to accept them would be to multiply Communist victory.

The Western European allies, still fearful that the Korean war would expand over all Asia, thereby playing into suspected Russian schemes for conquest of Europe, clung momentarily to hopes that Peiping would soften its demands. Strong sentiment for seating Communist China in the United Nations and recognizing its authority over Formosa had survived the events since June 25th, although the dangers of outright appeasement were recognized in European capitals. Peiping offered no concessions, however. The United States gradually won support for its unyielding stand. With promises of increased military help by the United Nations Allies, the Eighth Army faced the impending renewal of a long and possibly hopeless war in South Korea.

The major burden of carrying the United Nations flag in Korea still rested on the United States, but the Eighth Army was beginning to take on an international color. Britain had sent two brigades, totalling perhaps ten thousand troops, plus fleet surface and air units, and a marine commando detachment. Australia, France, Holland, Belgium (with Luxembourg), Greece, the Philippines, and Siam had furnished infantry battalions. A Canadian infantry battalion, the Princess Pats, was on the way, in the vanguard of a full brigade. Turkey's five-thousand-man brigade already was upholding the Turk's reputation among the world's best fighters. A New Zealand artillery battalion was added to the British Commonwealth Brigade. South Africa contributed a Mustang fighter squadron, Greece a fleet of transport planes, Sweden a field hospital. Denmark was preparing to send a hospital ship, and India a field ambulance corps. Britain, Australia, Canada, New Zealand, and France had placed ships under the control of the United States Seventh Fleet commander for Korean duty.

The United Nations ground force contingents were composed largely of professional soldiers or volunteers who bolstered their countries' prestige, despite their small numbers. They were attached to American divisions, where they generally set a high standard of performance under pressure. Still, their total strength represented only a little more than one division, as against the United States' seven

divisions. When United States air and naval forces, headquarters staffs and service units, supply, relief, and other
contributions were considered, America's disproportionate
burden was even more apparent. Some of the western allies
had heavy military obligations elsewhere, such as France's
fight against Communist-led revolt in Indo-China. Korea
also was competing for military strength with the rearmament of Western Europe, a high-priority operation for the
United Nations majority. Nonetheless, it was with some
justice that American military men in Korea cursed this
one-sided alliance as they waited for the Chinese bugles
to blow again.

All signs along the roads leading down to the Thirty-
eighth parallel pointed toward a massive Chinese onslaught
some time after Christmas. The tempo of increased Chinese
and North Korean military movements was matched by
the exultant voices of Communist radio propagandists who
threatened imminent destruction of the United Nations
forces.

The Eighth Army shifted and stretched its thin lines
along and just south of the Thirty-eighth parallel and
waited. Only a token defense force guarded the central
mountain invasion route, northeast of Seoul. New, untested
ROK divisions held some important sections of the line.
There were not enough men for the job, and everyone knew
it.

*A young sergeant from Arkansas squatted in the noon-
thawing mud beside a foxhole and poked at his canned
lunch of C-ration ham and lima beans. With him on this
bare nose of a hill near the Thirty-eighth parallel were nine
even younger men. The sergeant was the only member of*

*the squad who had come to Korea with the division five
months earlier. He had been a private then, and much happier.*

*"Got a moose\* in Osaka and I'm gonna get back over
there to see her pretty soon if I have to go over the hill,"
he was saying. "I wrote her I'd be there Christmas."*

*"You ain't goin' over no hill," grunted a rifleman who
was scraping the melting snow away from his tiny fire.
"You're gonna stay here and fight the . . . Chinks like the
rest of us."*

*"If them ROK's over yonder start running again this
time, none of us will have to fight," said the sergeant. "We
can just bug out and try to keep up with 'em."*

*"I'm buggin' out when they start blowing the bugles,"
said another, but he didn't pause in cleaning his rifle.*

At this moment in its variable fortunes, the Eighth Army
lost General Walker. Like his World War II boss, George
Patton, "Johnny" Walker died in a highway accident. He
was riding along a narrow, icy road to the British Twenty-
seventh Brigade command post north of Seoul on December 23rd when a ROK army truck pulled out of line into
the path of his jeep. The sixty-year-old general died almost
instantly. His death came just as a recommendation for his
promotion to the four-star rank of full general was being
prepared. The promotion was made posthumously.

Within hours, the Pentagon appointed Lieutenant General Matthew B. Ridgway as the new commander. Ridgway, whose name already was being mentioned as the next
United States Army Chief of Staff, had been forewarned
that the Eighth Army command might go to him in just

* Occupation GI slang for the Japanese *musume*, sweetheart.

such an emergency. At his desk in Washington, where he was deputy chief of staff for administration, he had closely followed every phase of the war and was ready on short notice.

A 1917 graduate of West Point, Ridgway had missed overseas service during World War I. In the second World War he had organized and led on its first combat jump America's pioneer paratroop division, the Eighty-second Airborne. From Sicily he took the division to England and jumped with it in the Normandy invasion. In early 1945 he commanded the Eighteenth Airborne Corps in the final drive into north-central Germany. Until Japan capitulated, he was scheduled to lead the airborne phase of the invasion of the Japanese home islands. He became commander of the United States Mediterranean theater in late 1945, United States representative on the United Nations Military Staff Committee in 1947, and commander of the Caribbean theater in 1948.

Ridgway now faced one of the most difficult assignments ever given a new field commander. The Chinese assault was expected within the next seven days. The Tenth Corps' battered forces were just landing at Pohang and Pusan and needed rest, replacements, and equipment before they could join the Eighth Army on the Thirty-eighth parallel. The situation also offered opportunity for spectacular performance if Ridgway had the genius required to rekindle fighting spirit and exploit the know-how Allied soldiers had gained in five months of war.

In the first minute after his arrival in Tokyo on the night of December 26th he demonstrated a sure sense of diplomacy. Coming to MacArthur's domain and bearing the label of "Washington's man," he took pains to declare that he had long cherished the ambition of serving under Mac-Arthur, "one of the greatest military leaders in history."

He was still wearing his Washington uniform blouse, without overcoat, when he stepped from his plane to the frozen Korean ground on December 27th, four days after General Walker's death. He changed quickly to the paratroop combat gear, grenade harness, and field cap which henceforth became his trademarks.

Minutes counted now, and Ridgway moved fast. The Tenth Corps was placed under his command on December 27th, ending the hotly disputed division of United Nations field forces. There was little time to make use of its one hundred thousand men. Its two ROK divisions moved up the east coast to the parallel, but the line was still too thin. Ridgway covered most of the Eighth Army's front positions during the next three days, bounding from his jeep and striding across hills with a pace that exhausted men of half his fifty-five years. To a British brigade officer who showed Ridgway his plans for use in the Eighth Army's next withdrawal, the general replied: "I'm more interested in your plans for attack." To President Rhee, he said: "I am pleased to be in your country, and I aim to stay."

Bold words could not alter the facts, however. The Chinese massed overwhelming strength along the Thirty-eighth parallel near Kaesong, and the Eighth Army was forced to bend its lines back along Imjin River, abandoning a large slice of South Korean territory, on December 28th. Massive attack buildups were reported all along the still relatively quiet front, and there were signs that the Red Army had spotted Allied weakness in the center of the peninsula and were shifting into position to exploit it.

MacArthur's headquarters now estimated, in an intelligence summary calculated down to the sixth digit, that 443,406 Communist troops faced the United Nations forces in Korea—exactly 276,173 Chinese and 167,233 North Korean troops and guerrillas. In addition the Chinese were believed to have in Manchuria six hundred and fifty thousand troops available for assignment to Korea, and two hundred and fifty thousand more en route to Manchuria from other parts of China. Against this potential enemy force of more than a million troops, the United Nations had about two hundred and fifty thousand ground troops, including South Koreans, plus absolute command of the air and sea.

Almost at the moment that Rhee was assuring his people that Seoul was safe and that the government intended to remain at its post, the National Assembly voted on Christmas day to move to Pusan. Hundreds of government officials joined the exodus. Half of Seoul's million inhabitants had fled southward across the Han when Ridgway reached his advance headquarters. The Eighth Army already had moved most headquarters operations out of Seoul back to the old stand in Taegu.

Once again, five months to the day after the first Communist invasion, South Korea was to become the battleground of a war born at Potsdam, kindled in Moscow, and fought over ideologies exported to Korea by the great powers.

# XI

## *Rebound*

THE BUGLES BLEW on New Year's Eve, and Chinese screaming "Kill GI!" spread across snow-blanketed paddy fields like noisy locusts. Allied outposts along the barren ridges thirty miles north of Seoul were engulfed minutes after the pre-attack artillery barrage lifted and the assault began. From across nearly the entire front, urgent reports to Eighth Army headquarters added up to the long-awaited, "This is it."

A major attack swept across the thin ice of the Imjin River east of Kaesong into and around unyielding South Korean strongpoints. A second thrust pointed straight at Seoul, down the historic invasion highway from Chorwon into American lines. Inexperienced South Korean troops broke before a central front attack aimed at severing the Chunchon-Seoul supply and retreat highway. A fourth blow, farther east, was concentrated on the reorganized ROK Seventh and Eighth Divisions, battered survivors of the Chinese breakthrough drive during the November offensive.

American artillery boomed a defiant answer and machine guns cut the Chinese down like wheat. More Chinese swarmed forward to fill the gap, not in separate "human waves" but in a continuous flood of men, firing rifles, "burpguns," and captured American weapons as they advanced.

128

An American machine gunner reported later that he had kept firing until a dazed and glassy-eyed Chinese had stumbled into the smoking weapon and knocked it down. Front-line Allied infantrymen ran out of ammunition and fled for their lives, many to be trapped in fire-blocks set astride the roads by infiltrating enemy squads.

By midnight it was clear that this was a major offensive, involving most of the two hundred and fifty thousand Communist troops massed along the Thirty-eighth parallel. The planned withdrawal began. Some South Korean units, bent on avenging the Chongchon River defeat and restoring faith in the ROK Army, clung to their positions until they were surrounded, left behind by American withdrawals from their flanks. ROK divisions astride and east of the central highway through Chunchon were ripped apart by a North Korean attack, cut off from their scheduled retreat routes, and forced to fall back in separate regimental and smaller movements through the hills.

Most of the Eighth Army broke contact rapidly, however, and pulled back in orderly stages, protected by rear-guard regiments, toward the Han River. It was becoming a familiar operation. "We ought to be good at this," said an Eighth Army staff officer. "We've had plenty of practice."

The rumble of trucks through Seoul's almost deserted streets began early New Year's Day. By dusk the engineer bridges across the Han were carrying an unbroken procession of the wheeled and tracked monsters which move modern armies.

Some three hundred thousand Koreans had remained in Seoul, many on the strength of President Rhee's assurances that the capital would be defended. Now the final wave of panicky flight to the uncertain safety of the south began.

Rhee and his cabinet held out until early on January 3rd, then abandoned the capital and flew to Pusan.

The United States Twenty-fifth Division and the British Twenty-ninth Brigade had the assignment of holding back the tide of attacking Chinese until the rest of the Eighth Army was safely across the Han. The Communists pressed the attack furiously, abandoning camouflage and ignoring losses from around-the-clock air and artillery bombardment in a desperate attempt to trap the road-bound Allied retreat against the river.

The Twenty-ninth Brigade commander, Brigadier Thomas Brodie, ordered his men to stand on their lines and hold: "If you meet him (the enemy), you are to knock hell out of him with everything you have got. You are only to give ground on my orders." The brigade held, and a company of Royal Ulster Rifles was surrounded, suffering heavy casualties in fighting its way out.

The Anglo-American rear guard fell back on the fourth night to the outskirts of the ghost city. Fires, set by vandals or by carelessness, whipped through the old "thieves' market" and many of the western-style buildings which had escaped September's holocaust of liberation. Rifles cracked at every moving shadow. There were rumors that the Chinese had already crossed the Han downstream and were encircling the city.

It was all over quickly on January 4th. The last two companies—one American, one British—raced across the bridges about 1:30 P.M. Demolition crews set off the charges which marked the climax of another Allied retreat. Already the red flag of Communist Korea was flying over the scaffolding-shrouded capitol dome.

Kimpo and Inchon followed. The Air Force set the torch

to half a million gallons of gasoline and twenty-three thousand gallons of napalm which could not be saved in the hasty evacuation from its big Kimpo Air Base. Bulldozers gouged deep furrows in the runways. Bombers completed the destruction with two-thousand-pound bombs which made Kimpo resemble a telescopic view of the moon.

Inchon's partially rebuilt dock installations again were destroyed. American, British, Australian, Canadian, and Dutch warships standing off Inchon took aboard seven thousand men from the abandoned supply base and sailed for Pusan.

The Chinese made a show of continuing the attack south of the Han, but the main force of the drive had waned—again at the end of five days. Prisoners reported that Chinese troops went into the attack carrying enough maize and millet to last that length of time. Chinese divisions had no effective means of obtaining a steady flow of ammunition and other supplies during action against an enemy who controlled the air. After exhausting their initial load, they were virtually disarmed. However, a second echelon of fully armed divisions, nearly as strong as the assault echelon, could be passed through the spent forces to renew the attack. (Although this potential was a constant threat, in five major Chinese offensives it was never employed on an important scale.)

The Chinese sent only two complete "armies," the Fiftieth and the Thirty-eighth, south of Seoul in immediate pursuit of the Eighth Army. Battalion-sized reconnaissance forces from these army corps (a Chinese "army" is composed of three divisions of eight to ten thousand men each, and is comparable to a small American corps formation) occupied Kimpo and Inchon and on January 7th entered Suwon.

There another important airfield fell into Communist hands. Past the first American battleground of the war below Osan, now healed by time and camouflaged by snow, the retreating column moved.

But there was a difference. This time the United Nations had more than two hundred thousand organized, battle-tested, and well-equipped men to answer the Communist challenge. General Ridgway held the United States First Corps on the main highway south of Suwon, and shifted the Ninth Corps into position along secondary roads to the east. The Tenth Corps, reorganized to include the Second Division, Seventh Division, and two ROK divisions, blocked mountain roads down the center of the peninsula. The Marines were in army reserve near Taegu.

The Second Division stood and fought at Wonju, forty-five miles south of the Thirty-eighth parallel and gateway to the mountain passes leading to Taegu and Pusan. The division, although still suffering from its punishment at Kunu in late November, smashed a North Korean break-through drive and rekindled hope in the Allied world. Two European infantry battalions, the French and the Dutch, fought beside the Americans and played major rôles in the timely victory. The scale of the action was small, but the psychological stakes were great.

The battle opened on January 5th when a Second Division rescue column opened an escape route for trapped South Korean regiments attempting to withdraw down the Chunchon-Wonju axis. Four North Korean divisions, sustaining their attack after the Chinese push in the west had slowed, rammed into the Second Division defense line at Wonju. Fifth Air Force planes and Second Division artillery blasted the white mountains ringing the town, and the defenders held their ground. Slowly the North Koreans closed a pincers grip from east and west and drove into Wonju from the north. Fighting and withdrawing, street by street, the Second Division pulled back to the inverted horseshoe ridge south of the town on January 8th and dug in for the next round.

Blinding snowstorms swept across the hills, and at night the temperature dropped as low as twenty degrees below zero. Fighter planes and artillery observers were grounded; the American, French, and Dutch infantrymen were on their own. The division stretched its lines southward in a wedge, holding the apex below Wonju.

Two North Korean divisions shifted east of Wonju and found a gaping hole in United Nations lines. They drove twenty miles southward and threatened to isolate the Second Division salient. At this critical moment the Second Division counterattacked, driving back into Wonju. The audacious move, ordered by the corps commander, General Almond, was matched by a shift of Seventh Division and ROK troops into the east-central mountains to block the flanking drive. As quickly as it had attacked, the Second withdrew, sucking the Communists back in. Weather cleared and B-29 bombers and lighter planes pulverized Wonju with a saturation bombardment which shook the hills for miles around.

Thereafter, the North Koreans were able to launch attacks only in battalion strength. The Second Division fell back ten miles and straightened its lines for the next move while other Tenth Corps troops mopped up scattered bands of North Koreans in the mountains to the southeast. Parts of one full Korean Communist division, the Tenth, infiltrated across the Soebek mountain range and assembled thirty-five miles north of Taegu; it did not present a serious threat, however. Isolated from regular supplies, it degenerated into a guerrilla band and was gradually destroyed.

The Wonju battle alone did not turn the tide; the real enemy remained the Chinese Army, but it was a badly needed success at a dark hour. It stuck the first pin into what General Ridgway later called the "inflated balloon" of Communist military might. It proved to Allied fighting men that they were not yet "washed up," and it revived faith in American fire-power.

Tokyo and the Eighth Army still expected another major Chinese assault below Seoul. The Eighth Army's divisions dug in along strong points across the peninsula roughly fifty to sixty miles south of the Thirty-eighth parallel, deploying their strength in depth. They anticipated further retreat and set up division rear headquarters far to the south, in or near the old Pusan beachhead.

General Collins, back in Korea on his second flying visit from Washington in six weeks, said the United Nations Forces "certainly will stay in Korea and fight." He refused to predict, however, that they would prove strong enough to stay permanently.

Official Lake Success, Washington, and London swayed toward appeasement with each gloomy report from Korea and Tokyo, then stiffened and reasserted their nearly abandoned principles when Ridgway's army began making hopeful news.

Peace at almost any price was the majority attitude at Lake Success in early January of 1951. The United States had promised in December to go along with the majority on Korean policy. On January 13th the General Assembly was called to a vote on a new peace plan which offered an

almost certain capitulation to Peiping on both Formosa
and United Nations membership in exchange for a Korean
settlement satisfactory to the West. This was in direct con-
tradiction to United States policy and Acheson's recent
statements, but the State Department directed delegate
Warren Austin to vote with the majority as a demonstra-
tion of American desire for peace and respect for the western Allies' views. While angry congressional and editorial
protest mounted in the United States, the General Assembly passed, 50 to 7,* a five-point proposal calling for:

1. An immediate cease-fire in Korea with guarantees
against use of the truce as a screen for mounting a new offensive.

2. Action during the truce on a permanent Korean settlement.

3. Withdrawal of "non-Korean" troops by "appropriate
stages."

4. United Nations-approved administration of all Korea during the truce.

5. Creation of a special United Nations agency, including Red China, Russia, Britain, and the United States, to
settle outstanding Far Eastern issues, including the future
of Formosa and Chinese representation in the United Nations.

Senator Robert Taft called point five of the plan "the
most complete surrender to which the United States has
ever agreed," and Democrats joined Republicans in de-
nouncing Secretary of State Acheson.

Now Peiping overplayed its hand. On January 17th,
Chou En-lai countered with a demand for all that the Gen-

* The Soviet bloc opposed the plan on the ground that Communist
China and North Korea were not parties to its preparation.

eral Assembly's proposal implied and much more. He called for a seven-nation conference on Korea and other Far Eastern issues to be held while the war continued. By rejecting the principle of cease-fire first, then negotiation, China sought to retain the club of its apparently crushing military superiority on the Korean peninsula—a club it could wield freely during the conference. In addition, Chou demanded a United Nations seat for Communist China effective with the opening of the conference. He proposed that the conference be held in China, and named Russia, Britain, the United States, France, India, Egypt, and Communist China as the seven participating nations.

Secretary of State Acheson quickly called Chou's reply a "complete rejection" of the United Nations proposal. He defended American participation in the offer, saying it had enhanced the United States' moral position and had served to unmask Chinese aggressive intentions. "We must face squarely and soberly the fact that the Chinese Communists have no intention of ceasing their defiance of the United Nations," he said. "The strength of the United Nations will lie in the firmness and unity with which we move ahead." Acheson instructed the United States delegation at Lake Success to press for a United Nations vote branding Communist China as an aggressor.

Britain and a bloc of Asian-Arab states led by India refused to consider Chou's reply a flat rejection of the conciliatory peace plan. Peiping encouraged their optimism by modifying its position to the extent of agreeing to discuss a cease-fire as the first item on the agenda of the proposed Far Eastern peace conference. The Chinese Communists continued, however, to demand United Nations membership as the price for even attending the conference.

More encouraging news now was coming from Korea;

the Chinese monster was beginning to seem less awesome. The United States began gaining ground in its campaign to name Red China as the aggressor in Korea and an enemy of the United Nations.

The day Chou En-lai rejected the best terms he was likely to get from the United Nations, General Ridgway's army took the first cautious steps along the road back.

All across the Eighth Army's front, American tank-infantry patrols poked tentatively northward into what intelligence reports had described as a growing Chinese "attack buildup." They found unexpected weakness. One armored force plunged sixteen miles back toward Seoul, dashed into Suwon and bloodied the nose of a surprised Chinese regiment, then withdrew without suffering a single casualty. Other strong reconnaissance patrols probed out five to fifteen miles across no-man's land before hitting a firm Chinese line. During the next seven days it became apparent that reports by air observers and intelligence agents of a massive Communist buildup south of the Han had been exaggerated.

General MacArthur was sufficiently encouraged to voice publicly on January 20th the conviction he had held for some weeks: "No one is going to drive us into the sea. This command intends to maintain a military position in Korea just as long as the statesmen of the United Nations decide we should do so."

Thus armed with encouragement, two weeks after it had offered a virtual surrender to Communist China, the General Assembly voted overwhelmingly to pin the label of "aggressor" on the Peiping régime.

The pendulum had swung a long way since New Year's Eve. Ridgway decided to act before it could swing back.

# XII

## *The Red Bubble Bursts*

RIDGWAY'S ANSWER TO Chinese numbers was delivered the day he started his fifth week in Korea. On division war maps it was labeled "Operation Killer." Its objective was to whittle down the Communist Army by killing Communist soldiers. It had no formal territorial objectives. Any piece of ground in Korea which the Eighth Army could use to its advantage in rooting out, killing, or capturing Chinese and North Koreans was to be sought. If successful, the operation also would score advances back toward North Korea, since it had to close constantly with the enemy. This would accomplish another Ridgway goal—reviving morale and confidence among his almost beaten men.

Civilized people who winced and protested when they read of "Operation Killer" demonstrated their misunderstanding of the assignment the United Nations Allies had given a small, outnumbered army of men in Korea. They apparently had not allowed the naked meaning of the term "war of attrition" to soak into their consciousness. Perhaps some had never understood the terrible meaning of war itself. Some Americans, while admitting the necessity of Ridgway's scheme, suggested that the bloodthirsty tone of its name would build ill will against the United States in

Asia. This protest possibly embodied a misunderstanding of the Oriental's capacity for realism, unhampered by the Christian ethics.

If the United States government's determination to persevere in Korea was to offer any hope of net gain for the free world, then it was necessary to improve the bargaining position of the United Nations majority. No recognized military authority, in Washington, Tokyo, or Korea, saw any chance of winning a complete military victory against the Chinese so long as operations were confined to Korea. (The Joint Chiefs of Staff later testified that they did not share MacArthur's belief that complete victory could be won even by a practicable extension of the war to China.) There was a reasonable chance, however, that by using Allied fire power and mobility to the maximum, the United Nations army could hurt the Chinese so badly in Korea that they would agree to an acceptable peace settlement. This hope sustained the Truman administration while it faced politically dangerous criticism for "condemning American soldiers to fight an endless war with one hand tied behind their backs." Ridgway approached his job with an enthusiastically demonstrated conviction that the required limited victory could be won.

On January 25th, heavily armed tank-infantry patrols moved out across the ten-mile-wide no-man's land south and southeast of Seoul. Hitting hard and fast, they rammed into Chinese and North Korean positions, opened fire, pulled back and called in artillery and air strikes by radio, then hit again. At night the patrols withdrew, but to a line which had advanced closer to the enemy. Larger armored "killing forces" went out the next day, and behind them battalion and regimental-sized infantry forces moved for-

ward into blocking positions to meet a possible counterattack. Tanks broke through Chinese outpost lines and shot
up Communist positions from the rear, then dashed full
speed back to safety. The blocking positions moved forward
each day. Almost imperceptibly, what had been hit-and-
run patrol action became a "limited offensive."

This, said veteran tankers, was the way armor was intended to be used. It took ex-paratrooper Ridgway to do it.

On the central front—east, west, and north of Wonju—
the burden fell more heavily on the infantryman. There
the roads for tank movement were fewer and smaller; the
mountains had made a great concession to farmers and soldiers when they permitted a valley to spread as much as
half a mile wide.

Over all fronts the Fifth Air Force enjoyed a gory picnic.
As the ground attack flushed out entrenched and camouflaged Communist pockets, F-80 Shooting Stars, F-84 Thun-
derjets, and F-51 Mustangs pounced on them with rockets,
machine guns, and napalm.* The Mustangs laid a carpet of
liquid hell across the front southeast of Seoul in a mass
napalm raid. The arrival of America's fastest jet fighters,
F-86 Sabrejets, best suited for dueling with the even faster
Communist MIG-15's along the northwest frontier, had
freed all other air force fighters for support of the offensive.

Vastly improved air-ground co-ordination brought the
fighters in on targets within minutes or even seconds after
they were sighted by ground controllers, advance army
units, or air spotters who hovered over enemy lines in light
observation planes.

The air force had been at work before the Eighth Army

* Jellied gasoline bombs which explode in a shower of liquid, burning at
about two thousand degrees Fahrenheit.

struck back. Under orders to destroy every suspected hiding place of the mysteriously invisible enemy, fighters and bombers had set out in early January on a systematic campaign of devastation. Nearly every village and clump of buildings in a broad belt north of the Allied line came under attack. Most of the South Koreans in the area had left their homes and fields and joined the refugee movement into the deep south. Many, however, remained to be killed, wounded, or made homeless by their allies. It was a tragic story to be often repeated, later with the variation that its victims became North Korean civilians as the battle moved back across the Thirty-eighth parallel. The air force and army argued that there was no alternative. Civilians had been warned to evacuate the battle zone, which for the air force stretched far to the north. Communist troops were known to be taking cover from observation, attack, and winter cold in farmhouses, schools, and churches—every type of building.

Advancing Allied troops found evidence of another tragedy along the roads. The bodies of Korean women and children, now frozen, lay beside blood-tinged blots in the snow. They had been refugees, fleeing toward safety down the same roads the Communist Army had taken. At five hundred miles an hour, a jet pilot could not distinguish them from the motley, often disguised troops of the pursuing enemy.

The Chinese abandoned Suwon on January 26th and the air force gained an excellent airfield minutes away from the front. Hoengsong, ten miles north of Wonju, fell two days later. On the east coast, South Korean troops, supported by naval gunfire, took Kangnung, twenty miles below the Thirty-eighth parallel. A week after the cautious offensive had opened, the First Corps' international force of Americans, British, South Koreans, and Turks was within nine miles of Seoul. More important, the Eighth Army Fifth Air Force offensive was killing an estimated one thousand Communist troops a day and wounding three or four times that many.

Resistance stiffened all across the front during the second week. Holed up in caves and bunkers, the Chinese and North Koreans withstood thundering artillery bombardment and direct fire from tanks. When it seemed that no living thing could have survived, rifle and machine-gun fire cracked from the hillside entrenchments. Allied infantrymen were compelled to climb and crawl up the hills and dig the stubborn ones out, sometimes with bayonets.

Nervously, intelligence officers and commanders watched for signs that the Chinese were reinforcing their two armies south of the Han or preparing a counterattack. Small groups did cross the Han from Seoul, and previously unidentified North Korean units began appearing on the line, but that was all on the western front.

On February 9th and 10th, the Twenty-fifth Division, the British Twenty-ninth Brigade, and the Turkish Brigade broke through the last tough crust of resistance and drove to the Han. Yongdungpo, Kimpo, and Inchon, names which revived memories of September's victories, were liberated for the second and last time. The green beer of Yongdungpo's brewery was still there, and a new group of thirsty GI's had one of those small treats which mean so much in the distorted world in which a soldier lives.

The advance in the west was a locked-elbows, solid front movement, with plenty of strength in depth to meet a counterattack. On the Tenth Corps' central front there were not enough men for such a cautious movement. The mountains here sided with the unmechanized Communists, but the enemy appeared to be largely North Korean, so less caution seemed required.

Five fingers of men probed northward in a fan-shaped advance north, east, and west of Hoengsong. One reached a point in the mountains twenty-five miles from the Thirty-eighth parallel. On the Eighth Army's war map the central front looked dangerously like October's race to the Yalu.

The Communists counterattacked on the night of February 12th. They mauled or cut off all five Allied fingers, attacking out of the mountains to the sides and behind the American and ROK task forces. Again the victims were the United States Second Division and the ROK Eighth Division. A battalion of the Thirty-eighth Infantry Regiment, Second Division, and supporting artillery batteries were cut off on the road above Hoengsong. The trapped American attempted to make a dash for safety through the crossfire of North Koreans lining the road; few survived to tell the story of that night in "Massacre Valley." Other Thirty-eighth Regiment battalions fared little better. The attached Dutch Battalion, standing at Hoengsong to hold open an escape route, was hit by infiltrators, then brought under full-scale attack. Its commander, Lieutenant Colonel M. P. A. den Ouden, was killed in his command post.

The Eighth ROK Division virtually ceased to exist.

The main Chinese attack came west of Hoengsong, against a four-thousand-man regimental combat team composed of the Second Division's Twenty-third Regiment and the attached French Battalion. Here the Chinese received more than they bargained for.

The Franco-American force pulled back into the mountain-ringed village of Chipyong and did not attempt to flee southward to safety. Four Chinese divisions surrounded the Chipyong garrison, attacking day and night for three days. They lobbed mortars into the center of the two-mile-wide Allied pocket and charged with bayonets and grenades. The French counter-attacked with their own bayonets. The American regimental commander, Colonel Paul Freeman, was wounded and evacuated—under protest—by helicopter. On the afternoon of the fourth day a relief column of the Fifth Cavalry Regiment tanks broke through the Communist cordon from the southwest. Its accompanying infantry company took heavy casualties; many wounded cavalrymen were captured. The siege of Chipyong lifted almost simultaneously with the arrival of the relief column. Withdrawing remnants of the four attacking divisions left hillsides literally covered with Chinese dead.

The slaughter at Chipyong was equalled on the front immediately northwest of Wonju. American artillery was "zeroed in" on every road and valley leading to Wonju and the lateral highway west of the town. Chinese and North Korean troops marched in suicidal column formation down the roads. Artillery opened upon them, and still more rigidly disciplined Communists advanced into certain death. The Tenth Corps claimed ten thousand casualties a day on February 14th and 15th.

The "Wonju Shoot" and the valiant stand at Chipyong broke the back of the Communist counteroffensive. A general Chinese retreat from the central front began on February 16th.

The Eighth Army already had demonstrated that it could advance against the vaunted Chinese Communist army and inflict casualties at a rate of ten or more to every allied loss.

At Wonju and Chipyong it proved to itself and to the world that it could meet and destroy a Chinese offensive.

*Standing before a floodlit relief map in Taegu, General Ridgway outlined plans for renewing the Allied attack. It was a confidential briefing for Allied news correspondents. He spoke with a quiet eloquence which few military men, other than MacArthur, can equal. Somehow I didn't expect this from a bounding, robust general who wore paratroop gear and the inevitable grenade at a headquarters one hundred miles from the battlefront.*

*It was not mere showmanship. What he had to say reflected a deep insight into the psychology of his own troops and of the enemy. What he had already done in helping the Eighth Army regain faith in itself recommended him for a place in the select company of the great.*

When "Operation Killer" jumped off again on February 20th, Allied front-line strength equalled the Communist army's front-line numbers for the first time since the "home by Christmas" débâcle. Intelligence estimated that nearly two hundred thousand Communist troops in six Chinese "armies" (two of which had been crippled in the western front drive to the Han) and remnants of three North Korean corps faced the Eighth Army. Almost exactly this number of Allied troops—all seven American divisions, four ROK divisions, and most of the smaller United Nations contingents—were on the line. Except for the United States Third and ROK First Divisions on the extreme western flank below Seoul, all were attacking.

American staff officers were loath to admit this numerical equality, because the enemy still had possibly two hundred thousand troops in reserve along and north of the Thirty-eighth parallel, while the Eighth Army was throwing almost every available unit into action. They also pointed out that, with a one hundred and ninety thousand men, the Chinese and North Koreans could put far more riflemen and machine gunners on the line than could the complex, supply-laden American army. This apparent disadvantage, of course, had been known and accepted by the authors of western military doctrine for decades. It was the price the American army had chosen to pay for tremendous artillery firepower, unrestricted flow of supplies and ammunition to the front, mobility, and sustained operations—all the applications of American industrial might and wealth which were cheered during World War II.

The renewed Eighth Army attack was planned in two phases. The first was to wipe out the sagging dip in United Nations lines left by the Communists' central front counter-offensive and to eliminate a pocket of Chinese still holding south of the Han River east of Seoul. The second was the critical test: it was to ram head-on into the main Chinese concentrations east and northeast of Seoul.

The first phase lasted two weeks and knocked out of effective action three North Korean divisions. The Chinese abandoned their bridgehead pocket south of the Han and pulled back into a fifty-mile-wide concentration between Seoul and Chunchon.

The United States First Marine Division, back in action, drove up the central highway through Hoengsong and "Massacre Valley," past the grotesque forms of men frozen in violent death. The United States Second and Seventh Divisions moved slowly through the east-central mountain wilderness, flushing out North Koreans and swinging northward in a wide arc. The Seventh, Third, and Fifth ROK Divisions attacked on the flanks of this movement.

The Communists gave ground stubbornly, but by March 6th the United Nations line ran almost straight across the peninsula from the banks of the Han below Seoul in the west to a point less than twenty miles below the Thirty-eighth parallel on the east coast.

Ridgway called his shots for the second and most important phase of the offensive in another off-the-record press briefing. The objective was the destruction in place of six Chinese armies dug in along the mountains east of Seoul. He would concentrate Eighth Army striking power against this enemy mass and ignore Seoul itself. The North Korean commander holding Seoul would think his forces threatened by an apparent flanking maneuver aimed at the city as the Eighth Army pushed northward against the Chinese. Finally he would probably decide to evacuate. A feint toward double envelopment might be required to hasten his decision. Without diverting forces from the main objective and without wasting an Allied soldier's life, Ridgway predicted he would recapture Seoul by "imposing a threat against the mind of the enemy commander."

Chunchon, an important road-hub city seven miles south of the Thirty-eighth parallel and exactly in the center of the peninsula, was believed to be the supply depot of the Communist Army in South Korea. Six weeks of intensive effort was reported to have gone into building up its stockpiles of everything the Chinese needed to resume their southward drive in the Spring. Ridgway proposed to capture Chunchon, possibly by an airborne operation or by use of armored task forces, before the Chinese could haul their supply hoard away.

At dawn on March 7th, massed American artillery served thundering notice on the Chinese that a pile-driver offensive was on. Twenty-fifth Division infantrymen climbed into rubber assault boats and a motley fleet of river craft and attacked Chinese positions on the north bank of the Han, fifteen miles east of Seoul. Farther east, the Twenty-fourth and First Cavalry Divisions rammed squarely into the Chinese mountain lair. Marines advanced up the central highway toward Chunchon. Below Seoul, Allied troops made menacing motions toward the city but did not attack. On the east-central front, the Tenth Corps renewed its hill-by-hill campaign against the North Koreans.

On the first day of the attack the Eighth Army claimed a new record toll of Communist casualties: 11,400 in twenty-four hours, exclusive of air force claims.

The enemy commanders reacted precisely as Ridgway had predicted. Under relentless attack, the Chinese fell back slowly through the mountains east of Seoul. The Twenty-fifth Division's bridgehead deepened and finally reached the Chunchon-Seoul highway. The North Korean First Corps commander ordered retreat from Seoul.

Five ROK foot patrols crossed the Han during the early evening of March 14th and entered Seoul. One very optimistic patrol leader carried a South Korean flag, little expecting to use it. They found only a few starving old people and ragged children. The North Koreans had fled, taking pro-Communists and all able-bodied men and women with them as bearers. The optimistic patrol leader snatched down the Communist flag which had flown over the capitol for ten weeks. Up went the red-and-blue banner of the Republic. The patrols pulled back to the river's edge for the rest of the night.

The next morning Seoul was firmly liberated by a patrol of eight Allied war correspondents; two American infantrymen and one British jeep driver went along to make it official. The United States Third and ROK First Divisions followed. They found the city about seventy-five per cent. destroyed—only slightly worse than on the Eighth Army's hasty departure on January 4th.

Almost simultaneously with the North Korean evacuation from Seoul, the Chinese began falling back across the entire west central front, leaving only a thin covering force to delay the Allied advance. Chunchon fell without a fight on March 21st to a First Cavalry Division armored task force. This time Ridgway's plans went awry. The great Chinese supply cache was not there. The Chinese probably could not have moved northward in two weeks—under day-and-night air attack—what they had required six weeks to assemble. Ridgway readily admitted that his intelligence had been faulty.

Now the Communists were in full retreat from South Korea. Ridgway tried to trap ten to twenty thousand North Koreans above Seoul in a three-armed pincers closed by a parachute drop and two great armored task forces. The 187th Airborne Regiment jumped near Munsan, twenty miles north of Seoul on the Imjin River on March 23rd. A tank column driving up the Seoul-Munsan highway was to chase the Reds into Munsan and reinforce the paratroopers for the clean-up. A second armored force drove into Uijongbu the next day and turned westward to close the last Communist escape route. The maneuver ran smoothly, but the North Koreans were not there. Only a few stragglers were captured; the bulk of the enemy forces, both Chinese and

North Korean, had escaped across the Thirty-eighth parallel.

Again, as the battleline inched back toward that discredited but symbolic border, the war of words—second front of the Korean war—flared into significant activity. This time it produced a major casualty: General Douglas MacArthur.

# XIII

## *The MacArthur Controversy*

At the top level of government, the realms of the military and of politics are merged, or at least blurred. At a level just below the top, a fine line of distinction between the functions of diplomacy and of military science can usually be drawn, but not invariably. American theater commanders waging the complex campaigns of World War II, leading international forces in operations which would reshape the political destinies of millions, were constantly required to make essentially political decisions. In the postwar years, the voices of military men have played a major rôle in guiding American foreign policy. General MacArthur in the Far East, and General Eisenhower and others in Europe, exercised authority which could be separated from policy-making only by the most precise definition.

In Japan, during a brilliantly successful occupation, General MacArthur had quickly assumed supreme power and exercised it in a manner generally applauded by both the American people and government. He was more than a subordinate in the executive branch of the American government. He was the representative of the Allied powers in Japan, and his responsibilities were political, economic, and to only a lesser extent military. To the Japanese he was

151

Democracy's Emperor, a demi-god of unchallenged authority. To Washington he often was a source of irritation, for he made it quite clear that he was steering his own ship and needed no help. He complied with all official orders, however, and his record of achievement was a credit to the United States Government.

Following the Communist conquest of China, MacArthur became increasingly outspoken in his criticism of American policy in Asia. A procession of visitors to his Tokyo headquarters, as well as news correspondents, freely obtained and made public his program for fighting Asiatic Communism. The general expressed his views on matters outside Japan only when they were solicited, and then only in a general, positive manner, rather than in negative criticism. Nevertheless, each revelation from Tokyo amounted to an attack on the adopted policies of his nominal superior, President Truman. Official Washington was frequently reported to be angered but did little to silence its chief representative and most effective critic in the Far East.

An intensely dedicated man, MacArthur acted only in what he regarded as the best interests of his country and the cause of freedom. Thirty years of high office and almost unbroken success had imbued him with great self-confidence. He had graduated from the military academy at West Point in 1903 with an academic average which still stands as the highest ever achieved. At thirty-seven, he was the youngest American division commander in World War I. At thirty-nine, he was West Point's youngest superintendent. At fifty, he was the youngest Chief of Staff. Some of his superiors in the Pentagon in 1946–1951 had been lieutenants and captains when MacArthur was a general.

When President Truman and the democratic majority

at Lake Success decided to go to the aid of invaded South Korea, MacArthur welcomed the opportunity to come to grips with Communist aggression. He believed that the Korean intervention and the parallel decision to protect Nationalist China's Formosa from Communist invasion represented a shift toward his viewpoint. In July he made an official visit to Chiang Kai-shek on Formosa and embarrassed the Truman administration by giving the public impression that the American alliance with Chiang was being revived. His critics were quick to charge that MacArthur was again trying to make policy, failing to draw that fine line between military and political affairs. This was the first of what became, in the eyes of the Truman administration, a new series of "MacArthur incidents."

In late August MacArthur provoked a second incident by criticizing the administration's "hands-off-Formosa" policy in a message sent to the Veterans of Foreign Wars convention. When Truman learned of the message before the delivery date he ordered MacArthur to withdraw it, but he could not stop its publication.

MacArthur's spectacular victory over the North Korean army overshadowed past disagreements. All hatchets apparently were buried at the very cordial Wake Island Conference in mid-October. When Allied fortunes and the personal prestige of General MacArthur plummeted following the Chinese Communist intervention in North Korea, Washington remained friendly and defended his conduct of the war.

The new situation in Korea demanded new decisions. When they were not immediately forthcoming, MacArthur began publicly to press his views.* He called for swift

* See pp. 117–118 *ante.*

retaliation against Communist China based on a recognition that the United Nations was already at undeclared war with the Chinese. He proposed complete reorientation of American policy around the concept of Asia, rather than Europe, as the current decisive battleground against Communist conquest. These proposals were not made openly and bluntly. They were advanced only by implication in a series of statements issued in late November and early December. All the statements were presented as a military leader's analysis of a military situation.

The policy decisions announced by President Truman on December 8th and subsequently elaborated upon at Lake Success were, in MacArthur's eyes, no decisions at all. Washington had decided that MacArthur's forces would fight on in Korea, without retaliating against the Chinese mainland or otherwise initiating any action to expand the war. MacArthur was to "resist aggression" but not to strike back at the nation which spawned that aggression. Limited war, leading at best to limited victory, was the policy. The bleak future this program offered to the men in Korea, MacArthur believed, was a prolonged war of attrition ending in a negotiated compromise with the aggressors. To the rest of the world, Washington believed, it offered a greater chance of avoiding atomic World War III. Europe remained the prime theater and Russia the number one enemy in Washington's strategy.

MacArthur was silent for a short time after receiving another warning on December 7th to clear policy statements with appropriate Washington authority. The order was addressed to all United States "officials overseas, including military commanders." It instructed them to "clear all but routine statements with their departments and to refrain from direct communications on military or foreign policy with newspapers, magazines or other publicity media."

The strong-willed general did not keep his silence long. He never abandoned his conviction that anything less than forceful retaliation against China was appeasement which only postponed that showdown fight in Asia which he believed inevitable. He bitterly resented being called upon to fight, in the closing moments of his illustrious career, a war he could not win. In January and February he again inserted in what his aides called "routine military announcements" thinly veiled protests against the "restrictions" imposed upon his air operations which gave the enemy a "privileged sanctuary" and "unprecedented advantage."

In March he thoroughly reopened the issue. The Eighth Army had survived the crisis and was driving back toward the Thirty-eighth parallel, destroying thousands of Communist troops. The distasteful war of attrition was succeeding, and Allied confidence was reviving. There was talk of pushing back into North Korea. MacArthur chose this moment to declare that the best his troops or the enemy could hope for was a fluid and endless stalemate, involving continuous bloodshed and destruction. Again he called for "vital decisions" on the governmental level to meet the "problem raised by Red China's undeclared war in Korea." He issued the statement at a press conference held at Suwon airstrip on March 7th, a few hours after the Eighth Army had jumped off in its renewed offensive.

*The general sat behind a folding wooden table at the end of a small command tent. He had shed an outer coat but still wore his battered leather jacket, with the unnecessary nameplate, "MacArthur," stenciled in gold across the left side. He read slowly and deliberately from a penciled manuscript, pausing to insure that he had been clearly understood. We soon realized that this was a statement which to him and to the world was of more than passing importance.*

"Progress of the campaign continues to be satisfactory," he said, "with all three services—army, navy and air—performing well their completely co-ordinated tactical missions. Designed to meet abnormal military inhibitions, our strategic plan, involving constant movement to keep the enemy off balance with a correspondent limitation upon his initiative, remains unaltered.

"Our selection of the battle area, furthermore, has forced him into the military disadvantage of fighting far from his base and permitted greater employment of our air and sea arms against which he has little defense. There has been a resultant continuing and exhausting attrition upon both his manpower and supplies. There should be no illusions in this matter, however. In such a campaign of maneuver, as our battle lines shift north the supply position of the enemy will progressively improve, just as inversely the effectiveness of our air potential will progressively diminish, thus in turn causing his numerical ground superiority to become of increasing battlefield significance.

"Assuming no diminution of the enemy's flow of ground forces and matériel to the Korean battle area, a continuation of the existing limitation upon our freedom of counter-offensive action, and no major additions to our organizational strength, the battle lines cannot fail in time to reach a point of theoretical military stalemate. Thereafter our further advance would militarily benefit the enemy more than it would ourselves.

"The exact place of stabilization is of necessity a fluctuating variable dependent upon the shifting relative strengths of forces committed and will constantly move up *or down. Even now there are indications that the enemy is attempting to build up from China a new and massive offensive for the Spring. There are the salient factors which must continue to delimit strategical thinking and planning as the campaign proceeds.*

*"This does not alter the fact, however, that the heavy toll we have taken of the enemy's military power since its commitment to war in Korea cannot fail to weaken his hold upon the Chinese nation and people and materially dampen his ardor for engaging in other aggressive adventure in Asia.*

*"Even under our existing conditions of restraint it should be clearly evident to the Communist foes now committed against us that they cannot hope to impose their will in Korea by military force. They have failed twice— once through North Korean forces, and now through the military might of the army of Communist China. Theirs was the aggression in both cases. Theirs had been the double failure. That they should continue this savage slaughter despite an almost hopeless chance of ultimate military success is a measure of wanton disregard of international decencies and restraints and displays a complete contempt for the sanctity of human life.*

*"No longer is there even a shallow pretense of concern for the welfare of the Korean nation and people, now being so ruthlessly and senselessly sacrificed. Through endless bloodshed it is apparently hoped to enforce either international banditry or blackmail, or both."*

*The general paused and looked up from his papers before reading the final paragraph, then continued:*

*"Vital decisions have yet to be made—decisions far beyond the scope of the authority vested in me as the military commander, decisions which are neither solely po-*

*litical nor solely military, but which must provide on the
highest international levels an answer to the obscurities
which now becloud the unsolved problems raised by Red
China's undeclared war in Korea."*

*The possible effects of this declaration on the morale of
Eighth Army's troops and on opinion in the United States
were evident to nearly every correspondent as we struggled
with telephone connections to army headquarters. We
called it MacArthur's "die for a tie" statement, because in
effect he was telling the troops that they were being called
upon to do just that because their governments had no
policy except to muddle through. MacArthur's remarks,
of course, were aimed at readers far from Korea.*

Five days later, General Ridgway took pains to put Washington's policy in a better light. Without flatly disagreeing with his five-star commander's military estimate, Ridgway viewed Allied prospects on a positive note, and he gave his troops assurance that they were winning an important victory.

"We didn't set out to conquer China," he told correspondents summoned to his advance command post. "We set out to stop Communism. We have demonstrated the superiority on the battlefield of our men. If China fails to throw us into the sea, that is a defeat for her of incalculable proportions. If China fails to drive us from Korea, she will have failed monumentally."

Already, he said, the United Nations forces had "let a lot of air out of the inflated balloon of Communist China's military might."

"The things for which we are fighting here are of such overwhelming importance I can't conceive of any member of our fighting forces feeling that there lies ahead any field of indefinite or indeterminate action.

"This war is positive from beginning to end, and the potentialities are positive."

Ridgway's statement won applause at Lake Success, where October's determination to unify Korea by force had been quietly replaced by hopes for a cease-fire somewhere near the Thirty-eighth parallel and a new try at political unification.

Two days later MacArthur pressed his campaign for a freer hand with an ever clearer statement of his views. In a message responding to a question submitted by President Hugh Baillie of the United Press, MacArthur said: "The problem (of future strategy) involved requires much more fundamental decisions than are within my authority or responsibility to make as the military commander—decisions which must not ignore the heavy cost in Allied blood which a protracted and indecisive campaign would entail."

On March 24th he went further. Washington had informed the Tokyo headquarters that a new statement of Allied peace aims and a proposal for a military armistice were being drafted for submission to the Chinese Communists. Before they could be issued, MacArthur stepped in with his own offer to meet the enemy commander and work out a cease-fire. He coupled with the offer—which he had not cleared with Washington—an implied threat that unless the Chinese accepted, the United Nations might abandon its "tolerant effort to contain the war to the area of Korea" and launch military operations against the Chinese mainland.

MacArthur dropped this bombshell as a special press release, distributed in Tokyo just as he was departing on a mystery-shrouded flight to Korea. He said:

"Operations continue according to schedule and plan. We have now substantially cleared South Korea of organized Communist forces. It is becoming increasingly evident that the heavy destruction along the enemy's lines of supply, caused by our 'round-the-clock massive air and naval bombardment, has left his troops in the forward battle area deficient in requirements to sustain his operations.

"This weakness is being brilliantly exploited by our ground forces. The enemy's human wave tactics definitely failed him as our own forces became seasoned to this form of warfare; his tactics of infiltration are but contributing to his piecemeal losses, and he is showing less stamina than our own troops under rigors of climate, terrain, and battle.

"Of even greater significance than our tactical success has been the clear revelation that this new enemy, Red China, of such exaggerated and vaunted military power, lacks the industrial capacity to provide adequately many critical items essential to the conduct of modern war.

"He lacks manufacturing bases and those raw materials needed to produce, maintain and operate even moderate air and naval power, and he cannot provide the essentials for successful ground operations, such as tanks, heavy artillery, and other refinements science has introduced into the conduct of military campaigns.

"Formerly his great numerical potential might well have filled this gap, but with the development of existing methods of mass destruction, numbers alone do not offset vulnerability inherent in such deficiencies. Control of the sea and air, which in turn means control over supplies, communications, and transportation, are no less essential and decisive now than in the past.

"When this control exists as in our case and is coupled

On April 5th, when the administration thought it had finally placed MacArthur in the position of either accepting his government's policies or resigning, Martin read the general's reply before the House of Representatives. It was a bluntly worded attack on President Truman's policies, issued to the leader of the opposition party.

"My views and recommendations with respect to the situation created by Red China's entry into war against us in Korea have been submitted to Washington in most complete detail," MacArthur wrote. "Generally, these views are well-known and clearly understood, as they follow the conventional pattern of meeting force with maximum counter-force as we have never failed to do in the past. Your view with respect to the utilization of the Chinese forces in Formosa is in conflict with neither logic nor this tradition.

"It seems strangely difficult for some to realize that here in Asia is where the Communist conspirators have elected to make their play for global conquest, and that we have joined the issue thus raised on the battlefield; that here we fight Europe's war with arms, while the diplomats there still fight it with words; that if we lost the war to Communism in Asia the fall of Europe is inevitable; win it, and Europe most probably would avoid war yet preserve freedom. As you point out, we must win. There is no substitute for victory."

President Truman read the letter a few minutes later when it was bulletined out on press association teletypes. He was later reported to have made up his mind at this moment that there was no way out except to dismiss MacArthur. The President believed that the general's outspoken disagreement with the policies he was required to support could never be resolved. He considered MacArthur's action a challenge to the tradition of civilian control of the military and a violation of the obligations which any man, especially a military officer, assumes when he enters government service. Secretary of Defense Marshall, Chairman Bradley of the Joint Chiefs, and Secretary of State Acheson agreed, although Acheson was later reported to have urged caution in dealing with the hero of the Pacific.

The military chiefs held an emergency meeting on Sunday, April 8th, and Washington buzzed with rumors that stern action against MacArthur was being planned. Congressional Democratic leaders saw the President and came away with the conviction that the last straw had been added. Still no announcement came from the White House. Newsmen and columnists, who had forgotten Harry Truman's courage in past emergencies, speculated that he would not dare fire the popular genius in Tokyo in defense of the unpopular State Department's policies. Republican leaders, sensing a crisis, took the offensive with demands for the dismissal of Acheson and a congressional hearing in Washington for MacArthur.

While the storm was brewing, Secretary of the Army Frank Pace, Jr., arrived in Tokyo on what was billed as a "routine" trip. It apparently was just that. When he left Washington there had been no formal decision on the dismissal of MacArthur. Pace said later that he did not forewarn MacArthur during his conferences with the general on April 9th.

Official Tokyo professed complete unconcern over news reports from Washington indicative of impending disciplinary action. Major General Courtney Whitney, MacArthur's longtime associate and closest adviser, told correspondents that differences with Washington were being adjusted amicably and that the storm was blowing over. An "informed source"—usually Whitney—predicted that MacArthur would win his demands for a freer hand in Korea. No one in MacArthur's official circle suggested any possibility that the general might back down and apologize to Washington.

On April 10th President Truman took the final plunge, fully aware of the political battle which lay ahead. Suggestions that a Presidential envoy be sent to Tokyo to deal with MacArthur, that he be given an opportunity to resign, or that he be ordered to Washington and reprimanded had been discussed and rejected. The decision, supported by all the President's high civilian and military leaders, was for outright dismissal.

The order to MacArthur and the Presidential announcement of it were prepared that afternoon for release at 1 A.M. on April 11th—just in time to "make" final morning papers in the United States. Through what apparently was a failure to allow sufficient time for delays in transmission, the official message to MacArthur arrived in Tokyo twenty minutes after the announcement had been broadcast in the United States and over the short-wave facilities of the Armed Forces Radio Service.

It was shortly after 3 P.M. in Tokyo, and MacArthur was finishing a late lunch at his American Embassy residence. A note quoting the radio bulletin was handed to him. Aides said he was astounded.

"With deep regret," the President's announcement said, "I have concluded that General of the Army Douglas MacArthur is unable to give his wholehearted support to the policies of the United States Government and the United

Nations in matters pertaining to his official duties. . . . I have decided that I must make a change of command in the Far East. . . . I have, therefore, relieved General Mac-Arthur of his command and have designated Lt. Gen. Matthew B. Ridgway as his successor."

In the order to MacArthur, the President said:

"I deeply regret that it becomes my duty as President and Commander in Chief of the United States military forces to replace you as Supreme Commander, Allied Powers; Commander-in-Chief, United Nations Command; Commander-in-Chief, Far East; and Commanding General, U.S. Army, Far East. You will turn over your commands effective at once to Lt. Gen. Matthew B. Ridgway. You are authorized to have issued such orders as are necessary to complete desired travel to such place as you select. . . ."

The emotional impact was instantaneous. Supporters of MacArthur's position and many Republicans who did not fully agree with him demanded Acheson's head and threatened impeachment proceedings against Truman. Democrats cheered Truman's "courage" and asserted that he had saved the American form of government and reduced the danger of a third World War. There was less hysteria in Korea, more concern over losing Ridgway as Eighth Army commander than over losing MacArthur. The Japanese were stunned, but they recovered quickly under assurances that American efforts toward negotiating a soft peace treaty for Japan would not be slackened.

The flood of telegrams to the White House following the announcement ran heavily against the administration. President Truman moved swiftly to meet the attack and focus attention on the issues, rather than on the personalities involved. He went on the air that night with his side of the case:

"In the simplest terms, what we are doing in Korea is this: We are trying to prevent World War III. So far, by fighting a limited war in Korea, we have prevented aggression from succeeding and bringing on a general war. And the ability of the whole free world to resist Communist aggression has been greatly improved. . . .

"We do not want to see the conflict in Korea extended. We are trying to prevent a world war—not to start one. The best way to do that is to make it plain that we and the other free countries will continue to resist the attack.

"But you may ask why can't we take other steps to punish the aggressor? Why don't we bomb Manchuria, and China itself? Why don't we assist Chinese Nationalist troops to land on the mainland of China?

"If we were to do these things we would be running a very grave risk of starting a general war. If that were to happen, we would have brought about the exact situation we were trying to prevent. If we were to do these things we would become entangled in a vast conflict on the continent of Asia and our task would become immeasurably more difficult all over the world. What would suit the ambitions of the Kremlin better than for our military forces to be committed to a full scale war with Red China?

"A number of events have made it evident that General MacArthur did not agree with that policy. I have therefore considered it essential to relieve General MacArthur so that there would be no doubt or confusion as to the real purpose and aim of our policy. It was with the deepest personal regret that I found myself compelled to take this action. General MacArthur is one of the greatest military commanders. . . .

"We are ready at any time to negotiate for a restoration

of peace in the area. But we will not engage in appeasement. We are only interested in real peace. . . ."

Then he outlined the basic requirements of a settlement:

"1. The fighting must stop.
"2. Concrete steps must be taken to insure that the fighting will not break out again.
"3. There must be an end of the aggression.
"A settlement founded upon these elements would open the way for the unification of Korea and the withdrawal of all foreign forces. . . ."

General MacArthur returned to the United States on April 17th for the first time in fourteen years. The ovations he received at Honolulu, San Francisco, and Washington were only samples of the emotional upsurge of respect, support, and curiosity that were to influence the forthcoming great debate. The general demonstrated in San Francisco his mastery of the situation: "The only politics I have," he said, "is contained in the simple phrase known well by all of you: God bless America."

Before a joint session of Congress on April 19th the seventy-one-year-old general stated his case with a dramatic eloquence which only those who had seen him in action in the Far East could anticipate:

"I address you with neither rancor nor bitterness, in the fading twilight of life, with but one purpose in mind: To serve my country. . . .

"The issues are global, and so interlocked that to consider the problems of one sector oblivious to those of another is to court disaster for the whole. . . .

"There are those who claim our strength is inadequate to protect on both fronts, that we cannot divide our effort. I can think of no greater expression of defeatism. . . .

"Any major breach (of the American island defense line around the western rim of the Pacific) would render vulnerable to determined attack every other major segment. This is a military estimate as to which I have yet to find a military leader who will take exception. For that reason I have strongly recommended in the past, as a matter of military urgency, that under no circumstances must Formosa fall under Communist control. . . .

"While I was not consulted prior to the President's decision to intervene in support of the Republic of Korea, that decision, from a military standpoint, proved a sound one . . . as we hurled back the invader and decimated his forces. Our victory was complete, and our objectives within reach, when Red China intervened with numerically superior ground forces.

"This created a new war and an entirely new situation, a situation not contemplated when our forces were committed against the North Korean invader; a situation which called for new decisions in the diplomatic sphere to permit the realistic adjustment of military strategy. Such decisions have not been forthcoming. . . .

". . . Military necessity in the conduct of the war made necessary:

"1. The intensification of our economic blockade against China.

"2. The imposition of a naval blockade against the China Coast.

"3. Removal of restrictions on air reconnaissance of China's coastal area and of Manchuria" and action to "neutralize the sanctuary protection given the enemy north of the Yalu.

"4. Removal of restrictions on the forces of the Republic of China on Formosa with logistical support to contribute to their effective operations against the Chinese mainland."

He said it was "my understanding that from a military standpoint the above views have been fully shared in the past by practically every military leader concerned with the Korean campaign, including our own Joint Chiefs of Staff."

"It has been said in effect that I was a warmonger. Nothing could be further from the truth. . . .

"War's very object is victory, not prolonged indecision. In war there is no substitute for victory. . . .

"The Soviet will not necessarily mesh its actions with our moves."

MacArthur closed by describing himself, in the words of the old Army ballad, "Old Soldiers Never Die," saying, "And like the old soldier of that ballad, I now close my military career and just fade away, an old soldier who tried to do his duty as God gave him the light to see that duty. Goodbye."

The issues MacArthur raised did not so quickly fade away. From May 3rd to June 25th the Senate Armed Services and Foreign Relations Committees jointly heard more than two million words of testimony on MacArthur's dismissal and the whole range of United States policy in Asia.

MacArthur told the committees that the administration's "lack of policy" in Korea would result in "perpetuating a slaughter such as I have never heard of in the history of mankind." President Truman replied that one atomic bomb dropped on an American city, during the war that the MacArthur program might start, could cause more casualties than the sixty thousand suffered by the United States up to that date in Korea.

Defense Secretary Marshall denied that the air and naval

retaliation against China which MacArthur sought would assure United Nations military victory in Korea. Air Chief of Staff General Hoyt Vandenberg also denied the validity of MacArthur's principal argument. Even if United States bombers destroyed all the big cities of Manchuria and southern China, he said, it would "not be conclusive" because of the great geographical dispersion of troops and supplies possible in Manchuria and because the chief source of important Chinese Communist supplies is Russia, not China.

Marshall argued that broadening the war, as MacArthur proposed, would increase rather than reduce United Nations casualties, intensify and solidify Chinese efforts, and probably draw Russia into the conflict under the terms of its military alliance with Peiping. He said the present campaign was "chewing up" the "trained fabric of the Chinese armies" to such an extent as perhaps to make possible a satisfactory peace settlement without complete United Nations military victory.

General Bradley said MacArthur's plan would involve the United States "in the wrong war, at the wrong place, at the wrong time, with the wrong enemy."

Public-opinion polls recorded a strengthening of the administration's position during the hearings; MacArthur's program suffered from an inability of the Republican Party to give it solid support. The Formosa issue lost significance before the debate started when the Defense Department disclosed plans to send a large military mission to the island and resume large-scale military-aid shipments to Chiang Kai-shek. Secretary Marshall in his testimony went far beyond previous policy statements in declaring his opinion that the United States government would never allow the island to fall into Communist hands.

The stiffening of American policy toward the Chinese Communists and the unqualified official assurances that there would be no appeasement of Peiping went a long way toward answering MacArthur's demands. There was no compromise, however, in the administration's determination to limit the war to Korea and work toward a negotiated settlement short of complete military victory. The policy of collective security—built around co-operation with the European democracies and recognition of Western Europe as the crucial theater, Russia as the main enemy—survived intact.

Events in Korea, almost as much as words spoken in Washington, served to sustain the Truman administration in meeting MacArthur's challenge. The Eighth Army was giving the Chinese a bloody beating.

# XIV

## *Men at Work*

THE RAINS CAME early in March, washing rotten snow from the mountainsides, flooding the ice-encrusted paddyfields, turning every gorge and gulch into a frenzied torrent. Deep-frozen roads became ribbons of mud. The American army's wheels and tracks, which have a mysterious ability to make mud even of barely damp earth, now mired deep into the melting ground. Bridges washed away. Ice floes tumbled down the rising Han and smashed the engineers' pontoon bridges, cutting the lifeline to the front.

Taking a leaf from the enemy's book, Eighth Army transportation and supply officers organized Korean "A-frame brigades" to keep supplies moving forward. Human pack trains of South Korean civilians took over where roads became impassable or non-existent.

The rains ushered in an early Spring, a feeble reawakening of this miserable land. Trees which had survived the scourge of war and generations of wanton deforestation added a touch of green to Korea's depressing "seven shades of brown." Blossoming plum and cherry trees struck a sharp note of contrast among the ugly scars where villages had been.

The season's best efforts could do little to change the drab monotony of the landscape or to shake off the atmosphere of despair which shrouded this land of hopeless poverty and desolation. Korea chilled a strong man's spirit and sapped his enthusiasm even when Spring was in the air and the enemy was in retreat. The country itself, rather than the indecisive nature of the "yo-yo war," was the great blight on a soldier's life. There were no prizes ahead, no fabled cities to be liberated, no rear-area resorts or night spots where a man could escape from the exile he felt in Korea. Beyond this barren pile of earth and rock—almost too low to be called a mountain, yet undeserving of the army's term, "hill"—was another just like it. Beyond this town named Chungpyong was another equally drab and devastated.

To provide a brief escape, the United Nations command began sending small groups of men to Japan for five days of "Rest and Rehabilitation." A man became eligible for "R & R" after six months in Korea. A permanent system of rotating veterans from Korea and replacing them with draftees and reserves from the United States was rumored, finally announced, and slowly put into effect. Now a man had a tangible goal, a chance of getting out before a bullet claimed him.

The Thirty-eighth parallel was not a goal, nor even a point of climax. The enemy was waiting just to the north when the Eighth Army approached, then crossed, the invisible line in late March. Less than half of the Communists' estimated fifty to sixty divisions had been committed in South Korea. Most of them had escaped, battered but intact, while expendable rear guards slowed the grinding Allied advance. A mighty Spring offensive, perhaps the Chinese army's supreme effort to destroy the United Nations forces, was expected momentarily.

It was an alert, professional army, without illusions of early victory, which inched across the old border for the second time. The Eighth Army had gone through the crucible and emerged hardened but flexible. What its men lacked in noble inspiration, belief in the cause, and faith in eventual victory was offset by personal and unit pride and a sure knowledge that for them the issue was survival. The fittest do not always survive in war, but the survivors under good leadership can use the lessons of experience to become the fittest. Some seasoned observers of two or more wars called Matt Ridgway's Eighth Army the best the United States had ever put in the field. A leavening of first-class fighting units contributed by the European Allies helped to make it so.

The Eighth Army's seven "American" divisions had become big, power-loaded outfits. Reinforced by United Nations battalions or brigades and by ROK soldiers integrated directly into the ranks, each division numbered approximately twenty thousand men. They had a full complement of tanks, including American Pershings and Pattons and the British Twenty-ninth Brigade's mammoth Centurions. Artillery battalions, many of them United States National Guard units, had landed at Pusan and moved up to the front with their 240-millimeter howitzers, 155-millimeter "long tom" rifles, track-mounted self-propelled 155s, and smaller howitzers. Korea's narrow mountain trails and dirt "highways" were ground alternately into mud and dust and often shelved away under the weight of this ponderous war machine.

The seven to nine frontline divisions of the American-advised, Korean-led ROK Army also presented a better appearance. The First Division had repeatedly proved its dependability under heavy pressure. In repelling the Chinese February counter-offensive, the Sixth Division had regained the respect lost in its Winter collapse in the northwest. The Third, Fifth, and Seventh Divisions had carried their share of the attack in the Tenth Corps' drive northward on the east-central front. Now, again, the light-footed Capitol Division was pacing the march back into North Korea, advancing far up the east coast.

The ROKs, however, had suffered heavy casualties— about a hundred and seventy thousand since June 25th— and their ranks were filled by green recruits. More serious, junior officers and non-commissioned officers had been lost almost as fast as they had gained experience. ROK regimental and division commanders still demonstrated abysmal ignorance of the mechanics of large-scale operations, failed to use their communications facilities, and shared the common Oriental indifference to precision in handling figures. "Thousands" of enemy troops in an ROK intelligence report could be several hundred. Claimed "annihilation" of an enemy regiment often proved to be no more than heavy casualties inflicted on an enemy battalion.

The South Korean divisions also were weaker in both manpower and firepower than their Allied counterparts; their strength was about ten thousand men each. They had little organic artillery. American artillery battalions were attached to the ROK divisions in more critical sectors, but often the ROK commander was forced to call on American corps artillery for heavy fire support. American tank companies and battalions worked with the ROK divisions when they needed armored striking power. Usually, however, the South Koreans had to fight the North Koreans and Chinese with only light infantry weapons.

All would be well when one ROK infantryman faced one better trained but no better equipped Communist infantryman. Disaster was almost inevitable, however, if numerically superior Communist forces attacked one of the greener ROK units. Consequently, the Allied command attempted to disperse ROK divisions on the line between strong American divisions or to give them small, less critical sectors where the enemy was unlikely to concentrate superior forces. These weaknesses were well known throughout the Eighth Army, but in taking on a Communist army potentially numbering half a million men, all available strength was needed.

The enemy likewise exhibited great weaknesses, and intimate knowledge of them was a source of Allied confidence as the hour of the enemy's Spring offensive neared. Raw manpower, coupled with a willingness to spend men like ammunition, was the only real weapon in the Chinese arsenal. It was a good shock weapon. Nothing—not even the finest instruments of death produced by American industry—will stop the initial attack launched by a horde* of well-disciplined infantrymen, armed with nothing larger than mortars and unsupported by air or artillery. This tactic, however, brings only momentary success against a cool-headed, mobile army which has learned to "roll with the punch." The Eighth Army had learned that it could absorb a deep Chinese penetration safely without holding back strong reserves, because the Chinese could not sustain the assault. When the opening attack collapsed for

* No professionally acceptable definition of "horde" has come out of the Korean experience, although some war correspondents used this arbitrary table of organization: three "swarms" equal a "horde," two "hordes" make a "human flood," and any number of "human floods" imply a "bottomless pit of Chinese manpower."

lack of re-supply and command co-ordination, the threat was over, regardless of the depth of the initial penetration.

Military experts often snorted over reports describing Chinese tactics as an adaptation of Russian procedure; a strong imagination was required to detect a similarity. The Chinese attack deserved the name "tactics" only because it was usually based on good intelligence information and consequently aimed accurately at weak ROK links in the Allied line. It also involved good use of infiltration and night movement, which helped to minimize the Chinese shortage of heavy weapons. But tactics imply continuing control and disposition of forces during an action; Chinese army commanders almost completely lost such control after their attacks had gained momentum.

Some Eighth Army officers considered the Chinese more proficient in defense than in their more publicized attacks. They were masters of camouflage and concealment; whole divisions could disappear from sight in barren mountain country. A flight over the Chinese buildup zone, where Communist troops presumably were teeming, often revealed less than a dozen brown-clothed figures which might be Communist soldiers. They executed withdrawals skillfully, seldom allowing a rear-guard unit to be trapped. They were willing to take casualties in a delaying action, but they reduced their losses by constructing along ridges deep log-and-rock bunkers which withstood heavy Allied pounding from bombs and artillery. In withdrawing, they often left small raider units behind in hills astride the main Allied advance routes. These forces raised havoc at night, and their raids frequently were mistaken for counter-attacks.

Given substantial Russian military aid—particularly artillery, tanks, trucks, planes, and aviation gasoline—the Chinese Army would have been as strong as its numbers implied. Without adequate logistics and firepower, it was a dangerous foe, capable of taking a heavy toll of Allied soldiers' lives, but in the long run completely outclassed by the Eighth Army.

It was not known in the early Spring, however, that the Russians again had failed to deliver the matériel which might have saved their Chinese allies from another bloody failure. Intelligence reports described a growing buildup of troops and supplies in the triangular plateau between Chorwon, Kumhwa, and Pyongyang. This hilly but mountainless area is fifteen to thirty miles north of the Thirty-eighth parallel in the heart of the peninsula. The best network of roads in central Korea made it an ideal assembly area. Correspondents quickly settled on the convenient name, "iron triangle." There, all reports indicated, the Chinese had cached their supplies, guns, and ammunition for a Spring offensive which might involve forty Chinese and fifteen North Korean divisions.

Prisoners of war and air reconnaissance supplied an ominous warning: the Spring offensive probably would be supported by a strong Communist air force. The planes would be Russian, but the pilots presumably would be Chinese. Prisoners said Chinese troops had been promised that they would not be thrown into another offensive without air support. Lieutenant General George Stratemeyer, commander of United States Far East Air Forces, reported that there was "unmistakable evidence" of preparations in both North Korea and Manchuria to launch air attacks against the United Nations ground forces. Allied intelligence believed the Chinese could mount five to six hundred sorties a day with the air strength which had grown rapidly at Manchurian bases.

Was one of the strangest aspects of this strange war to end? Almost from the beginning, Allied air force and naval aviation had roamed Korean skies at will, strafing and rocketing Communist troops, burning and blasting Communist bases, towns, and transport. American pilots were virtually assured of never meeting an enemy plane unless they flew deep into northwest Korea on a bombing or reconnaissance mission. There they dueled with Russia's best production-model jet fighter in a sort of "proving ground" battle which revealed the MIG-15 as the best airplane, but American fliers as the best gunners and pilots.

United Nations troops had almost never been required to dive into a ditch, or camouflage a position, or douse a light when planes were overhead; the air was ours. So accustomed to this tremendous advantage had the Allies become that a surprise enemy air attack could have caused tremendous loss of life and damage.

General Ridgway and Lieutenant General Earle E. Partridge, Fifth Air Force commander, decided to take precautions, but they did not enforce all the cumbersome restrictions which would necessarily follow if the Communist air threat materialized. Sandbag walls went up around key installations, blackout and air raid warning systems were tested, and tops were ordered removed from jeeps and trucks. Division headquarters and other intermediate forces dug air-raid bunkers and personal foxholes.

The Eighth Army advance did not pause in the face of anticipated Chinese assault. The orders were to press the attack into North Korea, closing with and killing Communist troops, probing into the enemy buildup zone. Unlike the October drive across the Thirty-eighth parallel, this attack had no territorial goals and was not calculated to score a deep penetration. (Any deep advance would require a new political decision, Secretary Marshall announced in Washington on March 27th.) "We are not interested in real estate," was Ridgway's favorite explanation. "Our mission is solely the destruction of hostile forces and the conservation of our own." By continuing to hit the southern fringes of the Communist buildup, Ridgway hoped to keep the enemy off balance, upset his timetable, and perhaps force him to strike before offensive preparations were complete.

The ROK Capitol Division crossed into North Korea on the east coast road on March 27th, and the United States Twenty-fifth and Twenty-fourth Divisions edged over the parallel on March 31st and April 1st. By the end of the second week of April, the entire Eighth Army attack line was six to eight miles inside North Korea, except on the east coast where it was deeper, and in the west where it bent back along the Imjin River northwest of Seoul.

General MacArthur's dismissal moved General Ridgway to Tokyo. Lieutenant General James A. Van Fleet replaced him in Korea on April 14.

*General Ridgway introduced his successor to the press during a very informal farewell party at the commanding general's four-room Taegu residence. The contrast between the two men was complete. Ridgway was the suave, polished field marshal, clearly destined for higher station. Van Fleet was the fellow next door back home, good-natured, unaffected, strong, but no world-beater at turning a phrase. It was not because I had read his personal history file that I thought of a football coach in uniform. Ridgway nursed along a single highball. Van Fleet, a teetotaler, had a "coke."*

Three years Ridgway's senior, Van Fleet was a member of the 1915 West Point class with Dwight Eisenhower and Omar Bradley—two classes ahead of Ridgway. He fought in the first World War as a machine-gun-battalion commander. In World War II combat he quickly gained the promotions which had passed him by in peacetime, while he was serving at Fort Benning and as ROTC instructor and football coach at the University of Florida. He landed on Utah Beach in the forefront of the Normandy invasion as a regimental commander. He became acting commander, then commander of the Fourth Infantry Division, then as a major general took command of the Ninetieth Division. On the final Allied drive into Germany Van Fleet paced the First Army's attack as commander of the Third Corps.

General Van Fleet came to Korea with two high recommendations: a brilliant combat record (he is the only army commander eligible to wear the combat infantryman's badge), and chief credit for the Greek victory over Communist guerrillas in a civil war not entirely different from Korea's. He headed the Joint United States Military Advisory and Planning Group in Greece which in two and a half years overcame political and financial obstacles, rebuilt the Greek Army, and helped stamp out the Communist-led minority revolt.

It was not easy to fit this big, plain-spoken man into the picture of all-around capacity which his record indicated. He was no more articulate a week later, at his first press conference. But he made a prediction there that gave a hint of what may be his secret. The Communist Spring offensive, he said, could be expected momentarily. The next *night it began. Later he again displayed this sure sense of timing and understanding of the enemy's intentions. In the field, with men and maps and tactical problems, he was at home—a cool, canny football coach with a head full of trick plays.*

# XV

## *The Balance Shifts*

It was a quiet enough Sunday, even at the front. Back along the sparkling Han River east of Seoul there was a GI regatta—won by a chugging engineer motorboat named *Queen Mary*. Out beyond the front, however, it was beginning to look like New Year's Eve.

The now-familiar signs had begun to appear late on Saturday. Air reconnaissance, then foot patrols reported columns of Chinese troops marching south from Kumhwa, moving into Chorwon and east from Kaesong toward the Imjin River. The Chinese brought artillery into position around Chorwon, within five miles of the Twenty-fifth Division's lines. This alone meant that they planned to retreat no farther. Patrols radioed back similar information on Sunday morning, April 22nd. British and Belgian patrols added a warning from a new sector, west of the Imjin and north of the Thirty-eighth parallel. For days that area, astride the highway to the Communist capital, had been deserted—a tantalizing invitation from the spider to the fly. Van Fleet had not fallen into the trap, but he had put patrol bases out and stretched his lines considerably along the middle Imjin, north-northwest of Seoul.

The Eighth Army had stopped in its tracks Saturday and Sunday except on the central front. There the ROK Sixth Division pushed northward on Sunday through the mountains west of Hwachon, and the Twenty-fourth Division on its left and the First Marine Division on its right brought up their flanks to keep abreast.

Late Sunday afternoon the ROK right flank regiment stumbled head-on into the first blows of the Chinese Spring offensive. A week later the story of what happened to that trusted ROK division was still being pieced together. For the moment there was silence.

Shortly before 7 P.M. an intense Communist artillery and mortar barrage opened along the entire front. Allied artillery answered, and air force fighters and bombers scrambled into the fading twilight. The Eighth Army braced for the attack. No one at headquarters knew that the Sixth ROK Division was at that moment in disorderly retreat, opening a ten-mile-wide hole in the center of the United Nations line.

The line-up was: the First ROK Division on the lower Imjin, the Twenty-ninth British Brigade on its right, the United States Third Division with attached Belgian and Filipino battalions on the northwest corner of the bent front, the Twenty-fifth Division and Turkish Brigade directly south of Chorwon and north of Seoul, and the Twenty-fourth Division to the right, southwest of Kumhwa. Next came the Sixth ROK Division. To its right stood the Marines, part of the Second Division, the Seventh Division, and four ROK divisions holding the extreme eastern end of the 140-mile front. Two-hundred thousand frontline Allied troops faced Communism's supreme effort in Korea. The First Cavalry Division was in reserve east of Seoul, ready to move to meet the greatest threat.

Green flares arched across the dusky sky, the bugles and whistles sounded, and the attack was on. Chinese infantry-

men struck the dangling flanks of the Twenty-fourth and
First Marine Divisions. At least three enemy divisions hit
the Twenty-fourth frontally; heavy assaults rolled against
the Twenty-fifth and the Turks. The Belgian battalion,
caught on the west side of the Imjin, was engulfed but
fought its way back to safety with American help. Tens,
then hundreds of Chinese waded the chest-deep Imjin near
Korangpo and spread like ants into the hills. British riflemen and machine-gunners mowed down dozens, but the
line was thin here and Chinese numbers were unbeatable.
Rapidly the Chinese attack spread to an eighty-mile front.
East of the Marines, the Second and Seventh Divisions
fended off lighter North Korean attacks and held their
ground.

The Chinese advanced through a curtain of flying steel.
Sweating American artillerymen fired through the night as
fast as they could load. By the light of a rising moon and
lazy, spiraling parachute flares, American bombers and
fighters blasted Chinese columns as they moved toward the
front.

Dawn brought no respite. From the central front came
hints of disaster. South Korean troops of the Sixth Division
were streaming southward, in trucks and on foot, abandoning guns and supplies. Marines tried to stop some of
them at gunpoint. Supporting American artillery battalions
were engulfed in the avalanche of fleeing ROKs. None of
the South Korean officers could explain what had happened. One lieutenant babbled to an infuriated Marine,
"Go Chunchon—vacation time—Chunchon." Marines on
the right and Twenty-fourth Division infantrymen on the
left turned to battle the riptide of Communists pouring
down the breakthrough corridor.

Twenty miles south of Sunday's central front, the British Commonwealth Twenty-seventh Brigade was celebrating. Its Middlesex and Argyll battalions had fought their last battle in Korea and were packing up to sail for Hong Kong. The Argylls already had started moving to Inchon for embarkation. Two other British battalions were sailing toward Inchon to replace them. When the brigade commander heard rumors of the ROK collapse he didn't wait for more details; it was a too-familiar story. He ordered his Australian, Canadian, and British (Middlesex) Infantry battalions into position to meet the attack, west of Chunchon. New Zealand artillerymen set up their guns and waited.

A second crisis was mounting on the western front. The Chinese expanded their bridgeheads on the east bank of the Imjin River, drove a wedge between the British Twenty-ninth Brigade and the First ROK Division, then surged around both flanks of the unyielding British Gloucestershire Battalion.

The three American divisions directly north of Seoul fought, fell back, and fought again, rolling with the punch. Their ceaseless gunfire piled Chinese bodies in the ravines leading into the United Nations line. Still more Chinese moved up to fill the ranks, and to die. The envelopment threats on the west and in the center forced a deeper withdrawal late Monday, however. The Turks, their bayonets freshly stained with Chinese blood, protested against withdrawing.

Now two hundred and fifty to three hundred thousand Chinese were believed to be in the attack, but not all the death and bloodshed was on their side. Loaded United States Army jeep-ambulances sped southward to collecting

stations, where bigger ambulances and helicopters picked
up the broken, bleeding bodies of terribly young soldiers
and carried them to overflowing field hospitals near Seoul.

The Gloucestershire Battalion was surrounded, and for
most of its wounded there was no way out. Under orders to
hold at all costs to protect the rear of the withdrawing
Third and Twenty-fifth Divisions, the British stood their
ground against five to ten times their number. Other battalions of the brigade fought their way southward or withdrew safely. Two attempts by relief columns to break
through and save the Gloucesters failed. The battalion ran
out of ammunition, food, and water; escape in small groups
was the last hope. On the Eighth Army's war map, the
Gloucesters were a tiny blue island in a sea of red. The sea
widened as the Eighth Army pulled back through Uijongbu
toward Seoul on Tuesday and Wednesday.

Only forty-one of the six hundred trapped Gloucesters
got out. Captain Maurice Harvey saved this tragic handful
by leading his company north, deeper into Communist territory, before turning south toward safety. While "chaps
were falling all around, marking the route like a bloody
paperchase," Harvey's dwindling band plunged through
Chinese lines to reach an American tank company supporting the First ROK Division.

Bright news came from the other British sector. The central breakthrough drive had been blocked and the threat
that it would spill over into the rear of the American divisions on each side of the corridor had ended. Australian and
New Zealand soldiers fighting on Anzac Day, anniversary
of their fathers' gallant stand on the shores of Gallipoli in
World War I, teamed with British and Canadian infantrymen, a regiment of the First Cavalry Division, American

Marines, and Twenty-fourth Division infantrymen in a clear defensive victory. They stopped the Chinese less than a mile north of the important Seoul-Chunchon lateral highway.

Two battalions of Chinese, however, did turn westward and knife behind the withdrawing Twenty-fourth Division. They laid an ambush for a long American column moving down a narrow valley road. A second and bloodier "Massacre Valley" episode was averted when the column turned under fire, withdrew northward, then took a detour around the Chinese pocket. The division reached a new defense line north of the Han intact, but not without heavy casualties.

By the fourth day the offensive was weakening. The Eighth Army pulled back all along the peninsula-wide front and dug in for the next blows. Chunchon was abandoned by the Marines. Although not seriously challenged, American and South Korean troops on the eastern front withdrew south of the Thirty-eighth parallel to shorten and straighten the line.

In the west, the Allies regrouped on a line four to eight miles north of Seoul and the Han River.

On the fifth day it was clear that the main force of the attack had been spent, but the Chinese had used only half of their estimated strength. Another three hundred thousand-man assault could follow. The long-heralded Communist air attack had failed to materialize, but this, too, could come at any moment. The Eighth Army might still be smashed against the Han by a second-round offensive.

General Van Fleet made a bold decision. In January General Ridgway had not dared to make a stand with the Han to his back. Retreat across the river would be costly, particularly in heavy equipment. Van Fleet not only decided to try it, but he ordered lumbering tanks and 155 mm. howitzers and "long tom" rifles into positions in the heart of Seoul. "It's good defensive terrain"—a good place to fight and kill Communists—was his only explanation. Retreat to the south bank of the river would only postpone the job of meeting and destroying the Red Army.

Chinese probing forces—and North Koreans in the extreme west—tested the new line before Seoul for two more days, then joined the general Communist withdrawal.

The first phase of the enemy's Spring offensive, launched with the announced goal of seizing Seoul and driving the United Nations into the sea, had ended in what the attrition-minded Eighth Army could call a resounding Allied victory. Van Fleet estimated that the Communists had paid seventy thousand casualties—about one-fourth of the attacking force—for their failure. Even with the British Twenty-ninth Brigade's heavy losses, United Nations casualties were less than one-tenth those of the enemy.

General Ridgway grasped the far-reaching psychological and political meaning of the Communist failure. "The crest of the Communist wave has been broken," he told General Van Fleet in a letter of congratulations.

Van Fleet allowed no time for victory celebration. He juggled his forces and put them to work building the nearest approximation of a static defense line that the United Nations had attempted in Korea. From the Han River northwest of Seoul to the mountains of eastern Korea, the Eighth Army strung thousands of miles of barbed wire and laid anti-tank and anti-personnel mines and trip-flares across all avenues of approach, except for narrow passageways left open for United Nations patrols. The big guns were zeroed in, and tons of ammunition were piled at each battery position. On the central front something new was added. Drums of napalm, used in air force fire bombs, were planted on the slopes of hills and armed with thermite explosive charges. When the Chinese attacked, a torrent of flaming, killing gasoline would flow down upon them. Diabolical? So is a bayonet or a bomb.

The Eighth Army did not remain in static defense. Tank-infantry patrols followed the withdrawing Chinese above Seoul, snapping at their heels. One regiment from each division on the line set up patrol bases as far as five miles out into the widening no-man's land. Patrols from these bases re-entered Uijongbu, then Chunchon. By May 10th they had dispersed Communist stragglers as far north as Munsan on the Imjin River. In the east they re-crossed the Thirty-eighth parallel and skirmished with North Koreans near Inje and the eastern end of the Hwachon Reservoir. The main Allied strength was held back along the defense line, however.

Air reconnaissance spotted a significant movement north of the parallel at the beginning of the third week of May. Chinese supply trucks and troops were shifting laterally eastward toward the Hwachon Reservoir. Patrols south of the thirteen-mile-long lake ran into Chinese troops for the first time in this area. Marines patrolling into Chunchon reported Chinese moving down the central highway. Growing troop concentrations were also reported north of Uijongbu and near Munsan in the west and along the Puk-han River west of Chunchon. These were danger signals which everyone had learned to recognize.

Round Two of the Communist Spring offensive opened late on the night of May 16th–17th. It was aimed directly

at the thrice-battered United States Second Division and
two ROK divisions on the Americans' right flank in the almost trackless mountains of east-central Korea.

Four Chinese corps—upwards of ninety-six thousand
men—swept across the mountains below the Hwachon
Reservoir, overran the Allied outpost line just south of the
Thirty-eighth parallel, and crashed against the main defense line. The ROKs were shattered, split into small
groups, and driven southward. The Second Division stag-
gered, held its ground, fell back, fought off encirclement
and infiltration, stamped out a dozen roadblocks, then
counter-attacked. The South Koreans retreated fifteen
miles before they were rounded up and thrown back into
the fight. Van Fleet pulled the Third Division out of reserve south of Seoul and moved it one hundred miles by
truck to the east, where it went into action to prevent a
deeper penetration.

The flood of Chinese swirled around the Second Division's exposed right flank, through the gap left by the ROK
collapse. One regiment and one battalion were surrounded
but kept on fighting. The division at one point was two-
thirds surrounded. A detailed map of the division's disposition, prepared in advance for the attack, was found on a
captured Chinese. The offensive apparently had been
aimed primarily at the destruction of the Second Division,
which the Chinese must have assumed was still crippled
from three bloody battles—at Kunu in November, Wonju
in January, and Wonju and Chipyong in February.

The Second held, and its commander, Maj. Gen. Clark L.
Ruffner, radioed: "We're killing Chinese faster than we
can count them." The attack collapsed amid a carnage un-
paralleled in the Korean War. Chinese bodies littered hill-

sides and actually filled ditches where artillery, napalm, mines, machine guns, and air attacks teamed in a gory slaughter. The Second Division alone claimed over thirty-seven thousand Communist casualties, and admitted losing 134 American, French, and Dutch killed and 826 wounded. ROK losses were lighter, but no official reports were disclosed. Most of the South Koreans escaped, just as the Sixth ROK Division had done in April. (The bulk of ROK losses appear in the "missing-in-action" column.)

Lighter attacks hit the ROKs near the east coast, the Marines below Chunchon, the Seventh Division farther west, and the Allied Han River bridgehead line. Again, the Chinese had failed to muster enough strength for a front-wide offensive, and again they had failed to force a general Allied withdrawal. The beaten remnants of the Chinese attack force broke off the attack on May 21st—another five-day effort—and retreated toward the Thirty-eighth parallel. Across the front they had lost fifty-eight thousand men in killed, wounded and captured, against less than thirty-five hundred admitted Allied losses.

The Eighth Army immediately went on the offensive in "hot pursuit" of the retreating enemy—a move armchair strategists had urged after every Communist attack. That it was able to strike back in May after absorbing the Chinese supreme bid for victory was proof that the tide had turned. Air power and artillery were the Eighth Army's salvation at several critical moments, but the decisive defeat was wrought by rugged, confident infantrymen and cool, professional leadership from the rifle squads up to the army commander.

Pursuing Allied columns wove a dragnet across Chinese escape routes from the east-central salient and raced north-

ward to block or engage retreating units all across the
front. Daily the bag of prisoners grew, reaching a peak on
May 26th and 27th when five thousand were captured in
one small pocket north of Chunchon. Fifth Air Force and
Navy fighters raked the fleeing Communist columns.

The Eighth Army crossed the Thirty-eighth parallel on
a solid front and kept the enemy on the run. By June 2nd,
the United Nations line was back to almost the exact positions hit by the offensive of April 22nd.

Van Fleet called off his "hot pursuit" counter-attack and
announced that the United Nations forces would continue
to "stop the enemy's unwarranted aggression against South
Korea and will, when necessary and profitable, meet such
threats within North Korea." The statement was widely interpreted as a suggestion to the Communists that now was
a good time to talk peace.

The Red Army's catastrophic losses spoke more loudly
to Peiping and Pyongyang than Van Fleet's words. Between
April 22nd and June 2nd the Communists suffered an estimated two hundred thousand casualties from all causes—
one-third of their assumed strength in Korea. It is probable
that the proportion was even higher, since intelligence estimates of enemy strength before the Spring offensive
credited a full complement of troops to identified Chinese
units.

All available supplies had been thrown into the offensive.
Months of laborious night movement under Allied air attack would be required to rearm and re-equip the troops
which survived. Russia again had failed to deliver the goods
which might have made all the difference—tanks, artillery,
and transport gasoline.

There was every reason to believe, despite lack of con-

crete evidence, that the Chinese military leadership was embittered against its Russian allies and reluctant to order
hopelessly outgunned Chinese troops into another suicidal
attack.

The United Nations forces emerged from the Spring ordeal as the dominant power in Korea. The balance had
swung dramatically against the Chinese five months after
they had driven the Eighth Army to the brink of defeat.

# XVI

## *Decision: Truce*

JUNE OF 1951 was the critical moment. If the Allied goals were a decisive military victory over the Communists and unification of Korea—or most of it—by force of arms, here was the best opportunity we were likely to achieve. If a truce based on the original United Nations objective of repelling aggression and preserving the Republic of Korea was the goal, here was a moment in which the United Nations could negotiate from strength.

"Big Jim" Van Fleet was to remember June as a time of lost opportunity.

The Red Army had taken a terrible pounding in two abortive offensives. Its front-line units were low on ammunition and food; its supply system had been unable to support a second Spring offensive, in May, on the same scale as the April assault. It had not yet begun to receive in large quantity the Russian artillery pieces which a year later equalized the firepower of the Communist and United Nations Armies. Its numerical superiority, cut by heavy losses, was no longer alarming.

Battered and pursued, it abandoned the Iron Triangle under sharp but far from maximum Allied blows. The Communist withdrawal was even more rapid on the east coast. It was not a rout, however. Van Fleet warned that a

196

"third-round" offensive might come at any hour during late June. The Red army was still formidable and the United Nations army had suffered in the Spring offensives losses which could not be replaced immediately. Three ROK divisions which crumpled during the Spring assaults required complete reorganization before they could be depended upon to hold front-line sectors again. The United States Second, Twenty-fourth, and Twenty-fifth Divisions and the British Commonwealth units had suffered heavy casualties.

Back home, in nearly every city and town, families were receiving the dreaded message from the Pentagon. Supply shortage also plagued the Eighth Army. Ammunition stocks dropped dangerously below minimum levels before the May offensive was repelled. Some types of ammunition were still short in June.

Geography imposed another problem for the Eighth Army. The Korean peninsula widens abruptly to the west above the Thirty-eighth parallel. No matter how it was planned, a general offensive would radically increase the width of the battlefront, forcing commitment of every available unit to blocking and holding and leaving no reserve strength available to exploit break-throughs. Clearly, a frontal drive up the peninsula was not guaranteed success.

Nearly two years later, after his retirement, Van Fleet told a Congressional committee that his plan had been an amphibious landing on the east coast coupled with a drive from the south to link up with the beachhead near Wonsan. The Communist forces on the central and western fronts, thus threatened with being cut off south of the peninsula's narrow waist, might be forced to withdraw. Van Fleet was willing to spare the First Marine Division from his southern battle line for the operation, despite the possibility of another Communist offensive. He would have needed at least two more divisions for the Wonsan landing. The newly reactivated Fortieth and Forty-fifth divisions—California and Oklahoma National Guard units—had recently arrived in Japan and might have been used in Korea, but they had not even completed unit training. Van Fleet reasoned that if a shoestring operation at Inchon had won the war against the North Koreans, a daring gamble might contain the formula for another victory.

Great victories require great risks and bold moves, but Van Fleet's proposal required more than that. It called for America to give the lives of thousands more of its youth for a cause beyond the original minimum objective of American and United Nations intervention: to save South Korea from Communist enslavement. It raised the specter of another Hungnam beachhead, another avalanche of fresh Chinese armies forcing yet another disastrous Allied retreat from North Korea. It could bring the Chinese Communist air force out of Manchuria to attack United Nations lines, resulting in American air retaliation and eventual bombing of Manchuria. It collided head-on with Washington's decision to avoid commitment of American military strength in a war to the finish with the Chinese. Even if the beachhead held, and the United Nations lines advanced to the "waist" above Pyongyang and Wonsan, no military man could guarantee the destruction of the Communist armies or the withdrawal of the Chinese Communists from the remainder of North Korea. As Ridgway in Tokyo and the Joint Chiefs of Staff in Washington saw it, Van Fleet's proposal offered, at best, the prospect of a new stalemate one hundred miles north of the current battleline.

The United Nations already had won a victory of sorts; most people at that moment were ready to settle for it and call a halt to an unpopular war. We had reacted with strength in 1950, at a moment when weakness would have led to world-wide disaster. We had restored the Communist-violated border of South Korea. We had shown the Kremlin that the free world would not allow piecemeal aggression to continue chipping away at its frontiers. We had met the challenge to the United Nations ideal of collective security and perhaps saved the United Nations itself from the fate of the League of Nations. In the process we had exposed the weakness of the United Nations, where ninety per cent. of the members were vocally opposed to aggression but only a few were willing or able to join the United States in supplementing that decision. Millions of Americans were disillusioned by the failure of the United Nations Allies to make sacrifices proportionate to America's effort.

We had virtually destroyed the North Korean Army, in one year inflicting an estimated six hundred thousand casualties, including nearly one hundred thousand military prisoners. The Chinese "People's Volunteers" had sustained more than half a million casualties, according to United Nations estimates. Communist Korea had been severely punished: its railways were wrecked, its industries ruined, its communications system destroyed.

These gains had cost more than eighty thousand American casualties, including twelve thousand known killed and nearly ten thousand missing. South Korea's losses were more than twice as heavy. A large proportion of America's ground, sea, and air power was tied down in Korea.

To refuse to settle for the major accomplishments and minimum victory already won and to gamble on an all-out drive to the Yalu would have required some unpleasant decisions. It demanded real mobilization, higher military spending, higher taxes, more borrowing, an end to the era of new cars, new television sets, and the pleasures of peacetime living. More important, it called for a sacrifice in blood and lives which no one could accurately estimate.

The issues raised in Van Fleet's offensive plans required no lengthy consideration in secret military councils, and they never became subject to public discussion. The great debate over MacArthur's recall centering around identical strategic questions, had just worn itself out after more than two months of Congressional hearings in Washington. The Truman administration and its military chiefs had held their ground and emerged with strong public support for their policy of limiting the Korean war and avoiding a commitment to unify Korea by force at all costs.

It came as no surprise to Van Fleet that his offensive plan was shelved.

The decision to end the shooting did not come suddenly, nor was the movement toward a truce unexpected. Peace feelers went out from both sides of the Iron Curtain as the United Nations forces advanced into North Korea for the third time. The MacArthur hearings closed with a clear and public definition of American official policy: to resist Communist aggression against South Korea but to rely on peaceful means to achieve Korean unification, Chinese military withdrawal, and a permanent solution to the Korean problems. In mid-June the State Department considered offering another cease-fire proposal to the Communists, but representatives of the sixteen United Nations countries active in Korea, meeting in Washington, decided against any new statement. Instead, "neutral" diplomats in Peiping made the American position known to the Communists. United Nations Secretary-General Trygve Lie declared that the time had come to talk peace. He said the Security Council's resolutions on Korea would be fulfilled if a cease-fire were arranged approximately along the Thirty-eighth parallel, provided the truce were "followed by restoration of peace and security" through political means. The Voice of America, quoting Lie's statement, asked Russia's United Nations delegation to "say the one word the whole world is waiting for."

The word came on June 23rd from Soviet chief delegate Jacob Malik. Speaking on the weekly United Nations radio program, "The Price of Peace," Malik assailed the United States and the North Atlantic Pact for a full fifteen minutes. Then, running overtime, he added: "The Soviet peoples further believe that the most acute problem of the present day—the problem of the armed conflict in Korea—could also be settled. This would require the readiness of the parties to enter on the path of peaceful settlement of the Korean question. The Soviet peoples believe that as a first step discussions should be started between the belligerents for a cease-fire and an armistice providing for the mutual withdrawal of forces from the Thirty-eighth parallel."

The United States was wary. A secret State Department memorandum inadvertently released in Tokyo three days later warned that Malik's proposal might have been a time-gaining "cover for military advantage," that a cease-fire was a more complex problem than the mere withdrawal of forces along the Thirty-eighth parallel, and that Malik's demilitarized zone need not necessarily be along the Thirty-eighth parallel. At the same time, American officials in Tokyo pointed out that the parallel did not provide good defensive terrain in many areas and that therefore a stable truce could not be achieved if the Russian plan were accepted too literally. General Ridgway let it be known that he had no intention of abandoning vital positions gained by the Eighth Army during its June advance into North Korea.

The issue of a Thirty-eighth-parallel cease-fire was to be among the first of many shoals on which the armistice conference was nearly wrecked. The truce negotiations had already started before a meeting was held.

There were other possible jokers in Malik's deck. The Peiping government repeatedly had demanded among its Korean peace terms such conditions as the grant of a United Nations seat for Red China in advance of any peace talks, withdrawal of all "foreign troops" from Korea, and "settlement of the Korean question by the Korean people." Peiping announced support of Malik's proposal. Were Malik's and Chou En-lai's plan one and the same? The American ambassador to Moscow, Admiral Alan G. Kirk, went to Soviet Foreign Minister Andrei Gromyko to find out. Gromyko assured the United States that the proposed armistice discussions could "be limited to strictly military questions without involving any political or territorial matters," the State Department announced the next day. "The military representatives would discuss questions of assurances against resumption of hostilities," according to Kirk's understanding of the Russian plan. The permanent political settlement would be left to a later conference.

The next day, June 29th, President Truman dispatched to Ridgway a directive from the National Security Council, instructing him to communicate with the Communist high command and to arrange for armistice talks. Early in the morning of the 30th, Ridgway's message was broadcast over every available radio station in Japan and Korea. Addressed to the enemy "Commander in Chief," it said: "I am informed that you may wish a meeting to discuss an armistice providing for cessation of hostilities and all acts of armed force in Korea. . . . Upon receipt of word from you that such a meeting is desired, I shall be prepared to name my representative. I would also at that time suggest a date at which he could meet with your representative. I propose that such a meeting could take place aboard a Danish hospital ship in Wonsan Harbor. . . ."

The reply came the following night, from two Communist commanders: North Korean military dictator Kim Il Sung, as supreme commander of the Korean People's Army, and Gen. Peng Teh-huai, commander of the "Chinese People's Volunteers." They rejected the Danish hospital ship, the *Jutlandia,* as the site of the conference, suggesting instead that it be held at Kaesong, one mile south of the Thirty-eighth parallel and about five miles beyond the United Nations outpost line on the western front. Allied patrols found "little enemy activity" in the Kaesong vicinity, and Ridgway mistakenly decided that it was a reasonably neutral site. Here trouble and disillusionment started.

On July 8th, three staff colonels from each side met in Kaesong to make arrangements for the armistice conference. United States air force Colonel Andrew J. Kinney, Marine Colonel James C. Murray, and ROK Lieutenant Colonel Soo Young Lee represented the United Nations. They found Kaesong populated with armed Chinese and North Korean troops who tolerated the presence of the escorted United Nations negotiators. It was far from a neutral meeting place in no-man's-land. The Communists had set the stage to show the world that the United Nations was suing for peace.

The Korean armistice negotiations formally opened on July 10th in a once-luxurious house on Kaesong's outskirts. The United Nations delegation comprised: Vice Admiral C. Turner Joy, commander of United States Far East Naval Forces; Major General L. C. Craigie, vice-commander of United States Far East Air Forces; Major General Henry I. Hodes, deputy chief of staff of the Eighth Army; Rear Admiral Arleigh A. Burke, commander of a cruiser division; and Major General Paik Sun Yup, South Korea's outstanding field general.

For the Communists: General Nam Il, 38-year-old "political officer" and long-time Soviet resident; Major General Chang Pyong San and Major General Lee Sang Cho of the North Korean army; Chinese Major General Hsieh Fang and Major General Tung Hua. Only Nam and Lee were on hand when the armistice finally was signed, two years, two weeks, three days, and millions of words later.

That morning at Munsan, the United Nations truce team's base camp, Admiral Joy refused to make any predictions on how long it would take to work out the cease-fire terms, but Allied newsmen watching the helicopter and jeep procession set out for Kaesong had already started a betting pool. The "pessimists" guessed six weeks.

# XVII

## *Stall and Rebuild*

THE FIRST THREE MONTHS of the war saw South Korea liberated from Communist occupation. In that time were compressed the withdrawal into the Pusan Beachhead, the desperate stand there while help slowly arrived, the planning and mounting of the Inchon landing, the breakout drives, the liberation of Seoul, and the Allies' hot-pursuit crossing of the Thirty-eighth parallel.

The first three months of the armistice negotiations produced exactly one agreement—on the agenda of topics to be discussed.

Were the Communists "stalling"? Yes, if that means stubbornly clinging to a position after it has repeatedly been rejected. Yes, if it means risking delays for the sake of propaganda advantage. But there were times when the shoe also fitted the United Nations command's foot.

The talks were deadlocked almost from their inception on the Communists' insistence that withdrawal of foreign troops from Korea should be the first order of business. Admiral Joy, making every move on signals called from Tokyo and Washington, said he was there to negotiate only a military armistice; withdrawal of the United Nations and Chinese Communist forces was a high-level political question for the peace settlement. The United States and the United Nations Allies had no intention of pulling out on the strength of a truce agreement, trusting virtually defenseless South Korea to the tender mercies of the North Koreans and their "volunteer" friends from across the Yalu. Many months later the Communists' troop-withdrawal plan won support from a strange quarter—South Korea's President Syngman Rhee. He violently denounced the United Nations for failing to make Chinese troop withdrawal—or the evacuation of all foreign troops if necessary—the key point of the armistice agreement.

The Reds dropped their demand at the ninth session, just as suggestions for a time limit on the truce talks began to appear in American news reports from Washington. The next day, Joy and Nam Il announced agreement on the following order of business: (1) fixing a military demarcation line to separate the opposing forces during a truce; (2) making concrete arrangements for a cease-fire and enforcement of armistice terms; (3) making "arrangements relative to prisoners of war"; and (4) filing "recommendations to the governments of the countries concerned" on the permanent settlement of the Korean conflict. The Communists reserved the right to insert their troop-withdrawal clause in these recommendations.

A new deadlock developed as soon as the first one was resolved. The Communists insisted that the demarcation line be on the Thirty-eighth parallel. They demanded that the United Nations army give up all the ground gained in two months of hill-by-hill advances into North Korea. Admiral Joy stood pat for a cease-fire "generally" along the actual battle line at the time a full armistice agreement should be reached. The Communists supported their contention by quoting recent statements by Secretary of State Acheson and United Nations Secretary-General Lie that a truce in the vicinity of the old border of South Korea would be a satisfactory way to end the shooting. The United Nations delegation argued that a cease-fire was exactly that— an agreement to stop shooting, not a territorial settlement. An armistice had no relation to pre-war boundaries the Communists themselves had sought to wipe from the maps on June 25th, 1950.

The deadlock produced a new twist in the conduct of international negotiations. On August 10th the white-haired American admiral opened the meeting by announcing that he was ready to discuss a cease-fire line and demilitarized zone "located generally in the area of the battle lines." Nam refused even to answer the offer. For two hours and eleven minutes of stubborn silence they glowered at each other, doodled, scribbled notes to other members of their delegations, and waited for the other man to weaken. Finally Joy called a recess and stalked out.

More than stubborn determination to hold on to a small chunk of North Korean real estate was involved in the United Nations stand. To accept the principle of a cease-fire along the Thirty-eighth parallel would have meant surrendering freedom to maintain ground pressure on the wounded, if not crippled, Red army during the truce negotiations. It would have given the Communists a virtual guarantee that there would be no major allied attack, for it would have been impossible to send United Nations troops into battle to die for North Korean hills already voluntarily relinquished and to be given up again on armistice day.

Tempers warmed as the deadlock tightened. Minor incidents occurring outside the conference room were treated with undue importance. Soon the propaganda war over violations of the neutrality of the conference site and air attacks on Communist truce delegation convoys was occupying the full time of the chief negotiators.

The "Battle of Incidents" began on the first day of the talks when the Communists set out to place the United Nations in the rôle of the vanquished suing for peace. Allied motor convoys were required to enter the "neutral" city of Kaesong bearing white flags, through lines of heavily armed Communist troops. Allied newsmen were barred from Kaesong. After two days of this propaganda staging, General Ridgway decided that it was time to show the Communists he would not play their game. He ordered the United Nations delegation to boycott the meetings until the situation was changed. In a radio message to the Red commanders he called for the creation of a truly neutral conference site. Ridgway's firm stand resulted in an agreement to "refrain from all hostile acts" within a five-mile radius of the center of Kaesong and to bar all armed troops except a limited number of military police from the area. Newsmen accompanied each delegation to the conference site—but not the meeting hall—as the talks resumed.

The next day the Communists filed their first of a long succession of protests, claiming that the United Nations army had violated the neutral territory by firing into it.

On August 4th, a company of armed Chinese soldiers marched openly past the United Nations staff house in Kaesong while Admiral Joy was having lunch. He noted it for the record at the afternoon session. General Ridgway took a sterner view. He suspended the negotiations and demanded an explanation from the Communist high command and a guarantee the incident would not be repeated. The Communists called it a "trivial" matter, but surprised everyone by admitting their guilt.

The Reds almost immediately set out to even the score. They claimed Allied aircraft were attacking clearly marked convoys of the Communist armistice delegation traveling between Kaesong and Pyongyang. Then they charged that United Nations troops had ambushed a Red military police patrol within the Kaesong neutral zone. The United Nations command denied the allegations and the talks droned on.

At 11:20 on the night of August 22nd, the Communist liaison officer called the United Nations base camp at Munsan by field telephone and claimed that an Allied plane had bombed Kaesong "with intent to murder the (Communist) delegates." United States Air Force Colonel Andrew J. Kinney arrived on the scene at 2 A.M. and found some damage which might have been caused by a variety of explosives other than an aerial bomb. He refused to concede, on the basis of a hasty inspection in the dark, that an Allied bombing had occurred. The senior Communist liaison officer, Colonel Chang Chun San, announced he was removing the evidence "for analysis." Then he declared, obviously with prior authority from the Communist high command, that all truce negotiations were "off from this time on."

Kim Il Sung and Peng Teh-Huai filed a blistering protest to the United Nations commander, who replied in kind. Ridgway told the Communists that their claims were "utterly false . . . preposterous and . . . obviously manufactured for your own questionable purposes." He rejected the bombing evidence as "malicious falsehoods."

Truce prospects cooled and the war became hotter as the suspension of negotiations continued through September and into October. The United Nations command proposed a change of scene and a fresh start at a new conference site. "When you decide to terminate the suspension of armistice negotiations," General Ridgway radioed the Communist commanders, "I propose that our liaison officers meet immediately at the bridge at Panmunjom to discuss selection of a new site." The Reds refused to budge and Ridgway refused to go back to Kaesong.

If the Communists were eager to end the shooting in July, why were they willing to risk a complete breakdown of negotiations in September? Military men believed the Reds' discovery that the United Nations command did not plan to launch a new offensive into North Korea accounted for their boldness. Diplomats attached more importance to the propaganda stakes: the Communists wanted to pin responsibility on the United Nations for the Kaesong bombing and, consequently, for the delay in achieving peace.

Whatever their reasons, the Communists finally agreed to shift the talks to Panmunjom, a village of four deserted mud huts about two-thirds of the way along the road from Munsan to Kaesong. Two weeks of liaison meetings there produced a complex agreement on neutral zones around the conference site, flanking the roads to Kaesong and Munsan, and around the opposing base camps. The armistice talks resumed there on October 25th, and the barometer of hope rose again.

The atmosphere in the Communist-supplied conference tent was businesslike during those early sessions at Panmunjom; solid progress was achieved. In the fourth session the Communists dropped their demand for a Thirty-eighth parallel truce; it was a concession which pessimists had believed impossible.

Soon it became apparent, however, that the Communists

wanted to put the cease-fire into effect immediately, while negotiations continued on the other provisions of the armistice agreement. They insisted that the demarcation line between the two armies be plotted on maps and declared final, regardless of subsequent changes in battle positions. While the shooting could continue, the practical effect would have been a paralysis of military action—a "de facto" cease-fire—such as would have resulted from fixing the Thirty-eighth parallel as the final demarcation line.

The Allies refused, insisting that the truce line be not actually fixed until the armistice was ready for signing. Admiral Joy's argument was based on sound foresight, but it was not easily defended. The United Nations delegation had agreed to the conference agenda, the first substantive item of which called for "fixing a military demarcation line" before taking up other business.

Just as a new deadlock was shaping up, the United Nations command offered a compromise: the Communists' "de facto cease-fire" scheme would be tried for thirty days. If complete agreement on the entire armistice could be reached within that time limit, the conditional demarcation line would become permanent, regardless of changes in the battle line which might occur during that period.

The war virtually stopped. United Nations and Communist staff officers agreed on the current line of contact, and on November 27th the race against the calendar was on.

"Home-by-Christmas" optimism enjoyed a brief revival. Pundits and plain people began accepting an armistice as practically achieved and again wondered aloud whether it was a good idea, after all. No one had a very clear notion of how a cease-fire could be converted into a real peace which would achieve the Allied political objective of Korean unification. Only the boldest optimists in the West dared predict that the Communists would accept unification of Korea, under a freely created government, without attaching an exhorbitant price tag to the transaction.

As it happened, there was no urgent need for peace-settlement planning in that hopeful pre-Christmas season of 1951. The drive for a truce in thirty days piled up one agreement on another, but it also revealed how big and time-consuming was the task of writing an armistice which, both sides realized, might be the last agreed word on Korea for many years. Christmas came, and the artillery boomed and whistled on. The deadline passed, and no end was in sight.

Suspicion—complete and unalleviated distrust—dominated every meeting across the green-topped table in the flapping tent at Panmunjom. It was the guiding principle of both delegations. In particular, it dictated Allied development of elaborate safeguards against military buildup under cover of the truce and against clandestine violations of the safeguards. Concessions on the most minor details were necessarily weighed as a military gamble.

Suspicion was justified. The Communists were using the relative lull on the battlefield to refill their ranks, stockpile supplies, and dig a labyrinth of bunkers which honeycombed not only the front-line ridges, but rear areas as well. Everything, from hospitals to headquarters, was going underground in apparent anticipation of a long war. Within three months after Russia proposed a Korean truce, General Van Fleet estimated that the Communist armies in Korea had not only replaced their Spring losses but had been expanded to 850,000 men. They were acquiring large numbers of Soviet artillery pieces and modern anti-aircraft guns. A formidable air force, equipped with as many as five hundred Soviet MIG-15 jet fighters and five hundred older planes, had come into being along the Manchurian side of the Yalu River by the end of 1951. These were strange preparations for a truce or the "peaceful settlement of the Korean problem by the Korean people."

The Communists found reason for suspicion, too. When the truce talks bogged down in the "Battle of Incidents," some prominent Americans called for a cessation of negotiation and "turning Van Fleet loose." Van Fleet did launch a series of "limited objective attacks" during the recess to gain dominating hills. Under Van Fleet's personal inspiration, the United States military advisory group organized an intensive retraining and rebuilding of the ROK Army. Syngman Rhee, whom the Communists regarded as an American puppet, used every opportunity to announce his disapproval of the truce talks and his belief that the Americans soon would see the necessity for a showdown battle for North Korea.

Still, progress was made in December, and the truce plan took shape.

The first task, after agreeing on the thirty-day trial ceasefire line, was to devise rules and machinery for insuring and enforcing a complete cessation of hostilities. The negotiations began poles apart.

The United Nations command proposed a set of rules designed to block any Communist plans to employ the truce period to prepare new aggression. The rules would have prohibited any increase in the number of foreign troops, planes, weapons, and other military equipment in Korea, ban airfield construction or rehabilitation, and provide for joint inspection behind the lines of both sides, including aerial survey, to enforce the agreements. The Communists opposed all these safeguards and returned to their stock solution, "withdrawal of foreign troops," a scheme no more acceptable to the United Nations in December than it had been in July.

Protracted, point-by-point bargaining started. The first major break came on December 3rd. The Communists accepted the principle of freezing foreign troop strength in Korea and, for the first time anywhere, agreed to admit inspection teams behind the Iron Curtain. Rather than joint military observation, they proposed that a group of "neutral" nations be asked to contribute members of neutral inspection teams to observe compliance with armistice terms behind the lines. Sub-committee meetings slowly narrowed the gap of disagreement on the other truce-enforcement issues. The Communists agreed to permit continuation of the "rotation" and replacement of troops at the end of their tours of duty in Korea so long as the total troop strength did not increase, but they demanded a limit on the rate of replacement. The Allies dropped six truce-keeping safeguards, including aerial inspection and the right of unrestricted travel by the inspection teams on the ground. They also gave up an effort to retain control of United Nations-occupied islands north of the cease-fire line. Disagreement continued on whether airfield reconstruction should be prohibited, on the number of ports of entry at which neutral inspectors would be stationed, and the monthly ceiling on troop rotation.

In an effort to give the world a Korean truce by the Christmas season, the United Nations Command had proposed simultaneous talks on the remaining agenda items—prisoner exchange and post-armistice "recommendations to the governments concerned." The Communists were reluctant to open additional negotiations before the truce-enforcement issue was completely resolved. But on December 11th they bowed to Allied pressure and sent representatives to a sub-committee meeting on prisoner exchange.

Here the real trouble began.

# XVIII

## *Prisoners*

THE KOREAN WAR never conformed to the well-known patterns. From the beginning it was a strange mixture of old-fashioned military conflict and an ill-defined new concept of collective security through international police action. It was compounded with a large portion of psychological warfare extending far beyond the Korean peninsula. It was an outgrowth of the cold war. Consequently, propaganda maneuvers often occupied the central battleground. The shift of emphasis to propaganda considerations increased as both sides accepted the fact of military stalemate.

It should have been no surprise, therefore, that negotiation of a cease-fire became entangled in ideological issues and propaganda by-plays only vaguely related to a purely military armistice. Panmunjom was not primarily a place for writing a truce agreement; it was a handy arena in the cold-war battle for men's minds.

When the prisoner-exchange debate opened on December 11th, 1951, the Allied casualty toll stood at 305,000, including 104,000 American, 192,000 ROK and nine thousand other United Nations troops killed, wounded, missing, and captured. Eighteen months later, agreement finally was reached on a prisoner-release and repatriation scheme. In those eighteen months of waiting for an armis-

216

tice, the United Nations forces suffered an additional one hundred and forty thousand casualties, including nearly nine thousand Americans killed. They died while negotiators of a military truce deadlocked over a political issue whether the Allies were obligated to repatriate fifteen thousand Chinese and thirty-five thousand North Korean prisoners of war who did not wish to return to Communism.

When President Truman made the firm decision to take a stand against forced repatriation, the free world applauded. No one could anticipate then that nine thousand American lives would be sacrificed in establishing a war prisoner's right to political asylum. Certainly, the highest officials at United Nations command headquarters did not expect that this issue would become the chief obstacle to an armistice. When the cost in blood became apparent, it was too late to decide that the objective was not worth the price. After holding in POW camps and listing as war prisoners Koreans who deserted to escape Communism, after cloaking the principle of free choice for war prisoners in the language of historic significance, after picturing it as an essential precedent for any future war with a Communist-enslaved people, we could not easily cast the principle aside to buy an earlier truce.

The Communists' equally stubborn refusal to compromise on their demand that every Red army captive be repatriated, at bayonet point if necessary, suggested to many officials and observers that delay was the Reds' objective. According to this theory, the prisoner-exchange controversy merely provided the most plausible excuse for delay; it was argued that, if the United Nations command had not raised the voluntary repatriation issue, the Communists would have found another issue on which to block an armistice. Such speculation is fruitless, because even in retrospect we lack real knowledge of the decisions taken in Communist secret councils.

Only this much is clear: for eighteen months neither side so desperately wanted a truce, or so clearly saw the way to converting the armistice into a peace favorable to its own interests, as to be willing to compromise after the prisoner-exchange deadlock developed. Later, too much "face" was involved; the repatriation issue had become a symbol.

It all started with the exchange of prisoner lists. For a week the Communist negotiators refused to reveal the number of Allied prisoners they were prepared to exchange until the United Nations command agreed that all captives then held would be repatriated. The Allied representatives refused to discuss the exchange rules until they knew how many Allied prisoners the Communists would exchange for the 132,000 Communist prisoners the United Nations held. Before making any commitments, the Allies also wanted to know how many prisoners had survived the ordeal of North Korean imprisonment. Already there had been reports from Korean agents and refugees of mass deaths among Allied prisoners resulting from starvation, medical neglect, brutality, and more vicious atrocities.

The lists were finally exchanged on December 18th. The Communists listed the names of only 11,559 Allied prisoners, including 7,142 South Koreans, 3,198 Americans, 919 British, 234 Turks, 40 Filipinos, 10 French, 4 Australians, 4 South Africans, 3 Japanese, and one each from Canada, Greece and Holland. The United Nations command furnished the names of 132,747 Communist prisoners.

American reaction, both official and public, was violent. During the first nine months of the war, the Communist

Pyongyang radio had broadcast official communiqués claiming capture of sixty-five thousand Allied troops. Possibly it was ambitious propaganda, but the figure did not exceed the number of men missing in action. More than ten thousand Americans were missing, and the Communists' prisoner list accounted for only one-third of them. Where were the missing fifty thousand South Korean troops?

The United Nations delegation and General Ridgway's headquarters studied the list and replied with specific and searching questions: Of the one hundred and ten prisoners reported by the Communists to the International Red Cross before all reporting was halted, why did the names of only forty-four appear on the latest list? Why were 1,056 Allied captives named at one time or another by Communist broadcasts and publications or identified as prisoners to Allied intelligence missing from the list? What had happened to the rest of the sixty-five thousand Allied prisoners the Communists had claimed nine months earlier? Of 585 Allied prisoners, mostly American, who were known to have reached rear-area prison camps safely, why were only 135 listed?

The implications were shocking. If the sample figures were representative, more than seventy per cent. of all Allied prisoners had died or disappeared.

The Communists admitted that 726 of the listed 1,056 had died or escaped or had been "released." They could not find records on the other 322. They wanted to forget about the sixty-five-thousand-prisoner boast but remarked that the low "resistance against climate and illness" of the captured Americans and South Koreans was one explanation for the small number of prisoners who survived.

Why were so few South Korean prisoners reported when

more than fifty thousand were missing? One explanation, the Communists said, was that captured Koreans were "re-educated" and "released at the front" in accordance with Chinese "revolutionary policy." Those so released had, strangely enough, volunteered to serve in the People's Army.

The United Nations Command also had engaged in an organized program of "re-education" among captured Communists. It also had offered political asylum to North Koreans and Chinese fighting with the Red Army who sought escape from Communism. Thousands had accepted this offer, made in leaflets and radio or loudspeaker broadcasts, and had voluntarily given themselves up, trusting the United Nations or the United States to live up to its promise. Unlike the Communists, the United Nations Command had not violated recognized rules of warfare by impressing into military service either those men who came into PW camps as anti-communists or those who subsequently turned against communism. They were still listed as prisoners and held in stockades in southern Korea.

In planning for the truce talks and the prisoner exchange, American officials had recalled the tragedy of forced return of anti-Communist political refugees to Russia and other Communist countries after World War II. The United States and most western countries had decided never again to take part in such wholesale violation of human rights. The 1949 Geneva Convention on treatment of prisoners of war did not, however, specifically apply this lesson of experience with civilians to the rules for repatriation of military prisoners. The principle of "voluntary repatriation" was not new, however. Russia had issued a surrender ultimatum to German troops during World War II offering them a choice of return to Germany or resettlement in the Soviet Union.

Against this background and in the face of Communist demands for return of every captive, the United Nations command formally introduced its plan for voluntary repatriation on January 2nd, 1952. American Rear Admiral R. E. Libby, head of the American sub-delegation negotiating the prisoner issue, stated the case for the United Nations viewpoint in a lengthy exposition which was to be rephrased and echoed by Allied delegates throughout the months of debate that followed. He then outlined the complex United Nations plan:

"1. POW's who elect repatriation shall be exchanged on a one-for-one basis until one side has exchanged all such POW's held by it.

"2. The side which thereafter holds POW's shall repatriate all those POW's who elect to be repatriated in a one-for-one exchange for foreign civilians interned by the other side, and for civilians and other persons of the one side who are at the time of the signing of the armistice in the territory under control of the other side, and who elect to be repatriated. POW's thus exchanged shall be paroled to the opposing force, such parole to carry with it the condition that the individual shall not again bear arms against the side releasing him.

"3. All POW's not electing repatriation shall be released from POW status and shall be paroled, such parole to carry with it the condition that the individual will not again bear arms in the Korean conflict.

"4. All remaining civilians of either side who are, at the time of the signing of the armistice, in territory under control of the other side, shall be repatriated if they so elect.

"5. In order to insure that the choice regarding repatriation is made without duress, delegates of the ICRC (International Committee of Red Cross Societies) shall be permitted to interview all POW's at the points of exchange, and all civilians of either side who are at the time of the armistice in territory under the control of the other side.

"6. For the purposes of paragraphs 2, 4 and 5, civilians and other persons of either side are defined as those who on 25 June 1950 were bona-fide residents of either the Republic of Korea or the Democratic People's Republic of (North) Korea.

"In summary, the UNC proposal provides for the release of all POW's including soldiers of the other side who may have been incorporated into the army of the detaining power. Thus, it is consistent with the first principle advanced by your side that all POW's be released. As regards repatriation, it permits freedom of choice on the part of the individual, thus insuring that there will be no forced repatriation against the will of an individual. It provides repatriation not for POW's alone but for those other victims of war, the displaced civilians. All those who desire it are permitted to return to their former homes. Finally, the proposal provides for a supervisory organ to interview the persons involved to insure that, whatever their choice, such choice will be made freely and without duress."

The Communists categorically rejected the United Nations proposal and sought to brand voluntary repatriation as a plot to detain Communist prisoners against their will for various evil purposes. They also rejected the one-for-one exchange formula, designed by the United Nations command to draw the maximum number of Allied prisoners and ex-prisoners out of North Korea. This was later modified and finally dropped by the American negotiators, but the deadlock over forced versus voluntary repatriation tightened.

The Communists found their strongest argument in the terms of the 1949 Geneva Convention, although they had never recognized it and had violated its requirements whenever convenient to do so.

Article 7 stipulates: "Prisoners of war may in no circumstances renounce in part or in entirety the rights secured to them by the present convention. . . ."

Article 118 provides: "Prisoners of war shall be released and repatriated without delay after the cessation of active hostilities. . . ."

The Communists insisted that the words had no other possible meaning than repatriation of every prisoner, regardless of his alleged personal desire to renounce his homeland. The United Nations delegation replied that this interpretation would "convert a document designed to aid the individual into one completely negating his rights. You are saying that the prisoner of war has a right to be handed over to you, and since he has that right he has the obligation to go back whether or not he wishes to. We cannot believe that the framers of the convention had any such purpose in mind."

Wearily and repetitiously, the debate continued through January, February, and March while staff officers meeting separately put non-controversial elements of the prisoner-exchange plan into draft form. Meanwhile, the truce-enforcement negotiations had lapsed into the same "no-progress" rut, lacking the pressure of a deadline or of progress in the key prisoner-exchange meetings. These talks made little headway in clearing the last two obstacles: United

Nations insistence on a ban on airfield construction and Communist nomination of Russia as a member of the "neutral" truce-inspection teams.

Progress was recorded, unexpectedly, on the final agenda item: "Recommendations to the governments of the countries concerned." The full delegations met seven times during February and agreed on a recommendation which laid the basis for a peace conference. Adopted on February 17th and entered into the armistice agreement as Article Four, it provided:

"In order to insure the peaceful settlement of the Korean question, the military commanders of both sides hereby recommend to the governments of the countries concerned on both sides that within three months after the armistice agreement is signed and becomes effective, a political conference of a higher level of both sides be held by representatives appointed respectively to settle through negotiation the questions of the withdrawal of all foreign forces from Korea, the peaceful settlement of the Korean question, et cetera."

Admiral Joy agreed on the recommendation with the qualification for the record that the Allies "do not construe the word 'et cetera' to relate to matters outside of Korea."

The brief display of harmony and progress encouraged no celebrations of an imminent truce. Many had come to think of a Korean truce as a phantom never to be snared. The prisoner deadlock strengthened this widely held conviction.

In a new effort to reach agreement on a prisoner-repatriation plan the problem was turned over to staff officers to negotiate in secret. It was felt that, free of the pressures of publicity and the demands of "face" and propaganda, the working-level colonels might find a compromise. Almost immediately this approach appeared to bear fruit. The Communist staff officer cautiously indicated willingness to negotiate the issue if the United Nations command would first disclose in round numbers how many Chinese and North Korean prisoners were seeking political asylum. The United Nations command could not answer even approximately, but proposed to interview all its prisoners and report back with the required figures. It also requested and obtained from the Communist command an official assurance to be given all prisoners that they would not suffer retribution for anti-communist leanings or activities in prison camp if they returned home.

The "screening" interviews touched off an explosion in the tense and teeming United Nations POW compounds on Koje Island. More than 132,000 prisoners of war and 38,000 civilian internees were concentrated on the small island off the southern tip of Korea. Nominally they were under the control of an American PW camp administration and a small ROK and United States guard detachment. Actually, they were being ruled by communist "commissars" and cadres within the compounds. During the Winter and early Spring, top Communists among the prisoners tightened their control over the five thousand or more men jammed inside each barbed wire enclosure. Under orders of trained communist agents, who, according to American intelligence, deliberately surrendered in order to get to Koje and organize rebellion, the compound commissars established unchallenged prisoner rule. A shortsighted and understaffed procession of American camp commanders, operating under a "soft" policy directive, did little to check the plot until it was too late to prevent a bloody and em-

barrassing showdown. Already there had been riots, mur-
ders, and savage episodes of "justice" for prisoners who
spoke out against Communism.

Into this hornet's nest came the screening teams with
their questionnaires and a plan to segregate the communist and anti-communist prisoners. Several compound
leaders effectively prevented their prisoners from taking
part in the screening. In other compounds there were
clashes between fanatical Communists and their back-slid-
ing countrymen. However, most of the prisoners and internees filed through the interview booths at the gates to
each compound and made their decisions. The questions
were designed to warn a man who chose self-exile that no
Utopia awaited him. Only those who persisted through all
the questions and declared that they would forcibly resist
repatriation were pulled out of the communist compounds
and sent to new mainland camps.

At the end of the day a startling fact emerged. Only
seventy thousand wanted to return to communism; two-
thirds of the Chinese "volunteers" said they would not
voluntarily go back. Nearly half the North Koreans interviewed and more than two-thirds of the civilian internees
chose certain hardship and isolation from their homes and
families rather than live again under Communist rule.
Later, after the toughest North Korean compounds were
broken up and the screening completed, the total who
would accept repatriation rose to nearly seventy-five thousand, but the picture of mass rejection of Communism remained.

It was a disastrous blow to the entire Communist world
and required an immediate counter-attack. When the
screening results were laid on the Panmunjom conference

table, the Communist colonel cried "fraud" and stormily broke off the secret sessions on April 25th.

The screening, tacitly endorsed by the Communist truce delegation before the results came in, was denounced as a vicious American scheme to hold one hundred thousand Koreans and Chinese in perpetual slavery to the Wall Street imperialists. The Peiping, Pyongyang, and Moscow radios and the entire Red propaganda machine charged in unison that threats, intimidation, and torture had been employed to persuade the prisoners to vote against repatriation— after they were first softened up through forced indoctrination by "Syngman Rhee and Chiang Kai-shek agents."

The United Nations command supported the validity of its screening and claimed, with the wording of the screening questions to support its contention, that if any pressure had been used it was to encourage Chinese and North Korean prisoners to go home. Privately, high United Nations headquarters officers in Tokyo said they had hoped that the screening would reveal so small a number of anti-communists that the Red truce delegation could compromise gracefully.

Admiral Joy called a full-dress session on April 28th and with a tone of finality proposed a "package solution" of all the remaining issues blocking an armistice:

1. Communist acceptance of the voluntary repatriation principle and the exchange of about seventy thousand Communist prisoners for about twelve thousand United Nations captives whom the Communists admitted holding. The United Nations would drop its demand for recovery and repatriation (on a voluntary basis) of the thousands of ROK captives impressed into the North Korean Army. To remove doubts about the fairness of the United Nations

screening, the Communists could observe a re-screening by a neutral agency such as joint Red Cross teams after the armistice was signed and before the prisoner exchange began. If any anti-Communist prisoners changed their minds, they would be free to go home.

2. The United Nations would drop its demand for restriction on airfield construction during the truce.

3. The Communists would drop their nomination of Russia to the Neutral Nations Supervisory Commission, and the United Nations would withdraw its nomination of Norway, making it a four-nation inspection commission of Sweden, Switzerland, Czechoslovakia, and Poland.

The Communists called a recess to consider the compromise proposal. They returned to the conference table on May 2nd and flatly rejected it.

Real negotiation stopped. The Communists hurled invectives at the United Nations delegation and propaganda at the entire world. The United Nations negotiators listened with growing impatience, occasionally restated the finality of the United Nations position, and called for a series of recesses in the hope of leading the Communists to advance a constructive compromise.

In May, General Ridgway succeeded General Eisenhower in Europe, and General Mark W. Clark took the United Nations and United States Far East commands. A towering, angular man, Clark brought to the job plainspoken frankness and a deeply ingrained sense of the team player who knows that the signals are to be called in Washington. He inherited the long-delayed task of bringing order to the Koje Island prisoner of war camp and restoring control over rebellious Communist prisoners. And he immediately found himself in the middle of a Syngman Rhee versus National Assembly political battle behind the lines in Korea—his first but far from last encounter with the single-minded old autocrat of South Korea who was to become the greatest thorn in Clark's, and America's, side.

At the Panmunjom conference table, Admiral Joy turned over the unenviable job of chief negotiator to Major General William K. Harrison, former Eighth Army chief of staff, who had been a member of the United Nations truce team for four months. Harrison, a Baptist lay preacher, abstained from profanity but found that no handicap in delivering a blistering public denunciation of his Communist opposites after the daily sparring sessions in the conference tent. Some observers feared his truculence would make it impossible for the Communists to initiate any compromise gesture. Later it was apparent, however, that Harrison's strong words had no influence on Communist policy.

A hard, unyielding deadlock which was to last a full year had begun.

# XIX

## *Stalemate*

More words than bullets were fired during the second year of the war. The prospect as the third year dawned was for a continuation of the same fare. But the bullets killed and maimed, and in the bloody mountain arenas where localized but fierce clashes erupted, men died in war which for them was still total.

The ground fighting itself had almost no influence on events. The lines of battle were fixed, first by the United Nations decision to sign a truce, then by temporary agreement on the demarcation line, and finally by the fact of military stalemate and the fear of tampering with the tantalizing hope for peace.

The "twilight war" flared into heavy fighting in the month-long battle of Heartbreak Ridge. There, during the September-October recess in the truce talks, two of the United States army's finest regiments—the Ninth and Twenty-third of the Second Division—and the attached French Battalion paid an appalling price for three towering, barren peaks which dominated the east-central front. After the thirty-day "Little Armistice" ending December 27th, 1951 and through the rest of the second year, localized but furious battles raged daily somewhere along the front on outpost hills which won fleeting fame in newspaper head-lines. The opposing armies dug deeper into shell-pocked ridges, probed and patrolled by night, and killed with ar-tillery on a 'round-the-clock schedule.

*Despite boredom and moments of seemingly purposeless suffering and death, a spirit of high adventure and good humor survived. Allied soldiers still tried to act like sol-diers.*

*An infantry lieutenant, who had lost an arm in the end-less "battle of the hills," ordered a soldier to go back and look for the missing limb. "There's a damned good Ma-sonic ring on the middle finger," he said.*

*Another infantryman, seconds away from death, asked with a wry smile in his final words, "Anybody know any good jokes?"*

*Hardly a dugout lacked a sign posted near the entrance —anything from "Waldorf Towers Basement" to "Home Sweet Home Hava-No" to "Marilyn Monroe Slept Here."*

*Signs, some new and some survivors of a year of shelling and weather, told the story of GI reaction to the war:*

*Planted by an outfit expecting orders to pull back under Red attack: "Look, Reds, don't throw trash in the area. We're coming back."*

*Fallen off a rickety bridge post near the Thirty-eighth parallel: "Gateway to Manchuria."*

*Along a road near the front, Burma-Shave style: "Heavy-Foot Harry . . . Passed a jeep on a grade . . . They picked up Harry . . . With a Broom and a Spade," and many more like it.*

*Name of a key outpost hill bearing twin, rounded peaks: "Jane Russell Hill." After months of artillery pounding had flattened its curves, some tried to change the name in an unflattering tribute to less amply endowed movie actresses.*

The great sustainers of high morale, and the chief subjects of conversation and hope, were "R & R" leave in Japan and "Big R," or rotation home. R & R had various official translations—Rest and Rehabilitation, Rest and Recreation, Rest and Relaxation. It was usually more aptly described by another name for the five-day plunge into the pleasures of Japanese civilization—"S & S" or Sex and Sake. About every six months an American could count on a five-day fling in Japan, where he either explored the fleshpots or struggled with his conscience and polished up lies to match the R & R reports of his less inhibited fellows.

For the army, Korean duty was measured not in battles or months but in points—four for every month at the front, three for intermediate areas, and two for non-combat areas. Thirty-six or thirty-eight points brought rotation home. The navy, air force, Marines and other United Nations units had different systems, but the sure prospect of going home after surviving a year of combat duty sustained all the men actually under fire.

The air forces carried as heavy a burden and against more effective resistance than they had during the first year of fluid warfare. The second year opened with an intensified and continuing Allied air offensive and closed on the same note. For North Korea there was no respite from bombs and fear until the truce was signed.

The Allied air assault smashed bridges, railroads, barracks and warehouses and took the inevitable toll of simple peasants' huts. This systematic aerial campaign against

Communist supply lines, called "Operation Strangle," raised the price in manhours and precious supplies that Communist China and Russia had to pay to support a massive army. The drain may have been so significant, as air enthusiasts claim, that it discouraged Red ambitions to try another offensive and weakened the entire Communist world, but it did not keep the Red army from rebuilding its strength rapidly. By mid-1952 it out-gunned the Eighth Army in artillery pieces by nearly two to one and had swollen to nearly one million men—twice its effective strength on the day the truce talks started.

A more clear-cut triumph for Allied airpower was scored by denying the Communists freedom to use their growing air arm against the United Nations forces. Immunity from air attack was one of the Eighth Army's greatest blessings and a significant military factor in the balance of numerically unequal ground forces. Supplies and troops moved in close convoys behind the United Nations front. Headquarters and installations beyond Communist artillery range could stay above ground, with a minimum of time and manpower spent in camouflage and anti-aircraft precautions.

Flashing Sabrejets ruled the skies to within sight of the big Communist air base at Antung, on the Manchurian side of the Yalu. Jet fighter-bombers of the Fifth Air Force and Seventh Fleet and propeller-driven warplanes of all services attacked Communist Korea at will behind the Sabres' protective screen. B-29 Superforts based in Okinawa and Japan, and Korea-based B-26 light bombers blasted big and minor targets by night. When the Superforts switched to night bombing, the Communists boasted that their MIGs had driven the B-29s from the daylight sky. The fact was that there were too few prime targets left in North Korea to justify even light losses. The MIGs, lacking radar tracking devices, were blind at night.

By the end of the second year, United Nations air force planes had inflicted in air-to-air combat a toll of 365 MIGs and 145 propellered Communist aircraft known destroyed against a loss of seventy-nine Allied planes shot down by MIGs. (Communist ground fire claimed about one Allied fighter-bomber per day, or an average of one per five hundred air force and navy combat sorties.) The American kill-loss superiority against the vaunted MIG rose steadily until it reached ten to one at the close of the war. For Sabre-jets alone, it reached nearly fourteen to one.

The second year ended on a shrill note of air alarm set off by a mass raid on the Yalu River hydroelectric plants. The biggest air strike of the war on June 23rd, 1952, carried hostilities back to the gateway of the "Manchurian sanctuary." Some five hundred United States navy, air force, and Marine planes hit the great Suiho Dam and three others, knocking out ninety per cent. of North Korea's power supply. The Manchurian border target was loaded with political dynamite. The all-American raid was carried out without prior consultation with the other United Nations Allies, and it briefly revived British fears that the impetuous Americans, their patience worn thin by the frustrating truce talks, were about to expand the war into China.

For two years Suiho Dam, powering both North Korea and Manchurian industry, had been "off limits" to Allied warplanes. Were other restrictions on American air operations also about to be lifted unilaterally by the United States government? While British on both sides of the

House of Commons protested, two hundred more American fighter-bombers returned the next day and finished off the job.

The tempest soon passed. The air offensive remained confined to Korea, and predictions of a tougher, more independent American war policy proved unfounded.

Summer brought the close of a year of frustrated hopes for peace, a year of half-war that seemed without end or purpose. The year-end balance sheet showed seven thousand more American lives lost while the armistice negotiations dragged on and the Communists doubled their military strength in Korea.

Summer also brought anniversaries, on June 25th and July 10th, and a soul-searching fear that indecision was giving the Communists victory. But it brought no climacterics, no emotional or practical cause for breaking off the truce talks and plunging into a fight to the finish. The armistice was being blocked by a single major issue, defined in American eyes as Communist delay in opposition to a humanitarian principle in the repatriation of war prisoners. The Communists might stall for months or forever, or they might give in and permit an armistice within hours. Was this a situation sufficiently clearcut or a cause so vital as to justify America's "going it alone" in a new and costly attempt to drive to the Yalu?

Washington's answer remained "No." The American public's answer came in the Presidential election campaign, where both parties discovered a strong popular demand to "do something" about the "Korean mess" but no mandate to spend more lives, risk world war, or draft more and spend more. MacArthur's theme, "There is no substitute for victory," had a brief revival in Republican convention oratory and the first weeks of the campaign, but party strategists were careful to insure that it did not become a clue to Republican intentions in Korea. They did not want the "war party" label.

The American Presidential campaign froze the pattern of life, death, and truce deadlock in Korea. Only a major decision by the United Nations or the Communist side, based largely on pressures outside Korea, could change the prospect of endless stalemate. The Truman administration could not reverse its Korea policy in the midst of the campaign and make the concession required to achieve a truce or the decision which would launch a bid for complete victory. After the Republican triumph, the "lame duck" Democratic administration was even more powerless to alter the course of events in Korea. On their part, the Communists were content to wait for the dust to settle in America before making their next move.

When candidate Eisenhower promised in the closing days of the campaign that he would go to Korea and seek a solution, the truce machinery had already stopped completely. The breakdown of negotiations had begun in May, when the Communists rejected a United Nations command offer to re-screen under Communist and neutral observation all prisoners refusing repatriation. In June General Harrison had seized the initiative in the propaganda battle and hammered on the theme that the Reds were afraid to face the truth of Communism's failure. The Communists replied with their most elaborate and successful propaganda campaign of the war—the charge, supported by "confessions" of captured American pilots, that the United States was waging bacteriological warfare against North Korea. The Panmunjom meetings also gave General Nam Il an audience for a less credible and more amateurish propaganda gambit. He accused the United States of blocking repatriation of all prisoners so as to use thousands of Chinese and North Korean captives in atomic bomb and germ warfare experiments.

General Harrison walked out on one of these tirades on June 7th and announced he would be back on June 11th. The Communists vainly demanded daily meetings to air their invective; the United Nations command refused. When no progress followed the recess, Harrison called another, and still another. One-week recesses became the rule; these were broken by a period of fruitless secret sessions in late July.

A series of staff-level meetings in August produced tacit Communist agreement to dropping Russia from the Neutral Supervisory Commission and United Nations acceptance of unrestricted airfield construction during the armistice. Only the prisoner deadlock remained.

On September 28th, the United Nations command made its final compromise offer. General Harrison gave the Communists a choice of three plans which would guarantee freedom of choice by prisoners and insure that no coercion was used by the detaining power to influence a prisoner's choice. Under one of the three alternative plans, all prisoners would be brought to the demilitarized zone in small groups, told which way the Communist and Allied lines lay, and released. The Communists once had boasted that this was what they had done with thousands of South Korean captives "released at the front." Now they rejected it and all other solutions short of forcible repatriation. General Nam announced the Red stand on October 8th, and the United Nations immediately called an "indefinite recess."

Harrison, in his parting remarks, laid down the United Nations terms:

"We will meet with you whenever you indicate that you are willing to accept one of our proposals or have presented in writing the text of any constructive proposals, designed to achieve an armistice, which you may desire to make. The plenary sessions now stand in recess."

It was the last meeting for six months.

# XX

## *Peace Offensive*

Korea was the battleground but seldom the scene or source of key decisions. The Korean powder keg was made in Yalta and Potsdam, not by Koreans. The signals which sent the North Korean Army across the Thirty-eighth parallel that fateful Sunday morning in 1950 undoubtedly were called in Moscow. The American and United Nations decisions to intervene were prompted more by the necessity of discouraging Communist aggression throughout the world than by the importance of South Korea itself. The decision that made the war a major and lasting conflict—Communist China's intervention—likewise originated outside Korea. The United States, the United Nations Allies and the United Nations Secretary-General suggested ending the fighting, over South Korea's official objections. Russia chose the moment and proposed an armistice conference. Two long-time Soviet residents, Nam Il and Lee Sang Cho, and several Chinese generals negotiated the truce for the North Korean side. Americans conducted the entire negotiations for the South, with a single ROK general serving on the delegation but without authority to influence decisions, which were made entirely in Tokyo and Washington.

In Korea, the United States met and negotiated by proxy with its global enemy, Soviet Russia. The military stalemate and the armistice deadlock were reflections of the global balance of titans, afraid of the consequences of bigger war and uncertain of the multiple effects of any settlement short of a clearcut conference-table victory.

Now, as snow and ice blanketed the nearly deserted Panmunjom conference site for a second winter, it was apparent that a deadlock-breaking move, if it ever came, was not likely to originate at Panmunjom and would not be merely a rephrasing of old proposals. A new factor had to enter the picture from outside—a new situation or new assessment of the world situation which justified compromising on the prisoner repatriation issue, plus a new formula for camouflaging the retreat.

A new formula came from the United Nations General Assembly in December. A compromise repatriation plan proposed by India was adopted with the lukewarm support of the United States and the votes of the entire anti-communist world. But the new conditions within the Soviet orbit had not yet developed, and Russia, seconded from afar by Communist China and North Korea, bluntly rejected the Indian effort.

On the American side, a new situation was developing with the election of a Republican administration and the rise to positions of Congressional leadership of men who had advocated a military showdown with Communist China, if necessary, to end the Korean stalemate. But the American elections also brought to power a government pledged to reduce taxes and balance the budget.

The most significant break in the pattern of global deadlock developed in Moscow. Josef Stalin died, and his successor as ruler of world communism, Georgi Malenkov, launched a new "peace offensive" abroad and turned more of the Communist world's energies, for the moment, to curing internal ailments. Again, at last, the pendulum of communist strategy swung toward peace. But that was in March.

No such dramatic answer to the Korean riddle could be anticipated in November and December when the United Nations General Assembly was searching for a formula to break the prisoner-exchange deadlock. The debate sounded and read like so many of the assembly's fruitless efforts to translate speechmaking into peace-making. Russia's Andrei Vishinsky and America's Dean Acheson lengthily restated the opposing arguments so well worn from repetition at Panmunjom. Vishinsky called for an immediate and unconditional cease-fire without a prisoner settlement, sidetracking the prisoner dispute to the proposed post-armistice political (peace) conference. The United States replied that the peace conference, lacking the pressure of ending the fighting, would be less capable of resolving the issue than the United Nations Assembly or the Panmunjom negotiators. The peace conference, it was argued, might debate interminably while all prisoners rotted in PW camps. The Russian scheme was soundly defeated and the Assembly gave its overwhelming endorsement to the American principle of voluntary repatriation. The score remained zero to zero.

India entered the picture in the rôle of the great Asian neutral. Indian delegate V. K. Krishna Menon offered a formula which avoided the injustice of indefinite captivity for those prisoners who wanted to go home and upheld the United Nations principle of free choice, but accepted the communist idea of referring the fate of non-repatriates to the peace conference.

The Indian plan provided:

1. All prisoners of war held by both sides would be turned over to a five-nation neutral commission in demilitarized areas.

2. All prisoners who told the neutral commission they wanted to go home would be repatriated immediately.

3. Decision on those remaining in the commission's custody after ninety days would be referred to the peace conference which, according to the final article of the draft armistice agreement, was to be held within ninety days after the cease-fire began. .

4. If the peace conference failed within a thirty-day time limit to agree on disposition of those who refused repatriation (the United Nations Allies at the conference would be free to block forced repatriation), they would be turned over to the United Nations for re-settlement.

This last point seemed vague to many. To the Communists, it was a scheme to leave their "intimidated and misled" captured soldiers forever in the hands of the enemy—the United Nations. The United States government believed reference of the dispute to the peace conference would be futile and was reluctant to agree to the four-month period of neutral custody for prisoners seeking political asylum. Nevertheless, the United States announced it would vote for the Indian plan.

The Indians had been confident that Moscow and Peiping would accept a reasonable compromise. Instead, Vishinsky violently denounced India's mediating efforts and added insult to injury by accusing the Indian chief delegate of joining the Anglo-American camp because he accepted the Allied doctrine of free choice. Despite the Soviet bloc's opposition, however, the United Nations Political Committee adopted the formula on December 1st and the Assembly voted approval two days later. Even before the proposal was officially transmitted to Communist China, the Peiping and Pyongyang radios parroted Vishinsky's scathing denunciation of India and rejected any compromise which did not include forced repatriation. Official rejection messages from the Russian and Chinese governments followed, apparently closing the door to peace within the foreseeable future.

Four months later a modified version of the Indian plan was suddenly presented by the Communists. The modifications could easily have been made in the General Assembly in December, sparing thousands of lives, if Russia had been seriously seeking a Korean armistice at that time.

What happened between December 1st and late March to account for the Communists' about-face? There was little that the new American government, coming into office in January, did or might have done in so short a time to cause the Communists to become eager for peace. From the moment his campaign-promised mission to Korea aroused popular hopes, President-elect Eisenhower took pains to warn of the realities of the complex Korean situation. The United States apparently faced three unpleasant choices: (1) to prepare rapidly for a big war in Asia, shooting for military victory or at least a truce on American terms; (2) to prepare for indefinite stalemate and a long border war, attempting to reduce the war's drain on American resources to a minimum; or (3) to concede defeat on the issue of political asylum for prisoners and settle for a truce which would give Communism a great propaganda victory.

Soldier-statesman Eisenhower knew that a fourth and better alternative was not likely to be discovered on a flying visit to Korea, and he publicly discounted the possibility that he might find a "trick solution." But politician Eisenhower felt compelled to fulfill his campaign promise, and soldier Eisenhower knew the value of an on-the-spot examination of a military situation even when spectacular results could not be expected.

The American President-elect, his defense secretary, Charles E. Wilson, his attorney-general, Herbert Brownell, and the chairman of the Joint Chiefs of Staff, General Omar N. Bradley, flew to Korea on December 2nd. In three closely scheduled days, General Eisenhower watched picked ROK troops in mock battle exercises, visited many units of the multi-nation United Nations forces, attended nearly a score of briefings, conferred with the American commanders in the field, and talked with President Rhee.

He reserved judgment on the military offensive plans outlined by Generals Clark and Van Fleet as possible alternatives to inaction. Clark made it clear that he would need more American divisions, more air power, more amphibious naval forces, and freedom to bomb Manchuria before he could undertake a major offensive with reasonable chance of success.

Eisenhower also was noncommittal after hearing Rhee's practiced recitation of the case for launching a new drive to the Yalu. In a tour-end speech to the press he reflected his determination not to start a bigger war to end this one: "How difficult it seems to be in a war of this kind," he said, "to work out a plan that would bring a positive and definite victory without possibly running the grave risk of enlarging the war." His attitude of caution doused South

Korean official hopes that the new Republican administration intended forthwith to begin rolling back the Iron Curtain in Asia.

The visit confirmed in Eisenhower's mind the wisdom of a decision made during his election campaign to speed the development of a big ROK Army and thus lighten the bloody burden borne by American troops. By replacing foreign troops on the battle line with South Koreans, the significance of the war in terms of the world balance of military power would be reduced and the West's ability to "wait out" a favorable armistice would be increased. It was also conceivable that such a long-range policy would lead the Kremlin to conclude that continuation of the war was no longer worth the cost, as it was not hurting America but was stimulating growth of a formidable South Korean Army. The fanfare given to the decision to expand the ROK forces suggested another possible aim: to keep alive in the Communists' minds the threat of a new United Nations offensive if they continued to block a truce acceptable to the Allies.

The effort to create a strong ROK Army was not new. Twice, in 1950 and again during the Communist Spring offensives of 1951, under-trained and poorly led ROK divisions had been reformed hastily after crumbling under attack. When the armistice talks began, only three or four ROK divisions of about twelve thousand men each could be regarded as dependable in the face of heavy attack. That Summer, for the third time in the Korean Republic's brief history, the process of building an army almost from scratch began. General Van Fleet made the task his major concern, closely supervising the enlarged United States Military Advisory Group in establishing American-style training schools and instilling an approximation of American tactical, logistical, and administrative methods. South Korea's induction machinery also was revamped and something approaching scientific, standardized selection of manpower was instituted.

Van Fleet had authority to rebuild the ROK Army to a maximum of ten light infantry divisions, equipped almost completely by the United States. Later, as heavy equipment became available and their training advanced, the ROKs were to get a full complement of American tanks and medium artillery. The job of dividing supply shipments among the front-line fighting units and the ROK training camps was left to the Eighth Army. Frequently Van Fleet was forced to resort to some unorthodox juggling of his ammunition stores to keep the ROK training program going at the pace he set.

The rebuilt ROK Army divisions passed their first battle tests in the outpost hill fighting of early 1952. Their new motto, "Stay and Fight," appeared to be more than bravado. With few exceptions, they were proving a match, man for man, for the Chinese and North Koreans.

Encouraged by these results, Van Fleet allied himself with President Rhee in calling for American support of a twenty-division ROK Army. The general conceded that the transformation of some of the original ten was not complete, and the entire ROK Army still had a critical shortage of both commissioned and non-commissioned officers. But he believed that nowhere else could the United States defense dollar buy so much.

The twenty-division plan was shelved at both the Far East Command headquarters and the Pentagon during the Spring and Summer of 1952. Washington had "top pri-

ority" arms-aid requirements all over the globe. The
United States simply had not mobilized on so grand a scale
as to take on the task of maintaining a twenty-division ROK
army without a complete overhaul of its defense program.
Van Fleet lowered his sights to sixteen divisions, then fourteen. Still Washington withheld approval.

The ROK buildup became a political issue when Mrs.
Van Fleet gave Republican candidate Eisenhower a copy of
an embittered private letter from her husband to a former
Eighth Army chief of staff, Major General Orlando Mood,
then assigned in the United States. Eisenhower used it to
support the charge that the Truman administration had
failed to exploit reasonable opportunities in Korea. The
Pentagon replied that further increases were planned, and
on the eve of the November elections Van Fleet received
authority to activate two new ROK divisions. They were
practically formed, except for equipment and public announcement, when the order came.

South Korean troops of the original ten-division army
were manning nearly two-thirds of the battle line when
Eisenhower visited Korea in December and confirmed his
decision to press the program further. In February, 1953,
two more divisions and a number of smaller, special units
were formed, and in May the ROK army's strength rose to
sixteen divisions and supporting forces—a total of nearly
four hundred thousand troops.

Van Fleet commanded a U.N.–ROK ground force of
nearly seven hundred thousand men when he stepped down
for retirement in February, after twenty-two months in
Korea. Bitterly disappointed that he had been denied the
opportunity to lead a second United Nations drive to the
Yalu, he told newsmen on his departure from Seoul that

the Allied forces then in Korea were strong enough to conduct a "successful" offensive. General Clark was amazed and angered by what he considered an irresponsible statement. "Van never had the means to conduct an offensive," Clark always insisted. Then and later Van Fleet encouraged and collaborated with President Rhee in a campaign to sell the idea of unconditional military victory as an easily attainable goal and the only honorable way out of the Korean war. Clark also preferred a military solution in principle, but not without far greater ground, sea, and air forces than he possessed—the kind of support which required major war mobilization in America. Knowing such mobilization and all-out war to be unacceptable to the United States government, Clark kept his silence.

A third move apparently calculated to make a Korean cease-fire more popular with the Reds occurred in February. President Eisenhower cancelled the Truman administration's "neutralization" of Formosa, theoretically freeing Generalissimo Chiang Kai-shek to invade the Red China mainland. The order relieved the United States Seventh Fleet of nominal responsibility for preventing Nationalist Formosa from starting a new round of warfare by landing in force on the mainland. As a possible forerunner to an American-supported Nationalist invasion, the order was an effective piece of psychological warfare. There was some evidence that it forced the Communists to strengthen coastal defenses and siphon off men and equipment which otherwise might have gone to Korea.

It is very unlikely, however, that the Formosa feint, the ROK buildup, and Van Fleet's call for a United Nations offensive were interpreted by the Communists as imposing an immediate military threat. Van Fleet spoke as a general who had abandoned hope that his battle plan would be heeded. The ROKs and the Chinese Nationalists were completely dependent on American logistical support, i.e., the American taxpayer. At that moment the United States government was committed to a course of reducing the defense budget and cutting taxes while increasing America's own military strength and paying a large share of the costs of western European rearmament. An offensive could not be launched on an economy-year budget. Furthermore, Eisenhower had publicly placed himself in the camp of those who sought to avoid spreading the Korean war or risking World War III.

No information available to the United Nations command through the end of February indicated that the Communists had changed their assessment of the Korean situation. Nor had conditions inside the Red orbit altered noticeably. The North Koreans were suffering from the cumulative economic effects of Allied air attack. The Chinese and Russians could anticipate a continuing strain in supporting the war so long as they refused to concede the repatriation issue. They had no hope of defeating the United Nations forces in Korea. However, these pressures for peace had existed a year earlier without producing communist concession on the single remaining obstacle to a truce.

Without a thought of setting off the delayed chain reaction which was to follow, General Clark renewed on February 22 the long-standing Allied proposal to the Red high command for an exchange of seriously sick and wounded prisoners during hostilities. Its timing, the general later confirmed, was not based on any secret information that the Communists were looking for a graceful way to return with concessions to Panmunjom. It was made on February 22nd, on orders from Washington, primarily because the United Nations General Assembly was to reconvene on February 24th. The executive committee of the League of Red Cross Societies had issued in December a new appeal for exchange of suffering or incapacitated prisoners, as required by the Geneva Convention. Before the Korea debate resumed at the United Nations, the unified command wanted to go on record again on the side of humanitarianism, once more putting the Communists on the defensive before the world.

The proposal was received in silence. It appeared destined to take a minor place in the United Nations command's thick file of futile efforts. Soviet Foreign Minister Vishinsky did not budge an inch from the communist position of December when he took the floor before the United Nations Main Political Committee on March 2nd.

Three days later Josef Stalin died. His death removed from power the author of the grave Korean blunder—the communist shift to military aggression which did more to unite the West and stimulate rearmament than any other Kremlin action since World War II. His death brought to power a Stalin disciple with a mind of his own, Georgi Malenkov, Communist Party boss whose training and interests foreshadowed greater attention to internal problems of the Communist world and a possible retrenchment in such foreign adventures as Korea. Stalin's death also brought relatively increased stature to China's Mao Tsetung, senior to Malenkov in the history of Communist revolution. This, too, increased the possibility of a Korean settlement, for Mao was hardly likely to be content with carrying indefinitely the burden of the Korean war for Malenkov.

Ten days after coming to power, Malenkov launched a "peace offensive" which went beyond the empty words of similar tactical shifts during the Stalin era. The new Soviet regime began reversing some of Stalin's authoritarian acts, removing some of the causes of friction with the West, and raising hopes that Russia wished to reduce world tensions —at least for the present. A Korean settlement met both the foreign and internal requirements of Malenkov's new policy.

It was believed that Communist China's Chou En-lai, during his visit to Moscow following Stalin's funeral, might have pressed and won Peiping's case for ending the war. However, too little is known at this time of the conflicts in Chinese and Soviet interests or of the weight given to China's viewpoint by the new Soviet regime to justify such speculation. The fact is that within three weeks after Stalin's death, the Communist world decided the time had come to make the minimum compromises necessary to achieve a Korean truce.

On March 28th the Communist commanders in Korea replied to General Clark's almost forgotten February 22nd appeal for a sick and wounded prisoner exchange. They agreed unconditionally—a major policy shift in itself. The significance of the Communist reply, however, lay in its third paragraph.

"At the same time," Kim Il Sung and Peng Teh-Huai wrote to Clark, "we consider that the reasonable settlement of the question of exchanging sick and injured prisoners of war of both sides during the period of hostilities should be made to lead to the smooth settlement of the entire question of prisoners of war, thereby achieving an armistice in Korea for which people throughout the world are longing. Therefore, our side proposes that the delegates for armistice negotiations of both sides immediately resume the negotiations at Panmunjom."

Years of frustrating negotiations with the Communists in Korea and Europe had taught American officials to eye the proposal with suspicion. Did the Communists intend to reopen the entire repatriation debate simultaneously with discussion of arrangements for sick and wounded exchange? What sort of trap were they laying? *The New York Times* commented editorially: "There is no better illustration of the confusion in which we are living than the fact that the Communist agreement to make an exchange of sick and wounded prisoners in Korea should have to be 'studied carefully' before a reply is made."

Chou En-lai added a mixture of clarification and confusion two days later when he formally outlined the Communists' terms for breaking the repatriation deadlock. In a statement broadcast by Peiping Radio and cabled to the United Nations General Assembly, Chou proposed that "after the cessation of hostilities those captured personnel of our side who, under the intimidation and oppression of the opposite side, are filled with apprehensions and are afraid to return home be handed over to a neutral state and that explanations be given them by the parties concerned, thus ensuring that the question of their repatriation will be justly settled and will not obstruct the realization of an armistice in Korea."

Chou prefaced his proposal by declaring that the Chinese and North Korean governments were ready to "take steps to eliminate the differences" between the U.N.C. and Communist truce delegations. But he raised new suspicions by adding, "It must be pointed out that in advancing the proposal we by no means relinquish the principle of release and repatriation of war prisoners without delay after the cessation of hostilities, nor do we acknowledge the assertion of the United Nations command that there are among the prisoners of war individuals who allegedly refuse repatriation."

The optimists among Allied diplomats interpreted this qualification as propaganda verbiage to camouflage a Communist retreat from forcible repatriation. However, at face value the words indicated that the Communists would insist on repatriation of all prisoners regardless of their wishes after the period of neutral custody and "explanations." If neutral custody was to be merely a way station on the road of forcible repatriation, there was no real concession in the Communist offer, no "constructive proposal designed to achieve an armistice" such as the Allies had declared a prerequisite to the re-opening of truce talks.

General Clark welcomed the Communist overtures. He insisted, however, that resumption of full-dress armistice negotiations be a "second order of business," after the Communists had proved their sincerity by agreeing to the terms of a fair sick-and-wounded prisoner exchange and had presented a satisfactory explanation of the contradictions in Chou's "over-all solution."

The Communists accepted the challenge. Their sharp-tongued Major General Lee Sang Cho, now abnormally agreeable and restrained, opened negotiations with American Rear Admiral John C. Daniel in special "liaison group" meetings at Panmunjom on April 6th. Tempers rose slightly only once, when the Communists announced that they had only about six hundred Allied prisoners eligible for repatriation as sick and wounded, a figure Daniel called "incredibly small." The United Nations command promised to deliver fifty-one hundred North Koreans and seven hundred Chinese. In terms of total number of prisoners held by each side, however, the ratios were nearly the same. After only five days of business-like negotiations, agreement on the sick-and-wounded exchange was announced. "Operation Little Switch" was set to begin the third week in April.

At the same time, the Communist armistice delegation complied in writing with the United Nations command's request for clarification of Chou En-lai's scheme to break the over-all prisoner deadlock. The letter, from Nam Il to Harrison, indicated that the optimists, for once, were right. The Chinese premier's insistence that the Communists were not abandoning their demand for one hundred per cent. repatriation began to look like a face-saving blind. Nam repeated Chou's words, but he made it clear that the Communists now were willing to rely on the power of their "explanations" to persuade anti-Communist Chinese and North Koreans to come home, rather than a specific requirement that the "neutral state" repatriate every captive.

"The Korean and Chinese side does not acknowledge that there are prisoners of war who are allegedly unwilling to be repatriated," Nam wrote. "Therefore, the question of the so-called forced repatriation, or repatriation by force, does not exist at all. . . . Captured personnel of our side who are filled with apprehension and are afraid to return home as a result of having been subjected to intimidation and oppression should be handed over to a neutral state, and through explanations given by our side gradually freed from apprehension, thereby attaining a just solution to the question of repatriation."

Through the North Korean's heavy-handed propaganda, a fuzzy but apparently substantial Communist concession emerged. The Allied governments agreed it was worth exploring further. That old familiar note of "cautious optimism" was back in the headlines on April 27th when, after a six-and-one-half month recess, the armistice conference reconvened in Panmunjom.

# XXI

## *The Rhee Revolt*

COMMUNIST PROPAGANDISTS LIKED to refer to Syngman Rhee as an "American puppet." American officials who collided with this strong-willed old revolutionary from the time of the United States occupation of South Korea through the war occasionally wished Rhee would accept that rôle. It was a futile hope; independence was his religion. For half a century he had fought foreign domination, whether Japanese or American. He owed almost everything to America—his own education at George Washington, Harvard, and Princeton universities, the military and economic salvation of his southern republic, the creation and support of his army—yet he remained an uncompromising nationalist. Korean independence was his single political cause. His driving ambition was to be known to history as the father and first president of a united Korean Republic.

From the beginning he was convinced that Korea would be unified only by force, that war between its communist and anti-communist halves was inevitable, and that any negotiated merger of the two Koreas on terms acceptable to the Communists would only pave the way for a Red coup drawing all Korea behind the Iron Curtain. For these reasons he opposed the abortive United States–Soviet unification talks in 1946.

256

Almost from the moment he was elected president of the southern republic following the United Nations-supervised National Assembly elections of 1948, he began laying plans to "liberate" North Korea. He regularly and frankly declared, up to the weeks before the Communist invasion, that only the staying hand of the United States had prevented him from launching the war of liberation. To insure against an ROK-precipitated war, the United States withheld tanks, heavy weapons, and warplanes from the South Korean armed forces and rationed their ammunition supplies. Nevertheless, Rhee's threats furnished a convenient smokescreen for North Korea's "defensive" invasion in June of 1950.

The United Nations Allies ignored Rhee's views when they accepted the Communist offer to negotiate an armistice. He consistently had denounced every suggestion of a conference-table settlement. From the start of the truce talks he publicly predicted their failure to achieve anything except dishonorable bargains which the Communists would break whenever expedient. He had no faith in the vaguely defined "peaceful political means" of achieving Korean unification which the United States proposed to employ after signing an armistice. Consequently, he regarded the projected armistice as the final—and totally unsatisfactory— outcome of the war.

During the long months when the armistice negotiations were in recess or on the verge of collapse, his clamorous denunciation of the truce plan gave way to occasional passive predictions that America would yet "come to its senses," break off the talks, and fight the Communists to the finish. But now the truce barometer was rising again. Events at Panmunjom soon challenged Rhee to make his supreme effort to block an armistice.

It was not merely to placate Syngman Rhee, however, that the United Nations delegation set out to drive a hard bargain when the truce talks resumed on April 27th. The highest Allied judgment was that the new Kremlin regime wanted a Korean truce, with a minimum of delay, and was prepared to make concessions to get one.

The Communists led off by explaining that Chou En-lai's proposal that the unrepatriated prisoners be "handed over to a neutral state" meant, literally, shipped out of Korea to internment camps in a neutral Asian nation. The period of "explanations" proposed by Chou to relieve turn-coat prisoners of "apprehensions and misunderstandings" and persuade them to come home was defined by Nam Il as six months. The Communists rejected the traditional neutrals, Switzerland or Sweden, nominated by the United Nations command, for the job of taking custody of prisoners who refused repatriation, and they refused to name their choice as the neutral custodian until the United Nations command agreed to the physical transfer of forty-nine thousand volatile, suspicious prisoners thousands of miles to an unnamed Asian "neutral" country. The Allied delegation bluntly refused, insisting that the prisoners remain in Korea, that the custodian be designated before anything else was considered, and that the period of authorized direct Communist efforts to persuade prisoners to come home be limited to two months.

On May 7th the Communists presented a compromise eight-point plan for prisoner repatriation similar to the United Nations General Assembly's "Indian plan," which they had curtly rejected five months earlier. It dropped insistence on moving the prisoners out of Korea. It proposed that unrepatriated prisoners be placed in custody of a five-nation neutral commission—the four supervisory neutrals, Poland, Czechoslovakia, Sweden, and Switzerland, plus India—at the existing sites of prison camps. Each member nation of the commission was to furnish troops for a custodial force. The plan also reduced the time for neutral custody and political "explanations" and reassurances for unrepatriates, from six to four months. (The Indian plan had not provided for access to prisoners by political agents of their home countries during the period of neutral custody.) The Indian plan had set a time limit of thirty days on consideration by the post-armistice peace conference of the disposition of prisoners who steadfastly refused to go home and specified that, if the peace conference failed to reach agreement, the final decision would be made by the United Nations. The communist plan made the peace conference the final authority, eliminating reference to the United Nations and providing no time limit to conference debate on the issue.

Without flatly rejecting any feature of the new Communist proposal, the United Nations delegation began asking a series of detailed and searching questions which had the effect of pointing up its complexities and impracticalities. It was clear that the Allies would not accept a scheme which would lead to indefinitely protracted argument in the peace conference on the same old prisoner issue, blocking action on the peace settlement itself. ROK officials also made it clear that the Rhee government would not tolerate the presence of armed Communist troops of Poland and Czechoslovakia around prison camps in South Korea.

Despite these objectionable features, however, the Communists' shift toward the terms of the Indian plan, which still was the United States government's official position, of-

fered sound evidence for the first time that an armistice
agreement was near.

Encouraged by this softening of the Communist negotiating line, and eager to produce something to soothe
Rhee's smouldering dissatisfaction, Washington ordered the
United Nations command to counter with a lengthy twen-
ty-six-paragraph repatriation plan in which was buried one
radical departure from both the Indian and Communist
plans. It proposed that all thirty-five thousand North Korean anti-Communist prisoners be freed in South Korea on
Armistice Day, and only "non-Korean" prisoners be turned
over to the neutral commission for custody and "explanations." In effect, it asked the Communists to declare that
they regarded North Koreans as expendable and sought
only to recover Chinese prisoners.

The maneuver was a major tactical error. Communist rejection was certain, and it came within minutes after General Harrison finished reading the lengthy document which
cloaked the key provision. The Communists were able to
demonstrate that it negated in large measure the basic principle of neutral internment of non-repatriates on which
the truce negotiations had been resumed. It was a position
from which the United Nations delegation inevitably
would have to retreat, and the retreat would serve to
strengthen the popular South Korean and American illusion of shameful appeasement by the United Nations command at Panmunjom.

Adamant and clearly final Communist rejection forced
the United Nations command to withdraw the proposal;
it thereupon called a three-day recess, then extended it five
more days, while Allied representatives conferred in Washington on a "final offer." Neither Rhee nor any member of

the ROK government was consulted on the new proposal—
another tactical error of the first magnitude. Rhee's views
were fully known, American officials argued, and were
taken into consideration by the Washington conferees.
However, the fact remained that Rhee was slighted and
treated as a second-class member of the alliance at a critical
moment when diplomatic courtesies might have at least
tempered his later actions.

Tokyo received the "final" United Nations plan from
Washington on May 24th and dispatched it to Munsan.
Early the next day Clark flew to Seoul and presented it to
Rhee an hour before Harrison began reading it to the Communists. The South Korean member of the United Nations delegation, Major General Choi Duk Shin, boycotted
the meeting after learning the contents of the Allied proposal; his decision won Rhee's immediate approval. A new
crisis was developing.

On Allied suggestion, the negotiations went into secret
session. As a consequence, the United Nations command's
"final offer" was presented to the world through slanted
"leaks" from General Choi and other ROK officials. Choi
denounced the United Nations offer as "complete surrender." Rhee declared that South Korea would not accept a
truce on the terms of the United Nations repatriation plan
and other previously drafted sections of the armistice agreement. Foreign Minister Pyun Yung Tae threatened that
ROK troops would fire on Indian guard detachments sent
to take custody of anti-communist prisoners and would bar
Polish and Czech "neutral" commission officials and communist indoctrination agents from South Korean territory.
Every day brought more impassioned charges of "sellout"
from the Rhee government.

The new United Nations proposal actually contained no unexpected compromises. It did not abandon the principle of free choice and political asylum for a prisoner who resolutely opposed return to his homeland. It followed the outlines of the American-supported "Indian plan," with the exception that it accepted the Communist amendment permitting Red political agents to come and talk to unrepatriated prisoners while they were in neutral custody. Agreement on this point had been implicit from the time the Allies decided to resume negotiations on the basis of the Chou En-lai formula.

The only United Nations retreat was from the ill-conceived experimental effort of May 13th to exempt North Korean anti-Communists from the neutral custody period and free them in South Korea. Expected or not, the South Korean government regarded this concession as a spineless compromise involving the lives of its citizens. (The Republic of Korea, on the basis of the United Nations General Assembly's 1948 declaration that it was the only legally constituted government in Korea, claimed sovereignty over the entire peninsula.) Rhee and his aides initially concentrated their verbal fire on this issue, but their attacks soon broadened to a sweeping denunciation of any negotiated truce. They named terms for an "honorable" armistice which involved political settlements which would have required rewriting the entire armistice document—the product of nearly two years' effort.

"No armistice that leaves Korea divided" was the theme of the ROK revolt against American truce policies. How a military armistice agreement could provide for unification or even assure it in the future was not made clear, but ROK officials offered one clue: Withdrawal of all Chinese Communist troops from North Korea was the basic provision that Rhee demanded in any cease-fire agreement.

On June 5th he outlined in an official government announcement minimum terms for a truce which he had earlier communicated to President Eisenhower: Simultaneous withdrawal of United Nations and Communist forces with the artlessly phrased "exception" that United States air and naval forces would remain and the United States army would be ready, under a defense pact, to rush instantly and automatically to South Korea's aid if the war resumed. (ROK government officials in Seoul made no effort to conceal their private understanding that these conditions would never be accepted by the Communists and that insistence upon them could only mean continued war.) In addition, Rhee demanded United States economic aid and logistical support of the ROK forces in peace or war.

Rhee's terms were announced just as the ROK-boycotted United Nations truce team compromised on the final disagreement over prisoner repatriation in secret sessions at Panmunjom. The Communists accepted the United Nations-proposed three-month time limit on the period of neutral custody and "explanations" to unrepatriated prisoners and a one-month limit on the subsequent peace-conference deliberations over disposition of those prisoners who still refused to go home. The American delegation agreed to drop the final phase of the Indian plan—disposition of prisoners by the United Nations if the peace conference deadlocked on the issue—in favor of direct resettlement by the neutral custodial commission. Only details remained to be worked out before the long-sought agreement clearing the last anticipated obstacle to a United Nations–Communist truce could be announced.

But Rhee's vehement opposition presented an unanticipated obstacle which American leadership belatedly recognized as very real. He could discredit and possibly block a truce merely by refusing to be bound by its terms. At the least, he could make a cease-fire agreement an unstable and dangerous undertaking for both sides. Furthermore, regardless of American protestations of innocence, the United States would be branded with responsibility and inextricably involved if the American-built South Korean Army did ignore the armistice terms and try to take on the Chinese Communists single-handed. Rhee exploited his bargaining position to the fullest.

Eisenhower had been reported drafting a new appeal for South Korean co-operation. While the message was en route, Rhee flamboyantly stiffened his stand and heightened the tension. He told his people in a radio broadcast that South Koreans must "continue the fighting and unify the country by driving north by ourselves." He promulgated a series of "extraordinary security measures" tightening police controls throughout the Republic. Symbolizing his mobilization for action and implying an imminent break with the United States, he ordered the recall from United States training schools of ROK Army Chief of Staff General Paik Sun Yup and other officers.

A few hours later on June 7th, General Clark arrived in Seoul from Tokyo with the American President's reply to Rhee's truce demands. Eisenhower promised to negotiate a purely defensive security treaty with South Korea *after* the armistice was safely signed. He assured South Korea of United States economic aid to repair the war's tragic destruction, and he guaranteed that the United States would make Korean unification its "central objective" in the political conference following the truce talks and would consult with the ROK government before and during the conference. But he warned Rhee that the United States would not condone or underwrite any "reckless adventure" prolonging the war and made clear that the policy of the United States government was to seek solutions of the Korean and other world problems through peaceful means.

Rhee immediately and publicly rejected Eisenhower's appeals and promises, removing all doubts that a serious crisis had been reached. He declared that "we will continue fighting by ourselves" and called on all South Koreans to "reassert our determination to risk our lives and fight on to a decisive end in case the United Nations accepts the truce and stops fighting." At the same time he predicted there would be "spontaneous demonstrations" against the United Nations, a prediction which the government-directed youth organizations, schools, and neighborhood associations began carrying out the next day.

The rumblings from Seoul went largely unnoticed inside the Panmunjom conference hut. The Communists apparently were convinced by their own propaganda that Rhee could be silenced by the United States when necessary. They were in no hurry to see him silenced. He was proving their best ally in spreading the impression that the armistice terms represented a great victory for Communism.

On June 8th, agreement was announced at Panmunjom on prisoner repatriation terms, informally reached three days earlier in secret sessions. The accord ended a dispute which had prolonged the war for more than a year at the cost of a hundred and forty thousand casualties and untold bloodshed and destruction in North Korea.

The agreement was in the form of Terms of Reference to

the Neutral Nations Repatriation Commission. It established firmly the principle of political asylum for war prisoners, a principle whose influence on the course of future wars between the Communist and anti-Communist worlds may be enormous. Its complicating effects on future armistice or peace negotiations are certain. The agreement provided for a complex series of steps designed to insure that each prisoner could make a free and sober choice for or against self-exile. In effect, it put on open trial the Communists' claim that none of their former soldiers voluntarily refused to return to Red China and North Korea, that all had been tortured, intimidated, and otherwise pressured by "Syngman Rhee agents," "Chiang Kai-shek agents," and Americans into pretending that they were anti-Communists. If these men had, as the United Nations command claimed, chosen self-exile only after being warned of its dangers and given opportunities to change their minds, then there was no reason to fear the Communists' efforts to persuade them to come home through "explanation" lectures and interviews. It was the Communists who were risking the greater propaganda setback by putting this embarrassing matter of mass defections to a fair and public test.

The South Korean government was not interested in the verdict of world public opinion. It saw the prisoner settlement as an intolerable admission of trained communist "brainwashers" into South Korea to indoctrinate good Koreans. Rhee and his cabinet members gave visitors the impression that they were honestly puzzled and alarmed by the United Nations command's willingness to agree to such a scheme. Rhee's subordinates again voiced threats to fight the Indian troops, members of the neutral commission, and

Communist "persuaders" scheduled to enter the prison-camp areas.

On July 9th "spontaneous" demonstrators protesting the truce terms carried banners and placards proclaiming a significant new slogan: "Free the anti-communist prisoners now." These giant banners invariably reflected government policy—or they did not remain up long. It was the first public warning of Rhee's most daring stroke against an armistice. Other veiled threats to attack the American-managed prison camps followed, in interviews, conferences, and written declarations by high ROK officials. Rumors of planned raids on the PW camps to release anti-Communist Korean prisoners circulated in Seoul.

Clark was confronted with the necessity of making a difficult decision. If he failed to take effective precautions and an ROK-assisted mass breakout occurred, the United Nations command would be guilty of violating its promise to deliver all the non-repatriates to the neutral commission. The result could be a complete breakdown of the armistice negotiations just as a cease-fire was assured. If he took all the steps required to guarantee against a breakout, he calculated he would have to withdraw a full American infantry division from the Eighth Army, relieve the South Korean military police guards with Americans untrained for prison duty at all the mainland camps, and give his troops orders to fire on both prisoners and ROK raiders if an escape were attempted. These precautions would demonstrate a complete lack of trust in the ROK government as well as lack of United Nations command control over, and authority to speak for, South Korea's forces on the armistice agreement. The prospect of mass slaughter of prisoners who, however misled, sought escape from Communist "brainwashing" was abhorrent to the United Nations commander and to the United States government. Shooting warfare between American and ROK soldiers would have been tragic.

Clark's decision was made easier by the Communists. On June 14th they launched their biggest attack in two years against the Fifth and Eighth ROK divisions on the east-central front. At least two Chinese divisions were committed to the main push down the upper Pukhan River valley, while pressure was stepped up generally along the front. Intense and almost ceaseless artillery barrages rained death on the ROKs as they fell back under the attack. Casualties were so heavy that neither of the two ROK divisions remained fully effective. The Communist assault had all the earmarks of a punitive operation designed to score a parting victory over the ROKs and impress South Korea's military leaders with the folly of Rhee's "on to the Yalu" notions. The United Nations command had no assurance of this, however. Clark dared not pull an American division out of the combat zone for prison-guard duty so long as there was a chance that the Chinese would follow up their initial penetrations.

Considering all these factors, and with Pentagon approval, Clark chose to take the calculated risk that Rhee was bluffing. He still had Rhee's written assignment of full control of all South Korean armed forces to the United Nations command. Furthermore, he had recently received new assurances from Rhee that he would not withdraw his forces from that Command except after advance notice and full discussion. Without outside help and collusion of the Korean military guards, a successful mass prison break was believed impossible. Clark alerted the American prison-camp administration and the reserve American regiment stationed at Pusan, but the ROKs were left on guard posts and orders against using fatal weapons against prisoners except in self-defense remained in effect.

Other matters were occupying the United Nations command's primary attention. Staff officers at Panmunjom were nearing completion of work on the last important detail of the armistice—fixing the final demarcation line on which a buffer zone between the two armies would be drawn. The mechanics of the prisoner-exchange, "Big Switch," were blueprinted. Tent and warehouse villages for receiving returned Allied prisoners were coming to life at Munsan as processing staffs arrived and began rehearsals. Transportation for some twelve thousand Allied and seventy-five thousand Communist prisoners was being assembled and scheduled. American Major General Blackshear M. Bryan and other senior officers were appointed United Nations members of the Military Armistice Commission. The last details were falling into place. On the night of June 17th Clark predicted privately that the armistice would be signed by the war's third anniversary, June 25th.

Before dawn of the 18th, Rhee scuttled these hopeful plans. More than twenty-four thousand anti-Communist Korean prisoners streamed out of four mainland PW camps in a well-rehearsed mass escape. ROK guards either actively aided or offered no serious resistance to the fleeing prisoners. ROK national police were waiting to meet the escapees, lead them to safe hiding places in the hills, and furnish them residents' certificates and clothing. At 6:30 A.M. the South Korean Provost Marshal, Lieutenant General Won Yong Duk, announced in a radio broadcast that he had directed the ROK guards, who technically were detached members of his command, to release all thirty-five thousand anti-Communist North Korean prisoners. He called on the people to "help and protect these patriotic youths." Shortly thereafter Rhee announced that he had ordered the entire operation without consultation with the United Nations command, to rescue the anti-Communist prisoners from the continued detention and communist "brainwashing" contemplated under the armistice agreement.

Eisenhower dispatched a personal protest and Clark fired off a blistering message to Rhee. "I must inform you with all the sincerity which I possess," Clark wrote, "that I am profoundly shocked by this unilateral abrogation of your personal commitment, which was so freely and voluntarily given at the time. I cannot at this time estimate the ultimate consequences of this precipitous and shocking action on your part, nor can its effect on the common cause for which we have sacrificed so much during these past several years be forecast at this time." Clark's official language was strong, but it was mild in comparison with his off-the-record denunciation of Rhee. From this moment, the United Nations Commander treated Rhee more as a treacherous adversary than an ally.

The United Nations command began replacing ROK prison camp guards with Americans, but that night about two thousand more prisoners escaped. Nearly one thousand more broke out of camps scattered throughout South Korea before the epidemic ended. Only 8,329 of the original 35,421 anti-Communist North Koreans remained behind barricades.

Rhee had long threatened to ignore a truce; the prisoner-release was his first concrete act to block one.

The Communists almost immediately broke off the truce negotiations, and in a formal letter to Clark, Kim, and Peng accused the United Nations command of conniving with Rhee in his scheme to wreck the armistice just as it was about to be realized. They characterized the releases as "forced detention" of North Koreans for the purpose of pressing them into service in the ROK army. They demanded that all the prisoners be recaptured and held for repatriation or neutral custody as promised in the draft agreement. Lastly, they demanded to know whether the South Korean government and forces were under the control of the United Nations command and would be bound by truce terms.

Clark obviously could not recover all the prisoners, now scattered among the Korean populace and protected by ROK police and troops. If the Communists insisted on their recovery as a prerequisite to proceeding with the armistice, there would be no truce. Neither could the United Nations command guarantee South Korean compliance with the truce terms. Repeated and lengthy visits by Clark and American Ambassador Ellis O. Briggs and at least three messages from President Eisenhower had failed to swing Rhee into line.

A new approach was urgently needed. The White House dispatched a special mission headed by Assistant Secretary of State Walter S. Robertson to Seoul with orders to break down Rhee's suspicion of an American "sell-out" and convince him that the interests of the anti-Communist world, including South Korea, would best be served by a cease-fire followed by a peace conference.

Rhee began moderating his position before Robertson arrived. With Washington's authority, Clark again flew to Seoul and served notice that the United States government had decided to sign an armistice without South Korea's endorsement if the Communists would agree. He made it plain to Rhee that the United States would not come to South Korea's aid if Rhee continued fighting or broke the cease-fire. This was the only leverage Clark could apply on Rhee. Until the Communists indicated that they were willing to sign such a shaky truce, it had had no spectacular effect on Rhee's stand, but it may have played a rôle in the slight moderation of attitude which followed.

In a war-anniversary address before the capitol in Seoul, shortly before Robertson's mission arrived, Rhee indicated that he was reducing his terms for accepting a truce. In press interviews two days earlier he had defined his price as: withdrawal of all foreign forces, a security treaty with the United States, a three-month time limit on deliberations of the peace conference, and advance agreement among South Korea and the United Nations Allies to resume the war if no political settlement achieving the goal of unification had been reached by the three-months deadline. In his June 25th speech, however, he proposed two alternative sets of conditions: (1) Chinese Communist withdrawal and a U.S.–ROK defense pact, or (2) the defense pact plus a U.S.–ROK agreement to walk out of the peace conference and resume the war if satisfactory progress toward Korean unification had not been achieved after three months of debate.

Plan one could not be considered seriously by the United States, as it stood no chance of acceptance by the Communists and could not be put into effect without rewriting the armistice agreement. Plan two did not require changing the armistice terms. In effect, it called for breaking the armistice after approximately six months if the peace conference was not making progress. Technically, the draft armistice terms contained no time limit and thus might be interpreted as permanently binding regardless of the outcome of the peace conference. However, a truce is inherently an interim agreement between opposing military commanders, not a permanent political settlement. One danger in plan two was the rigidity of its advance commitment to resume fighting after ninety days of unproductive peace-conference debate, regardless of other world considerations at that time. It also would have given Syngman Rhee a larger voice in involving the United States in war or peace than any foreign ally had a right to demand. Another difficulty with Rhee's second plan was his insistence that a defense pact be negotiated and signed (some ROK statements also added the term "ratified") before he would give his guarantee to abide by the armistice. This would have placed the United States in the position of negotiating under pressure while the war continued, with needless loss of lives.

These, in outline, were some of the issues to be thrashed out by Presidential envoy Robertson with the shrewd and stubborn old champion of Korean nationalism. The soft-spoken Virginian soon discovered that conferences with Rhee could not be confined to the immediate issues. Hopeful progress toward agreement was followed by lengthy arguments which returned to original positions.

While Rhee and Robertson sparred at the Seoul Presidential mansion, the Communists sat back and enjoyed the spectacle of the Korean tail wagging the American dog. The United Nations command sought to get the truce talks back on the track and thus strengthen Robertson's position with Rhee.

In a reply to the Red high command's protest letter of

June 20th breaking off the truce negotiations, Clark on June 29th called on the Communists to resume the conference and sign the truce as written despite the prisoner-releases. He admitted that he could not guarantee ROK compliance with the truce terms, but he promised that the United Nations command would, "to the limits of its ability, establish military safeguards to insure that the armistice terms are observed." He said it was "impossible" to recover the twenty-seven thousand freed prisoners, just as it would be impossible for the Communists to recover fifty thousand South Korean prisoners "released" by the Reds during hostilities.

Clark had waited nine days to give his reply. The Communists, apparently not inclined to appear eager for a truce, waited as long before agreeing to return to Panmunjom.

The American decision to proceed with the armistice and call Rhee's bluff was made personally by President Eisenhower, according to highest officials in Tokyo. It carried out recommendations submitted by Robertson, Clark, and Ambassador Robert D. Murphy, who had concluded that the ROK government would never compromise so long as it held the power to block an armistice merely by talking. By accepting Clark's call for renewed sessions at Panmunjom, the Communists co-operated with the American maneuver to neutralize Rhee's negotiating power.

Robertson's solid progress in winning assurances of ROK compliance with the truce terms dated from July 8th, when Kim and Peng announced that, although not entirely satisfied with Clark's assurances and explanation of the prisoner-release, they were ready to resume negotiation "prior to the signing of the armistice agreement."

Two years to the hour after the first truce conference began in Kaesong, the Communist and ROK-boycotted United Nations delegations met at Panmunjom on July 10th to complete the armistice.

That afternoon Rhee and Robertson came to terms in Seoul. They formally confirmed the agreements the next day. Rhee pledged that he would not obstruct implementation of the armistice; there was no reference to a time limit on this pledge. However, in a separate section of the agreements he reserved the right to withdraw from the peace conference and take whatever action he deemed necessary if he were dissatisfied with its progress and prospects after three months of negotiation. Robertson agreed that the United States would consult with Rhee after the conference had run ninety days and, if it were obvious to the United States as well as to Rhee that the Communists were not negotiating in good faith, the American delegate would try to end the conference. This neither committed the United States to walk out of the peace conference after ninety days, nor bound it to fight again, or assist Rhee in resuming the war, if the conference collapsed. In fact, Robertson orally made it clear that the United States government had no intention of renewing the war if the first peaceful efforts for unification of Korea failed.

On its side of the bargain, the United States began discussion of the defense treaty which Rhee demanded as advance payment for his limited pledge to abide by the truce. But Robertson won the point that the treaty would not be signed and ratified until after the armistice had gone into effect. Robertson also pledged economic aid, reiterating Eisenhower's assurances on this point.

The details of Rhee's reservations on abiding by the

cease-fire were given to the public piecemeal, after Robertson had returned to Washington. The first public announcement of their agreements was a vaguely worded joint statement issued on Robertson's departure from Seoul. In American bureaucratic prose it declared only that "these discussions have cemented our determination to continue and extend in the post-armistice period the close collaboration for our common objective . . ." and "we wish to emphasize our determination to work together for the realization within the shortest practical time of our common objective, namely a free, independent, and united Korea." Robertson added outside the statement that the United Nations command now had sufficient assurances of ROK co-operation to proceed to sign an armistice.

To assure themselves that Rhee actually would not be tempted to "go it alone," the Communists chose more direct methods. On the night of July 13th they aimed the Red Army's heaviest attack in two years directly at three South Korean divisions in and at the base of the Kumsong "bulge" —a central front sector where United Nations lines jutted northward in a salient to the hills immediately south of Kumsong. General Clark interpreted the Red offensive as purely "politically inspired"—to show Rhee he lacked the capability to sustain either offensive or defensive action alone.

The Eighth Army reported that ten Chinese divisions were committed in the offensive, which swept over and around some ROK defense positions and sent other South Korean units into pell-mell retreat far outstripping the pursuing Communists. American Third Division troops on the western end of the attack front held firm and prevented the entire central front from buckling. The ROK Third

Division also fought valiantly and fell back only under orders. The ROKs retreated as much as eight miles, however, before they were re-assembled and re-inforced on a new line. The Eighth Army ordered them to move back northward and regain contact. The advance regained up to five miles of territory occupied only by Communist patrols and outpost units. When it reached the new Chinese lines it bogged down in a series of vicious, see-saw hill battles which continued almost until the last shot of the war was fired.

The ROKs again had taken a bloody beating, but by numerically superior forces. Some South Korean officers may have re-acquired a sense of realism as a result of the experience, but there was no indication that Rhee's belligerence was dampened thereby.

In Panmunjom's renewed secret negotiations, the Communists demanded specific guarantees that South Korea would honor the armistice. Nam Il's price for signing a shaky truce was a clear and public acceptance of responsibility by the United States for any breach of the cease-fire by Rhee's forces. In a week of persistent questioning, he set out to obtain detailed guarantees that the United Nations command would honor the armistice indefinitely and would see to it that Rhee did likewise. Out of Harrison's straightforward answers, the Communists were building a case for the record. Harrison assured the Communists:

1. "We have received from the ROK government necessary assurances that it will not obstruct in any manner the implementation" of the armistice.

2. "The ROK forces will cease fire and withdraw" two kilometers from the demilitarized zone within twelve hours after the armistice agreement is signed, along with all

United Nations and Communist forces, as provided in the draft armistice agreement.

3. "The U.N.C. will not give support during any aggressive action of units of the ROK army in violation of the armistice." If the Military Armistice Commission were unable to deal with any ROK violation of the truce, "the injured side can . . . take such military action as it deems essential."

4. The U.N.C. would withhold support from the ROKs in case they attacked and would continue to abide by the armistice terms while the Communist side took necessary and defensive action against any ROK aggression.

5. "There is no time-limit to the armistice" and the ROK government would abide by "all provisions of the armistice agreement for the entire period and not for a temporary period."

6. The U.N.C. would insure the safety of neutral and Communist representatives serving in South Korea in supervisory, repatriation, and Red Cross commissions under the terms of the armistice.

7. No more anti-Communist war prisoners would be allowed to escape and the U.N.C. would do what it could to recover the twenty-seven thousand already set free by ROK guards.

These were not off-the-cuff answers. The United Nations command deliberately and with forethought declared that the U.N. allies would stand aside and let the Communists and ROKs fight it out if Rhee ever initiated another round of warfare. It is doubtful that Clark and Washington had a right to make this "no-time-limit" commitment on behalf of the ROK government; Rhee's written agreements with Robertson did not fully justify it. Rhee had reserved the right to violate the armistice after all its scheduled steps had been completed and after the peace conference had been given a three-months' trial. Every requested assurance except a guarantee to recover the escaped prisoners was given the Communists.

The Communists broke the secrecy of the Panmunjom sessions on July 19th to disclose Harrison's detailed assurances. Reserving the right to reopen the issue of the escaped prisoners at the peace conference, Nam Il announced that he had accepted the United Nations command's specific truce guarantees and was ready to make final preparations for signing the armistice.

The Seoul government again protested, with considerable justification, and Rhee again set the record straight. But the Communists had no need to worry about ROK threats; Rhee could not go far without American support, and the United States was publicly saddled with responsibility for keeping him in line.

Talk could not block a cease-fire now. The feverish pace resumed at Panmunjom. Staff officer groups re-charted the final demarcation line and worked out the mechanics of the prisoner-exchange. To reduce chances of friction between the South Korean populace or government and the Indian troops and Communist officials, it was agreed that the unrepatriated prisoners would be confined in new camps built in the neutral zone and operated by the Indian forces.

Even in the final hours of the negotiations, however, there was no harmony. The Communists nailed giant blue-and-white Picasso "peace doves," symbols of international Communist propaganda, over the entrances to the straw-mat building they had constructed for the armistice-signing ceremony. Colonel Murray, the American liaison officer, blocked this crude move and demanded that the doves be hauled down. Another unexpected clash caused more delay. The Communists revealed that their brave leader, Kim Il Sung, was afraid to appear in public at Panmunjom for a joint armistice-signing ceremony with Clark unless all South Koreans and Chinese Nationalists were barred from the area and all newsmen were prohibited from witnessing the ceremony itself. Clark refused to make this final concession to the Red police-state mentality. Plans for a joint appearance by the opposing commanders were cancelled; they would stay at their Korean headquarters and sign. The ceremonial signing was to be done by the chief negotiators, Harrison and Nam.

The last tedious checking of maps, and of English, Chinese, and Korean-language copies of the armistice and related agreements, the final details of closing the books on two years and two weeks of negotiation, were completed on Sunday, July 26th.

The end that was not quite an end came on July 27th. At 10 A.M. the United Nations and Communist armistice delegations filed into the T-shaped straw-mat and tar-paper "peace pagoda" and took their places behind a straight row of tables. Without a word or a glance at each other, Harrison and Nam began signing the 18 copies of the armistice document, nine in blue covers prepared by the United Nations command, nine in red leather backs prepared by the Reds. Within ten minutes the job was done. There were no softening, hypocritical amenities; nothing new could be said. When they finished signing they rose and walked out.

Twelve hours later, at 10 P.M., the guns were silenced. Thirty-seven months of killing and destruction were over

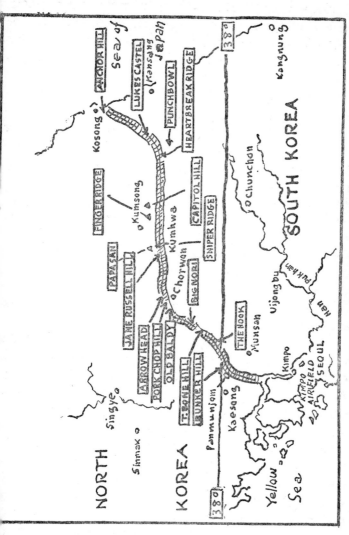

4. The Final Cease-Fire Line

281

# XXII

## *Big Switch*

NEVER HAS THE end of a major war been greeted with less enthusiasm. There was no dancing in the streets. There was sober relief among the men at the front who could at last be sure of living to see another day; there was even exultation among their families back home, whether in Paducah or Pohang-Dong. But most people could not feel a sense of climax or accomplishment in the armistice.

Perhaps unconsciously grasping for that concrete and final achievement on which a proper war should end, the American press and public made its own climax in the return of prisoners. "Operation Big Switch," as the army named the prisoner exchange, became the emotional windup of an often forgotten and uninspiring war. It was an unprecedented episode in the history of modern wars—and of journalism. After World Wars I and II, thousands of Allied captives had come home in anonymous multitudes, without ceremony or fanfare and almost unnoticed unless their names were famous. There had been little mystery about where they had been confined, who and how many had survived, or whether they had been converted to the enemy's ideology. More momentous events had gripped the world's attention, for the end of the fighting in 1918 and 1945 brought sweeping political and economic changes in the affairs of nations and in the lives of millions.

The end in Korea was different. The little war was only suspended, shelved in a warehouse full of TNT. The big war still loomed, and the tension of the arms race continued. The armistice might lead to something more stable and hopeful, but for the moment the only certainty was that freedom for some thirteen thousand Allied prisoners of war and six times that many Communists was assured.

There were other reasons for the unusual concentration of interest in the prisoner exchange. Prisoners, more than combat divisions, were the central figures in much of the war. The elusive truce had been snagged for a year and a half over the fate of prisoners. In the latter half of the war the ideological struggle for the minds of captive soldiers often had overshadowed the fighting itself. Korean war prisoners had been used by both sides for propaganda advantage in the world-wide war of words. The North Korean prison camps held the secrets of hundreds of American "confessions" to germ warfare and assorted other war crimes which the Communists had charged against the United Nations forces. Their inmates knew the answers to Allied suspicions of wholesale atrocities perpetrated against United Nations captives. These men were coming from behind the Iron Curtain, out of a place of mystery from which the International Red Cross and other neutral observers had been barred.

Not all was mystery when the armistice began, however. Sick and wounded prisoners had been exchanged during "Operation Little Switch" from April 20th to May 3rd. The Allies had handed over 6,670 lame, ill, or otherwise disabled Chinese and North Korean prisoners and received 684 United Nations and ROK captives in the exchange. In press and official interviews at Munsan's Freedom Village and in Tokyo's army hospitals, these first repatriates had broken the secrecy surrounding life in the Yalu River valley prison camps.

Many of the Americans and British freed in "Little Switch" had relatively minor ailments. Some of them had told of progressively improving treatment as the Chinese took over administration from the less humane and poorly equipped North Koreans. A few had been noncommittal about their experiences and their relations with the Communists; among the healthier-looking "sick and wounded," twenty-two Americans and about half a dozen British returnees were tagged by fellow prisoners as "favorites" or fellow-travelers of the Reds.

Most of the returned Allied prisoners had spoken freely and often vehemently of Communist maltreatment (tempered by sporadic improvement in conditions as the armistice negotiations took hopeful turns), of mass deaths from starvation, neglect, and brutality during the first Winter of 1950–51, of death marches from the front to North Korean PW camps in late 1950 and early 1951, of intensive political indoctrination, forced propaganda broadcasts, spurious confessions, and unrelenting "mental pressure."

Many educated westerners, particularly Europeans, had developed a sophisticated skepticism toward atrocity stories during the war years. Were these stories told by young American soldiers to headline-seeking newsmen a fair appraisal of Communist treatment of prisoners? Were these young repatriates, men generally ignorant of Asiatic standards, able to distinguish hardships, misery, and wholesale death caused by their captors' shortage of medical facilities, food, and western comforts from actually deliberate communist atrocities? How much of their reports was based on hearsay, exaggerated by the PW camp grapevine and embellished in retelling? These were the questions waiting to be clarified by the twenty-times larger group of Allied prisoners scheduled for repatriation in "Big Switch."

The sick and wounded exchange also had shed no light on the mystery of the germ-warfare confessions of captured American pilots, broadcast in infinite and convincing detail by the Communist propaganda machine, "confirmed" by Communist-picked medical investigating delegations to North Korea, and just as convincingly denied by the United States. These pilots were presumably among the 3,313 Americans listed by the Communists high command as awaiting repatriation.

Mystery also surrounded the question of whether many Allied prisoners, like nearly half of the Red Army captives, had turned against their own countries during imprisonment. Had the Communists succeeded in converting American soldiers to Communism; would any choose self-exile in the Communist world rather than return to the United States?

More than eleven thousand Americans were listed as missing in action or as prisoners, and nearly eight thousand of them would not be coming home. Communist refusal to comply with the civilized practice of communicating through the International Red Cross the names of prisoners and of men who died in PW camps had even made a mystery of who was to be freed.

Against this background, the prisoner exchange could not fail to produce significant revelations and suspense-charged drama. Following tedious months of armistice negotiations and stalemate war, it was the natural emotional climax. But like everything else in Korea, it was not to be done in a day.

Lack of transportation and administrative facilities limited the number of prisoners the Communists could receive at one time from the United Nations command; this necessitated a protracted schedule of daily deliveries. Big Switch began on August 5th, nine days after the cease-fire, and was scheduled to last thirty-two days, with the U.N.C. receiving about four hundred repatriates a day and delivering twenty-four hundred North Koreans and/or Chinese daily to the Communists.

At 9 A.M. on August 5th, the Iron Curtain parted and the Allied prisoners started coming home. The first to be freed were a truckload of twenty-three Turks, smiling, tough, unchanged men. Then came Americans, led by the inevitable Texan, some of them shouting and waving, some quiet and apparently dazed by the experience. South Koreans, many of them emaciated and coughing tuberculosis victims, and a sprinkling of other United Nations prisoners followed. The first days brought most of the sick and wounded, on litters or hobbling on twisted limbs or make-shift crutches, some recently captured and wearing untended bandages. The scene was repeated at Panmunjom daily through August and the first week of September. Ambulance convoys carried the repatriates to the Freedom Village processing center near Munsan, and helicopters took seriously ill or wounded men to hospitals. After the first few days there was little business for the helicopters standing by at Panmunjom; most of the men were bronzed and well-fed, thanks, the ex-prisoners said, to a radical improvement in general treatment during their last six to nine months in prison camps and particularly after the truce negotiations had resumed in April.

Big Switch launched a journalistic marathon. News

agencies and radio and television networks, with the un-stinting assistance of army signal and public-information officials, delivered the names, addresses, and other vital statistics of every repatriated Allied prisoner to his home town within a few minutes after his release at Panmunjom. Nearly every released United Nations prisoner and a large sampling of the South Korean repatriates were interviewed, and their stories spread around the world. When it was all over, an army censor calculated that 1,800,000 words of press copy on the exchange had been filed from Korea by the United Nations press.

Gradually the ex-prisoners' stories fell into a pattern unmarred by serious conflict in detail. They added up to a damning indictment of Communist inhumanity com-pounded by bestiality in which the North Koreans were the chief culprits. They confirmed and added new chapters to the earlier repatriates' accounts of the death marches of 1950 and 1951 in which American and South Korean pris-oners were herded northward without food or medical care, often stripped of their boots and parkas, abandoned to die along the way or crowded into squalid huts where dysentery-wracked skeletons of men gave up the fight to live. Physical and mental strength and a will to survive brought a handful through. Some veteran prisoners brought back carefully compiled lists of fellow-prisoners who died at Pyoktong and other far northern PW camps during the terrible first Winter of 1950–51.

After eliminating all possible duplications in their ac-counts, the United States Defense Department concluded that 6,113 Americans and 5,509 other Allied troops, mostly South Koreans, died after falling into Communist hands, nearly half of them after reaching organized prison camps.

There were unspeakable atrocities—the panicky slaughter of both American prisoners and anti-Communist North Korean civilians during the North Korean army's hasty retreat in the Fall of 1950; torture executions by both Chinese and North Koreans of unco-operative Allied captives, and isolated cases of brutality by PW camp guards. Most of the prisoner deaths, however, resulted from shortages of food, transportation, shelter, and medical facilities over which the Communist military had no control but for which the Communist governments had inescapable responsibility. Many returned prisoners emphasized that their captors had fared no better than they themselves, but had been better equipped by habit and physical immunities to survive intense cold, coarse and impure food, and other hardships.

In the Spring of 1951, as the Communists' supply situation improved and the Chinese took over administration of all camps for non-Korean prisoners, the death rate dropped sharply. After the armistice talks started, relatively decent living conditions prevailed for a time. Most British Commonwealth prisoners were captured during or after this period of improving conditions and given especially favorable treatment.

Simple physical torture was the occasional but not continuous fate of Allied captives after the PW camp organization was stabilized. For men who defied authority, refused to obey orders, organized resistance to Communist political indoctrination, or became the targets of informers and "rats," the punishment ranged from solitary confinement in cramped, unheated cages and dank "turnip pits," to starvation rations and denial of medical care, or transfer to hard-labor camp and special work details. Some died under punishment. The constant threat of it was enough to keep all but the most stubborn or foolhardy prisoners in line, for these men who had cheated death more than once wanted above all to survive. "A man could do what he was told, sit through the Communist lectures without falling for their line, mind his own business, and get along fairly well"—this was the almost uniform conclusion of the more mature prisoners interviewed at Freedom Village.

A little negative co-operation with the Communists bought relative safety, and more enthusiastic co-operation often won small favors and special privileges. Inevitably, there were some prisoners who sought the best deal they could get, a few who were exposed successfully to the strange and plausible theories of Marxian Utopia because they lacked maturity or a background of political education. (These men were as young as eighteen and their average age was barely twenty at the time of capture.) The Communists rewarded such "progressive" tendencies, and the prisoners who accepted or pretended to accept Communist doctrine became known in all prison camps as "progressives" or "pro's." Those who steadfastly rejected Communist indoctrination were branded "reactionary." Thousands of American repatriates proudly announced at Freedom Village that they were and always would be "reactionaries." Two more good words in the English language were forever ruined by Red distortion.

"Pro" was an ill-defined term, just as "leftist" is in America. One repatriated prisoner would declare that in his company half the men were "lousy pro's." Another man from the same PW camp company would report that "only three or four were real pro's," meaning confirmed Communists. The most conservative estimates of newsmen who kept a cross-check tabulation throughout the interviews at Freedom Village and the Inchon port processing center indicated that about fifty Americans accepted, at least temporarily, the Communist propaganda line on the Korean war and about half of these were converted in large degree to the Communist ideology. The latter group included a few soldiers who came from pro-Communist or Communist families in the United States. Several of them came home during "Little Switch." Others made up the hard core of eight or ten Communists among the twenty-three Americans who for a variety of reasons initially rejected repatriation and chose self-exile. One English soldier and 335 South Koreans also initially renounced their homelands and stayed with the Communists. Fear of punishment for collaboration or for PW camp crimes against fellow-prisoners apparently was the chief motivation of some noncommunist Americans and many of the 335 South Koreans who remained with the Reds.

There was wide disagreement in the stories told by repatriates on the question of whether the Communists tried to persuade "progressive" prisoners to renounce their right to repatriation. Some ex-prisoners told of glowing promises of advanced education in Communist China and Russia, wealth, women, and high position made by Red political agents to their converts. Many claimed that the Communists assured these prisoners they would be trained for government service and sent to the United States in about five years to help lead the Red revolution and organize the new "people's democracy" in Washington. But there were also reports of specific instances in which the Chinese camp commander announced that all men should accept repatriation and return home, and cases of the camp authorities individually urging "pro's" to go back to America and take up immediately the Communist cause there. Both accounts may have been true because, while an American Communist is likely to be of greatest use to the Kremlin in America, the Communist high command could not overlook the propaganda advantages of having some dependable Allied converts renounce their capitalist homes and rebuff the Allied "explanations" during neutral internment.

The most telling indictment of the Communists during the prisoner exchange was scored by the Reds' chief propaganda tools—the pilots who had confessed waging bacteriological warfare. They were the last to come home—"pardoned" from a scheduled war crimes prosecution, magnanimously released from special confinement, and returned at Panmunjom on the final day of the exchange on September 6th. These were the men whose names and statements had been used in one of the most elaborate and successful propaganda campaigns ever launched by the communist world. More than a hundred American air force prisoners had been accused and thirty-six had signed confessions, twenty-five of them detailed and lengthy depositions which were used by the Red propaganda machine. They had given names, dates, and technical and code terms allegedly employed in bacteriological warfare operations, summaries of instruction on handling and dropping germ bombs, the wording of orders on "BW" bomb missions, reports of staff conferences and private discussions on the project, and a mass of other details, all in convincingly American military idiom. These depositions had been broadcast by Communist radios, read by some of the confessing pilots in documentary movies, photographed, quoted by the Soviet delegation at the United Nations, and generally distributed throughout the world. The Communist world believed, as did millions in the "neutral" countries of Asia. Many anti-Communists were troubled and alarmed.

The free world had learned to expect masterpieces from Communist experts in the arts of brainwashing and forced confessions. The Soviet purge trials of the mid-1930's and the more recent people's court convictions in eastern European satellite capitals had proved that strong men could be made to say and write what their Red interrogators wanted. The United States air force and the United Nations command at first counted on this popular knowledge to dismiss the germ warfare propaganda as a magnificent fraud. When the campaign continued, American newsmen were given unqualified and categorical denials by the highest United States military authorities and finally by the President and Secretary of State. Still, American officials refused to be drawn into furnishing proof the Reds were lying by picking factual holes in the pilots' confessions. To do so, it was argued, might endanger the lives of pilots who had tricked the Communists with patently false details. In time, the United States government was confident, the "big lie" would be exposed and the ambitious propaganda campaign would fall flat.

The Communists' prize exhibit was the six-thousand-word confession of Colonel Frank Schwable, forty-five-year-old Naval Academy graduate and former chief of staff of the First Marine Air Wing in Korea. Shot down July 8th, 1952, Schwable signed the first draft of his deposition nearly five months later. Early in 1953 he recited his confession for a Communist propaganda movie and radio broadcast. His was the ultimate in confessions. Grey and haggard, he returned to freedom at Panmunjom in the final hours of Big

Switch. The next day at Inchon he told his story, similar in basic outline to the experiences of the other men who had signed.

Like other pilots selected for a rôle in the germ warfare hoax, the Marine colonel was segregated from regular prisoners. Taken deep into North Korea, he was thrown into a wooden lean-to built against the side of a farm hut. Almost immediately he was charged with the crime of bacteriological warfare and ordered to confess and co-operate with his captors. Cramped into an unheated 3 x 7-foot space, he was forced to exist in miserable filth and slowly reduced to the level of a mangy dog, robbed of all self-respect, broken in mind and body.

"It was the last couple of days in November that I gave up," Schwable recounted to newsmen after his repatriation. "I was cold. I was damn cold. My hand was frozen. There was no question in my mind. I knew they weren't going to let me stand up in front of a firing squad. They were going to leave me there all Winter. I knew I'd never make it . . .

"I think slow mental torture over a long period of time is worse than quick physical torture," Schwable continued. "You sit there day in and day out, day in and day out. Your choices are very limited. You either confess or you stay there."

"I had to decide whether I could better serve my country above the ground or below the ground."

He said his interrogator told him: "You will clear this problem or you will never leave this valley—not even after peace is signed."

"I couldn't take it any longer."

He said the Chinese ordered him to write a detailed confession and a plan of bacteriological warfare "as practiced by the United States." For three months he wrote and re-wrote his statement, changing parts which didn't fit the Communists' over-all propaganda scheme or which sounded unreasonable to them.

"Once you do this thing you've got to play it both ways," the colonel continued. "You've got to make it both realistic and ridiculous. I hope to God—I pray to God—I achieved that aim.

"I knew military people would understand. I don't know about the public. . . . But it is fantastic that anyone can believe that anything of that sort was used. I once told my interrogator that I would stand before God and swear it was never used. I told him that in our religion that's a pretty strong oath. But they never tried to make me swear it was true."

He had no doubts that his "confession" convinced many people that the United States was engaging in the most dia-bolical form of warfare against innocent civilians. "They have a good case for their people," he admitted. "I can only hope now that some of our people who are doubtful will be reassured."

Schwable's experience and his reaction were similar to those of other pilots, except that some agreed to write phony confessions after less persuasion, and many—at least forty and possibly some of the thirty-one other accused pilots who died—refused to sign. These men who refused to be used were among the real heroes of the war.

Some pilots reported that they were taken to a place near Pyongyang which the prisoners called "Pak's Palace." There, they said, Soviet Russian officials directed the staff of Chinese and North Korean interrogators and appeared to be responsible for the regulated system of mental and physical torture through which signed statements were extracted.

The official United States government report to the United Nations charged Russia with responsibility for master-minding the "big lie" of germ warfare in Korea and directing the propaganda campaign based on false confessions. American delegate Dr. Charles W. Mayo summed up before the U.N. General Assembly's Political Committee the repatriated pilots' accounts of the system used: "It is a method obviously calculated by the Communists to bring a man to the point where a dry crust of bread or a few hours' uninterrupted sleep is a great event in his life. All the prisoners victimized were subjected to the same pattern of intimidation, deprivation of basic physical needs, isolation and physical and mental torture. . . . The techniques varied only in detail . . . the total picture presented is one of human beings reduced to a status lower than that of animals, filthy, full of lice, festered wounds full of maggots, their sickness regulated to a point just short of death, unshaven, without haircuts or baths for as much as a year, men in rags, exposed to the elements, fed with carefully measured minimum quantities and the lowest quality of food and unsanitary water, served often in rusty cans, isolated, faced with squads of trained interrogators, bulldozed, deprived of sleep and browbeaten with mental anguish. . . ."

The Kremlin's super-collosal propaganda show flopped badly after a strong first act. The United States followed up its advantage by proposing that impartial commissions selected by the United Nations investigate the Communists' germ-warfare charges and the American reports of Communist atrocities. Russia's spokesmen blustered and changed the subject.

# XXIII

## *The Last Best Hope*

THE KOREAN ARMISTICE day was not a time for victory celebrations, but neither did the facts justify the guilty, self-reproachful feeling which seemed to dominate American reaction.

Two years of alternately hopeful and frustrating negotiations for a truce had taken the edge off the real thing when it finally came. Bitter experience at Kaesong and Panmunjom had made hard realists of millions who earlier had hoped that political negotiations could produce a peaceful solution of the Korean problem once the fighting stopped. Syngman Rhee's vehement attack on Allied truce-seeking as a cowardly sell-out for "peace at any price" had had its effect on large groups of Americans. Commentators in America exploited this gnawing doubt into something approaching national shame over "the compromise armistice terms."

Were the armistice terms shameful? No. If it was wrong to sign this truce, it had been wrong to negotiate an armistice from the beginning.

The armistice terms were in large measure a victory for the United States and its United Nations Allies. They provided for a cease-fire on the actual battleline, rather than at the Thirty-eighth parallel as originally demanded by the

Communists. They provided for joint inspection of truce compliance in the buffer zone between the two armies and neutral policing of the agreements behind the lines of both sides—a major victory of principle for the United Nations Allies, as well as a practical safeguard. The truce terms guaranteed the right of a war prisoner to choose either repatriation or political asylum, another triumph for Allied negotiators. The complex scheme of implementing this right through neutral custody of unrepatriated prisoners and political "explanations" to them was hardly the perfect solution, but this did not tarnish the victory. A totally unexpected additional benefit was later derived from this scheme, however, when India, acting as administrator and middleman of the Neutral Nations Repatriation Commission, belatedly learned some valuable lessons about dealing with the Communists and developed greater sympathy for the western powers as a result.

Armistice terms could be no more than a reflection of the military situation—itself a reflection of failures on both sides. The Communists had failed in their brazen gamble for conquest of South Korea and, eventually, Japan. The United Nations had failed to muster the strength and find a practical way to destroy the aggressors or solve finally the explosive problem of a divided Korea.

The final balance sheet, however, was not a neatly equalized stalemate of failures. We had set out to thwart the North Korean Communist invasion and to preserve the independence of the southern republic. We had succeeded. We had thrown back the aggressors, inflicted terrible punishment on all North Korea, more than restored the violated border, and brought the Korean Republic the greatest security it had ever known. We had called the Kremlin's biggest bluff. In doing so, we had saved the United Nations from extinction as a practical peace-keeping agency and at the same time had exposed its weaknesses. We had reassured the many small and vulnerable nations living on the periphery of the Communist empire in both Asia and Europe.

Even in our failure to win a conclusive military victory there was a compensating factor on the credit side which history may rate higher than traditional raw courage. In rejecting the "total victory" course which, after Red China's entry, would have forced major war mobilization in the United States, sent American bombers over China, and brought death to hundreds of thousands of soldiers and civilians, we had demonstrated a will for peace and a high sense of responsibility for averting atomic war. We had shown that we meant it when we said we sought peace and opposed the use of war to settle international disputes. We had strengthened our claim to moral leadership in the eyes of millions of Europeans and Asians who had viewed the United States with distrust. In this frequently damned policy of limited war, we may have done more to achieve our ultimate objectives of free world solidarity and peace than we could have accomplished in a successful offensive to the Yalu River.

Of course, we may also have served to contribute to an enormous increase in the prestige and influence of the Peiping regime among its neighbors. Hadn't the mighty capitalist-democratic nations of the West been unable to drive the Chinese Communists out of North Korea? The final judgment on this question will not come from today's statesman or "expert," but from the actions of governments and peoples, particularly Asians, in choosing between nervous neutralism and boldly anti-Communist alignment with the democracies. In the first half-year after the Korean armistice was signed, the verdict of opinion appeared to be on our side.

There were more valid doubts, however, to dampen the celebration of truce in Korea; had we merely deluded ourselves with hypocritical talk of a "peaceful solution" which we knew to be unattainable? Had we falsely raised hopes for peace, tied our hands with an armistice of unlimited duration, given the Communists time to retrench and rebuild at home and surrendered the initiative to the Kremlin?

These critical questions could be answered partially by citing the alternatives to an armistice, partially by recalling that "unconditional" victories in World War II—the nearest approach to total war and total victory the world has known—did not bring lasting peace and security or even relaxation of tension. A bigger and more dangerous delusion than the hope for a Korean peace without total victory may have been the assumption that any war, particularly one short of a global fight to the finish, could produce a neatly packaged and money-back-guaranteed peace. The Korean war, no matter how fought or ended, could hardly have been expected to make possible such a doubt-free settlement.

Certainly there was no guarantee of peace in the armistice plan. It recommended a high-level political (peace) conference "of the countries concerned on both sides," convened within three months after the cease-fire to "settle through negotiation the questions of the withdrawal of all foreign forces from Korea, the peaceful settlement of the Korean question, et cetera." No one familiar with the conflicting interests involved could forecast success for the peace conference. Syngman Rhee predicted its complete failure.

The Allied objective at the conference was to be the creation, through United Nations-supervised elections, of a unified and stable government of all Korea, at least strongly non-Communist and preferably anti-Communist and democratic in political leanings, but correct and unthreatening in its essential relations with Russia and Red China—a reliable, independent buffer state between the Communist mainland and Japan.

The announced South Korean objective was the absorption of the North into Rhee's Republic of Korea, preferably through new elections held only in the North, with all Communists barred from political life. Coalition with the Communists meant eventual conquest from within, Rhee insisted, and he had the evidence of Czechoslovakia to support his contention. The United States government, operating on the same theory, could hardly disagree.

All plans provided for the ultimate withdrawal of the United States, United Nations, and Chinese forces from all Korea.

As North Korea's population had dropped to about one-third or one-fourth that of South Korea's twenty-one million, the inevitable result of these unification plans would have been the formation of an anti-Communist all-Korean government, probably headed by Rhee, aligned with the United States and capable of massing a formidable army on the Yalu River border of Red China. This obviously was an unacceptable prospect to the Communists.

There was no evidence on armistice day or six months later that the Communists intended to permit creation of a unified and popular government of all Korea. Before the war Moscow had blocked all efforts to restore a unified nation on the peninsula. The Soviet-American negotiations on unification during the dual occupation of Korea collapsed after the Russians repeatedly increased their price, finally demanding, in effect, guarantees that conservative parties would have little chance of winning control of the first unified government. The United Nations General Assembly's unification efforts in 1948 failed when Russia and its satellite North Korean government refused to permit United Nations-supervised free elections in the North. Such elections to create a representative government were certain to be required in any agreed unification scheme; there was no reason to suppose that the Communists could stomach free elections in 1954 any better than in 1948.

Unification under any formula acceptable to South Korea and the United States spelled defeat and retreat for the Communists, for it meant rolling back the Iron Curtain and, at least symbolically, turning the tide against Communist expansion in Asia. To the Red leadership, this was a stiff price for Korean peace, if, indeed, peace was the Communist aim.

The announced Peiping-Pyongyang peace plan for Korea left many questions unanswered, but it stressed withdrawal of all foreign troops, including the Chinese, "nonintervention in Korea's affairs," and "peaceful settlement of the Korean question by the Korean people." Among American officials in Tokyo and Seoul there were at least three schools of thought, during the first months of armistice, on the Communists' actual plans and objectives:

1. That the Communists planned to obstruct or prevent convening of the peace conference until Rhee's patience

was exhausted and he openly violated the cease-fire, carrying out his "fight-to-the-death" threats to invade North Korea. The United States would be bound by unequivocal promises made at Panmunjom not to support a truce-breaking Rhee offensive. Consequently, the Chinese could safely roll with the ROK punch, wait until the South Korean Army had committed itself deeply and exhausted its six-day supply of American ammunition, and then systematically destroy Rhee's best troops. If this maneuver succeeded in rendering as many as ten ROK divisions ineffective, the Communists conceivably might then declare the armistice ended by Rhee's action and push their counterattack across the truce line in a fourth attempt to drive the United Nations forces into the sea. If, however, the South Korean attack force pulled back from North Korea without serious losses, the Communists could limit themselves to a purely defensive action, pushing back only so far as the buffer zone and demonstrating that they were the "true lovers of peace" and the original "victims of the Syngman Rhee aggression." If Rhee failed initially to carry out his threatened "go-it-alone" offensive, his bluff would be called and the only significant threat forcing China to tie down large armies in North Korea would thereafter be eliminated.

2. That the Communists eventually would come to a peace conference but insist in the conference on withdrawal of all foreign troops followed by formation of a coalition government of united Korea, with North Korea guaranteed freedom to elect Communists to legislative and executive positions in the new regime. When the conference broke down, Rhee would be tempted to fall into the trap outlined in the first hypothesis.

3. That the Communists would attend a peace confer-

ence but would reject all proposals for a democratically created government of a united Korea except at the price of United Nations membership for Peiping, military "neutralization" of Korea, and possibly other concessions in a general Asian "deal." They could certainly be expected to demand large-scale concessions in some area outside Korea in return for surrendering North Korea. At least so long as the blood of aggression was fresh on Communist China's hands and Mao Tse-tung had not proved elsewhere his claim to peaceful intentions, any such deal was certain to be rejected by the United States.

Experience with the Communists in Europe and Asia, and particularly in Korea, dictated this suspicious analysis of their intentions. The facts as known in the first half-year after the cease-fire permitted little hope for Korean unification.

Incomplete and possibly distorted reports of competition between Moscow and Peiping for dominant authority in North Korea suggested another reason for suspecting that a peace settlement involving early withdrawal of Chinese troops was not an immediate possibility. So long as the "Chinese People's Volunteer Forces" remained as a virtual occupation force, Mao rather than Malenkov exercised primary influence and control over North Korea. The apparent race of the two great Communist nations to outdo each other in announcing tremendous economic rehabilitation aid for North Korea within three months after the armistice was signed reflected this internal struggle for power and position.

The Communists' solidification of ties with the North Korean government and its proclamation of long-range economic-aid programs followed the United States government's announcement in early August of a five-year, billion-dollar rehabilitation program for South Korea and the initialing at the same time of a U.S.–ROK mutual-defense treaty.

Both American assistance measures were subject to revision or cancellation in the event of an agreement on Korean unification at the peace conference. But both reflected —as did the Communist agreements with North Korea— official skepticism over any early peace settlement. The American defense pact and the economic-aid program, the first $200,000,000 of which was immediately allocated, were prompt fulfillment of Eisenhower's promise in exchange for Rhee's acceptance of the armistice.

Secretary of State John Foster Dulles flew to Seoul on August 5th to conclude these arrangements and obtain from Rhee a firm agreement to assure the peace efforts a reasonable chance. Their four-day series of conferences produced a public elaboration of the earlier Rhee-Robertson agreement. The South Korean president promised "to take no unilateral action to unite Korea by military means for the agreed duration of the political conference." Dulles confirmed that the "agreed duration" was a reference to an earlier passage in the statement which said the United States and ROK delegations would walk out of the conference after ninety days if "it becomes clear to each of our governments that all attempts to achieve these objectives (creation of a unified and free government for all Korea) have been fruitless and the conference is being exploited by the Communist delegates . . ." Rhee agreed that, before taking precipitate military action, he would consult further with the United States "regarding the attainment of a unified, free and independent Korea." Dulles made it clear that renewal of the war was not among the methods the United States would consider in these consultations, while Rhee steadfastly insisted that war was the only way.

A high American official summed up the situation: "At least we have agreed on the areas of our disagreement and we will have a chance to reason with the ROK government if the political conference fails. We know we can count on at least six months of truce, possibly more, and we hope in that time peace will become a habit." That was the best hope within the bounds of reality as the highly unpromising negotiations to arrange a peace conference began.

Chances of convening a conference and agreeing on an agenda were small; chances of American agreement at a peace conference to the Communists' expected price for surrendering North Korea were nil. But the possibility of another round of warfare also was becoming remote. The Chinese Communists needed relief from the burden of fighting in Korea. The North Koreans had had enough of suffering and nightly disaster. The new Russian regime apparently had shifted tactics and sought a period of relative peace to permit greater attention to domestic ills. The United States government was committed to an economy based on a long-range defense buildup to meet the threat from a single great enemy, Russia. Consequently, war in Asia was to be avoided at almost all costs.

To further insure against Communist-initiated war, the United States and its fifteen fighting allies in Korea served notice in a joint declaration adopted in Washington on Armistice Day and made public two weeks later: "We affirm in the interest of world peace that if there is a renewal of the armed attacks, challenging again the principles of the United Nations, we should again be united and prompt to resist. The consequences of such a breach of the armistice would be so grave that in all probability it would not be possible to confine hostilities within the frontiers of Korea."

Considered together with the statements of American military leaders, the meaning was clear: If the Communists broke the truce by renewing their aggression in Korea, they could expect American bombs to fall on Chinese cities. There would be no more proxy war for Russia and Red China in Korea. We had done everything possible to prevent Korea from exploding into world war; such restraint in the cause of world peace could not be expected again in the face of a renewed Communist assault. The declaration represented a policy shift in London and other Allied capitals in favor of the tougher American viewpoint—a shift which could have occurred only as a result of the truce and in recognition of America's earnest struggle for peace through the trying armistice negotiations. As such, it was more important for the future than was the warning it conveyed to the Red capitals, because most military and political experts believed the Communists were unlikely to set off a new war in Korea in the foreseeable future.

Through this analysis, Allied leaders and unofficial observers arrived at the virtually unanimous conclusion that Syngman Rhee alone posed a threat of renewed war. Those who discounted the sincerity of Rhee's convictions felt that he kept this threat alive solely to assure himself the strongest bargaining position with the United States. That government could not operate on the assumption that Rhee was bluffing, however. It sent a procession of generals, ambassadors, and congressmen to Rhee's Seoul mansion to pound home the warning that the United States and the other United Nations Allies would not be a party to renewing the war to attain Korean unification and would not condone or support an independent offensive by the ROK forces. On the positive side, the promise of one billion dollars in reconstruction aid to South Korea was a tempting reward for co-operation.

Still, no one could be sure that Rhee was permanently dissuaded from reopening the war. Despite his commitment to give an eventual peace conference a chance, he remained openly dedicated to the proposition that an all-or-nothing fight for Korea with the Communists was the only practicable way to unification and peace. As time slipped by and even the chances of agreement on convening a peace conference became remote, the challenge to Rhee to prove to himself and his people that he was not bluffing became acute. Yet, he let the first clear challenge pass, when preliminary diplomatic talks at Panmunjom between the United Nations allies and the Communists collapsed over the issue of whether Russia should attend the peace conference as a neutral. Would he let another climacteric pass? American government leaders believed he would, but they could not be certain.

If Rhee wanted it so, the Republic of Korea could live and rebuild with bounteous American aid in as great security as any nation on the fringe of the Communist empire can expect—greater than most such nations now enjoy. For his nation now was guarded by the firm assurance that the United States, at least, would retaliate beyond the border of Korea against the sources of any future Communist invasion. If the global atomic showdown with Soviet Communism came—as Rhee firmly expected—he could also be assured that in the world which survived there would be a united Korea.

This was the future the United States proposed to an aged and fanatically devoted Korean nationalist whose time for realizing his last great ambition was slipping away. No one could expect him to accept it gladly without reservations. No one could be surprised if he rejected it. And no one, probably including himself, could predict far in advance what he would do.

If Rhee held his fire, the prospect was permanent division of Korea along and generally north of the Thirty-eighth parallel. The armistice would become a de facto peace, freezing the border of the Communist world along the jagged line where the shooting stopped on July 27th. A succession of international debates and conferences on Korea was inevitable, and out of them might come a "phasing-out" of the armistice machinery, a tacit relaxation of the truce restrictions, or even a joint withdrawal of United Nations and Chinese armed forces coupled with renewed truce guarantees. The advantages of withdrawal of American and Allied ground forces from Korea, dramatizing an openly declared reliance upon long-range air power to insure against new Communist aggression, were receiving increasingly serious consideration by the highest American military officers.

This was the best that a democratic alliance engaged in cold war could offer the Republic of Korea—rescue from extinction; peace without unification; economic patches and crutches, but no chance for economic independence without the North's industrial and mineral resources; security guarantees but no absolute respite from the latent threat of war. So stated, it was less than a glorious culmination of a three-year war into which Korea had poured its lifeblood and its friends had given selflessly in a cause far from home. But it was little worse than either the present or the future of some European nations with far greater claim to economic, political, and strategic importance than the southern half of the impoverished Korean peninsula. And it was perhaps as bright a prospect as this unhappy land had known in a history of wars and foreign occupations.

For the free world, the net balance of cost and accomplishment was good. America, England, Canada, Turkey, and all the other nations, large and small, which gave the lives of their sons to restore and defend the independence of the Korean Republic could be justly proud. More important than South Korea, they had preserved and strengthened the world's best chance for peace—the united resolve of the free nations to stand up to the Soviet challenge wherever presented.

# *Appendix A*

## ARMISTICE AGREEMENT

### VOLUME I

## TEXT OF AGREEMENT

AGREEMENT BETWEEN THE COMMANDER-IN-CHIEF, UNITED NATIONS COMMAND, ON THE ONE HAND, AND THE SUPREME COMMANDER OF THE KOREAN PEOPLE'S ARMY AND THE COMMANDER OF THE CHINESE PEOPLE'S VOLUNTEERS, ON THE OTHER HAND, CONCERNING A MILITARY ARMISTICE IN KOREA

## PREAMBLE

The undersigned, the Commander-in-Chief, United Nations Command, on the one hand, and the Supreme Commander of the Korean People's Army and the Commander of the Chinese People's Volunteers, on the other hand, in the interest of stopping the Korean conflict, with its great toll of suffering and bloodshed on both sides, and with the objective of establishing an armistice which will insure a complete cessation of hostilities and of all acts of armed force in Korea until a final peaceful settlement is achieved, do individually, collectively, and mutually agree to accept and to be bound and governed by the conditions and terms of armistice set forth in the following Articles and Paragraphs, which said conditions and terms are intended to be purely military in character and to pertain solely to the belligerents in Korea.

310

# ARTICLE I

## MILITARY DEMARCATION LINE AND DEMILITARIZED ZONE

1. A Military Demarcation Line shall be fixed and both sides shall withdraw two (2) kilometers from this line so as to establish a Demilitarized Zone between the opposing forces. A Demilitarized Zone shall be established as a buffer zone to prevent the occurrence of incidents which might lead to a resumption of hostilities.

2. The Military Demarcation Line is located as indicated on the attached map (Map 1).

3. The Demilitarized Zone is defined by a northern and a southern boundary as indicated on the attached map (Map 1).

4. The Military Demarcation Line shall be plainly marked as directed by the Military Armistice Commission hereinafter established. The Commanders of the opposing sides shall have suitable markers erected along the boundary between the Demilitarized Zone and their respective areas. The Military Armistice Commission shall supervise the erection of all markers placed along the Military Demarcation Line and along the boundaries of the Demilitarized Zone.

5. The waters of the Han River Estuary shall be open to civil shipping of both sides wherever one bank is controlled by one side and the other bank is controlled by the other side. The Military Armistice Commission shall prescribe rules for the shipping in that part of the Han River Estuary indicated on the attached map (Map 2). Civil shipping of each side shall have unrestricted access to the land under the military control of that side.

6. Neither side shall execute any hostile act within, from, or against the Demilitarized Zone.

7. No person, military or civilian, shall be permitted to cross the Military Demarcation Line unless specifically authorized to do so by the Military Armistice Commission.

8. No person, military or civilian, in the Demilitarized Zone shall be permitted to enter the territory under the military control of either side unless specifically authorized to do so by the Commander into whose territory entry is sought.

9. No person, military or civilian, shall be permitted to enter the Demilitarized Zone except persons concerned with the conduct of civil administration and relief and persons specifically authorized to enter by the Military Armistice Commission.

10. Civil administration and relief in that part of the Demilitarized Zone which is south of the Military Demarcation Line shall be the responsibility of the Commander-in-Chief, United Nations Command; and civil administration and relief in that part of the Demilitarized Zone which is north of the Military Demarcation Line shall be the joint responsi-

bility of the Supreme Commander of the Korean People's Army and the Commander of the Chinese People's Volunteers. The number of persons, military or civilian, from each side who are permitted to enter the Demilitarized Zone for the conduct of civil administration and relief shall be as determined by the respective Commanders, but in no case shall the total number authorized by either side exceed one thousand (1,000) persons at any one time. The number of civil police and the arms to be carried by them shall be as prescribed by the Military Armistice Commission. Other personnel shall not carry arms unless specifically authorized to do so by the Military Armistice Commission.

11. Nothing contained in this Article shall be construed to prevent the complete freedom of movement to, from, and within the Demilitarized Zone by the Military Armistice Commission, its assistants, its Joint Observer Teams with their assistants, the Neutral Nations Supervisory Commission hereinafter established, its assistants, its Neutral Nations Inspection Teams with their assistants, and of any other persons, materials, and equipment specifically authorized to enter the Demilitarized Zone by the Military Armistice Commission. Convenience of movement shall be permitted through the territory under the military control of either side over any route necessary to move between points within the Demilitarized Zone where such points are not connected by roads lying completely within the Demilitarized Zone.

## ARTICLE II

## CONCRETE ARRANGEMENTS FOR CEASE-FIRE AND ARMISTICE

### A. GENERAL

12. The Commanders of the opposing sides shall order and enforce a complete cessation of all hostilities in Korea by all armed forces under their control, including all units and personnel of the ground, naval, and air forces, effective twelve (12) hours after this Armistice Agreement is signed. (See Paragraph 63 hereof for effective date and hour of the remaining provisions of this Armistice Agreement.)

13. In order to insure the stability of the Military Armistice so as to facilitate the attainment of a peaceful settlement through the holding by both sides of a political conference of a higher level, the Commanders of the opposing sides shall:

a. Within seventy-two (72) hours after this Armistice Agreement becomes effective, withdraw all of their military forces, supplies, and equipment from the Demilitarized Zone except as otherwise provided herein. All demolitions, minefields, wire entanglements, and other hazards to the safe movement of personnel of the Military Armistice Commission or its

Joint Observer Teams, known to exist within the Demilitarized Zone after the withdrawal of military forces therefrom, together with lanes known to be free of all such hazards, shall be reported to the Military Armistice Commission by the Commander of the side whose forces emplaced such hazards. Subsequently, additional safe lanes shall be cleared; and eventually, within forty-five (45) days after the termination of the seventy-two (72) hour period, all such hazards shall be removed from the Demilitarized Zone as directed by and under the supervision of the Military Armistice Commission. At the termination of the seventy-two (72) hour period, except for unarmed troops authorized a forty-five (45) day period to complete salvage operations under Military Armistice Commission supervision, such units of a police nature as may be specifically requested by the Military Armistice Commission and agreed to by the Commanders of the opposing sides, and personnel authorized under Paragraphs 10 and 11 hereof, no personnel of either side shall be permitted to enter the Demilitarized Zone.

b. Within ten (10) days after this Armistice Agreement becomes effective, withdraw all of their military forces, supplies, and equipment from the rear and the coastal islands and waters of Korea of the other side. If such military forces are not withdrawn within the stated time limit, and there is no mutually agreed and valid reason for the delay, the other side shall have the right to take any action which it deems necessary for the maintenance of security and order. The term "coastal islands," as used above, refers to those islands which, though occupied by one side at the time when this Armistice Agreement becomes effective, were controlled by the other side on 24 June 1950; provided, however, that all the islands lying to the north and west of the provincial boundary line between HWANGHAE-DO and KYONGGI-DO shall be under the military control of the Supreme Commander of the Korean People's Army and the Commander of the Chinese People's Volunteers, except the island groups of PAENGYONG-DO (37°58'N, 124°40'E), TAECHONG-DO (37°50'N, 124°42'E), SOCHONG-DO (37°46'N, 124°46'E), YONPYONG-DO (37°38'N, 125°40'E), and U-DO (37°36'N, 125°58'E), which shall remain under the military control of the Commander-in-Chief, United Nations Command. All the islands on the west coast of Korea lying south of the above-mentioned boundary line shall remain under the military control of the Commander-in-Chief, United Nations Command. (See Map 3.)

c. Cease the introduction into Korea of reinforcing military personnel; provided, however, that the rotation of units and personnel, the arrival in Korea of personnel on a temporary duty basis, and the return to Korea of personnel after short periods of leave or temporary duty outside of Korea shall be permitted within the scope prescribed below. "Rotation" is defined as the replacement of units or personnel by other units or personnel who are commencing a tour of duty in Korea. Rotation personnel shall be introduced into and evacuated from Korea only through the ports of entry enumerated in Paragraph 43 hereof. Rotation shall be conducted on a man-for-man basis; provided, however, that no more than thirty-five thousand (35,000) persons in the military service shall be admitted into Korea by either side in any calendar month under the rotation policy. No military personnel of either side shall be introduced into Korea if the introduction of such personnel will cause the aggregate of the military personnel of that side admitted into Korea since the effective date of this Armistice Agreement to exceed the cumulative total of the military personnel of that side who have departed from Korea since that date. Reports concerning arrivals in and departures from Korea of military personnel shall be made daily to the Military Armistice Commission and the Neutral Nations Supervisory Commission; such reports shall include places of arrival and departure and the number of persons arriving at or departing from each such place. The Neutral Nations Supervisory Commission, through its Neutral Nations Inspection Teams, shall conduct supervision and inspection of the rotation of units and personnel authorized above, at the ports of entry enumerated in Paragraph 43 hereof.

d. Cease the introduction into Korea of reinforcing combat aircraft, armored vehicles, weapons, and ammunition; provided, however, that combat aircraft, armored vehicles, weapons, and ammunition which are destroyed, damaged, worn out, or used up during the period of the armistice may be replaced on the basis of piece-for-piece of the same effectiveness and the same type. Such combat aircraft, armored vehicles, weapons, and ammunition shall be introduced into Korea only through the ports of entry enumerated in Paragraph 43 hereof. In order to justify the requirement for combat aircraft, armored vehicles, weapons, and ammunition to be introduced into Korea for replacement purposes, reports concerning every incoming shipment of these items shall be made to the Military Armistice Commission and the Neutral Nations Supervisory Commission; such reports shall include statements regarding the disposition of the items being replaced. Items to be replaced which are removed from Korea shall be removed only through the ports of entry enumerated in Paragraph 43 hereof. The Neutral Nations Supervisory Commission, through its Neutral Nations Inspection Teams, shall conduct supervision and inspection of the replacement of combat aircraft, armored vehicles, weapons, and ammunition authorized above, at the ports of entry enumerated in Paragraph 43 hereof.

e. Insure that personnel of their respective commands who violate any of the provisions of this Armistice Agreement are adequately punished.

f. In those cases where places of burial are a matter of record and graves are actually found to exist, permit graves registration personnel of the other side to enter, within a definite time limit after this Armistice Agreement becomes effective, the territory of Korea under their military control, for the purpose of proceeding to such graves to recover and evacuate the bodies of the deceased military personnel of that side, including deceased prisoners of war. The specific procedures and the time limit for the performance of the above task shall be determined by the Military Armistice Commission. The Commanders of the opposing sides shall furnish to the other side all available information pertaining to the places of burial of the deceased military personnel of the other side.

g. Afford full protection and all possible assistance and cooperation to the Military Armistice Commission, its Joint Observer Teams, the Neutral Nations Supervisory Commission, and its Neutral Nations Inspection Teams, in the carrying out of their functions and responsibilities hereinafter assigned; and accord to the Neutral Nations Supervisory Commission, and to its Neutral Nations Inspection Teams, full convenience of movement between the headquarters of the Neutral Nations Supervisory Commission and the ports of entry enumerated in Paragraph 43 hereof over main lines of communication agreed upon by both sides (See Map 4), and between the headquarters of the Neutral Nations Supervisory Commission and the places where violations of this Armistice Agreement have been reported to have occurred. In order to prevent unnecessary delays, the use of alternate routes and means of transportation will be permitted whenever the main lines of communication are closed or impassable.

h. Provide such logistic support, including communications and transportation facilities, as may be required by the Military Armistice Commission and the Neutral Nations Supervisory Commission and their Teams.

i. Each construct, operate, and maintain a suitable airfield in their respective ports of the Demilitarized Zone in the vicinity of the headquarters of the Military Armistice Commission, for such uses as the Commission may determine.

j. Insure that all members and other personnel of the Neutral Nations Supervisory Commission and of the Neutral Nations Repatriation Commission hereinafter established shall enjoy the freedom and facilities necessary for the proper exercise of their function, including privileges, treatment, and immunities equivalent to those ordinarily enjoyed by accredited diplomatic personnel under international usage.

14. This Armistice Agreement shall apply to all opposing ground forces under the military control of either side, which ground forces shall respect the Demilitarized Zone and the area of Korea under the military control of the opposing side.

15. This Armistice Agreement shall apply to all opposing naval forces, which naval forces shall respect the waters contiguous to the Demilitarized Zone and to the land area of Korea under the military control of the opposing side, and shall not engage in blockade of any kind of Korea.

16. This Armistice Agreement shall apply to all opposing air forces, which air forces shall respect the air space over the Demilitarized Zone and over the area of Korea under the military control of the opposing side, and over the waters contiguous to both.

17. Responsibility for compliance with and enforcement of the terms and provisions of this Armistice Agreement is that of the signatories hereto and their successors in command. The Commanders of the opposing sides shall establish within their respective commands all measures and procedures necessary to insure complete compliance with all of the provisions hereof

by all elements of their commands. They shall actively cooperate with one another and with the Military Armistice Commission and the Neutral Nations Supervisory Commission in requiring observance of both the letter and the spirit of all of the provisions of this Armistice Agreement.

18. The costs of the operations of the Military Armistice Commission and of the Neutral Nations Supervisory Commission and of their Teams shall be shared equally by the two opposing sides.

# B. MILITARY ARMISTICE COMMISSION

## 1. COMPOSITION

19. A Military Armistice Commission is hereby established.

20. The Military Armistice Commission shall be composed of ten (10) senior officers, five (5) of whom shall be appointed by the Commander-in-Chief, United Nations Command, and five (5) of whom shall be appointed jointly by the Supreme Commander of the Korean People's Army and the Commander of the Chinese People's Volunteers. Of the ten members, three (3) from each side shall be of general or flag rank. The two (2) remaining members on each side may be major generals, brigadier generals, colonels, or their equivalents.

21. Members of the Military Armistice Commission shall be permitted to use staff assistants as required.

22. The Military Armistice Commission shall be provided with the necessary administrative personnel to establish a Secretariat charged with assisting the Commission by performing record-keeping, secretarial, interpreting, and such other functions as the Commission may assign to it. Each side shall appoint to the Secretariat a Secretary and an Assistant Secretary and such clerical and specialized personnel as required by the Secretariat. Records shall be kept in English, Korean, and Chinese, all of which shall be equally authentic.

23. a. The Military Armistice Commission shall be initially provided with and assisted by ten (10) Joint Observer Teams, which number may be reduced by agreement of the senior members of both sides on the Military Armistice Commission.

b. Each Joint Observer Team shall be composed of not less than four (4) nor more than six (6) officers of field grade, half of whom shall be appointed by the Commander-in-Chief, United Nations Command, and half of whom shall be appointed jointly by the Supreme Commander of the Korean People's Army and the Commander of the Chinese People's Volunteers. Additional personnel such as drivers, clerks, and interpreters shall be furnished by each side as required for the functioning of the Joint Observer Teams.

## 2. FUNCTIONS AND AUTHORITY

24. The general mission of the Military Armistice Commission shall be to supervise the implementation of this Armistice Agreement and to settle through negotiations any violations of this Armistice Agreement.

25. The Military Armistice Commission shall:

a. Locate its headquarters in the vicinity of PANMUNJOM (37°57′29″N, 126°40′00″E). The Military Armistice Commission may relocate its headquarters at another point within the Demilitarized Zone by agreement of the senior members of both sides on the Commission.

b. Operate as a joint organization without a chairman.

c. Adopt such rules of procedure as it may, from time to time, deem necessary.

d. Supervise the carrying out of the provisions of this Armistice Agreement pertaining to the Demilitarized Zone and to the Han River Estuary.

e. Direct the operations of the Joint Observer Teams.

f. Settle through negotiations any violations of this Armistice agreement.

g. Transmit immediately to the Commanders of the opposing sides all reports of investigations of violations of this Armistice Agreement and all other reports and records of proceedings received from the Neutral Nations Supervisory Commission.

h. Give general supervision and direction to the activities of the Committee for Repatriation of Prisoners of War and the Committee for Assisting the Return of Displaced Civilians, hereinafter established.

i. Act as an intermediary in transmitting communications between the Commanders of the opposing sides; provided, however, that the foregoing shall not be construed to preclude the Commanders of both sides from communicating with each other by any other means which they may desire to employ.

j. Provide credentials and distinctive insignia for its staff and its Joint Observer Teams, and a distinctive marking for all vehicles, aircraft, and vessels, used in the performance of its mission.

26. The mission of the Joint Observer Teams shall be to assist the Military Armistice Commission in supervising the carrying out of the provisions of this Armistice Agreement pertaining to the Demilitarized Zone and to the Han River Estuary.

27. The Military Armistice Commission, or the senior member of either side thereof, is authorized to dispatch Joint Observer Teams to investigate violations of this Armistice Agreement reported to have occurred in the Demilitarized Zone or in the Han River Estuary; provided, however, that not more than one half of the Joint Observer Teams which have not been dispatched by the Military Armistice Commission may be dispatched at any one time by the senior member of either side on the Commission.

28. The Military Armistice Commission, or the senior member of either side thereof, is authorized to request the Neutral Nations Supervisory Commission to conduct special observations and inspections at places outside the Demilitarized Zone where violations of this Armistice Agreement have been reported to have occurred.

29. When the Military Armistice Commission determines that a viola-

tion of this Armistice Agreement has occurred, it shall immediately report such violation to the Commanders of the opposing sides.

30. When the Military Armistice Commission determines that a violation of this Armistice Agreement has been corrected to its satisfaction, it shall so report to the Commanders of the opposing sides.

## 3. GENERAL

31. The Military Armistice Commission shall meet daily. Recesses of not to exceed seven (7) days may be agreed upon by the senior members of both sides; provided, that such recesses may be terminated on twenty-four (24) hour notice by the senior member of either side.

32. Copies of the record of the proceedings of all meetings of the Military Armistice Commission shall be forwarded to the Commanders of the opposing sides as soon as possible after each meeting.

33. The Joint Observer Teams shall make periodic reports to the Military Armistice Commission as required by the Commission and, in addition, shall make such special reports as may be deemed necessary by them, or as may be required by the Commission.

34. The Military Armistice Commission shall maintain duplicate files of the reports and records of proceedings required by this Armistice Agreement. The Commission is authorized to maintain duplicate files of such other reports, records, etc., as may be necessary in the conduct of its business. Upon eventual dissolution of the Commission, one set of the above files shall be turned over to each side.

35. The Military Armistice Commission may make recommendations to the Commanders of the opposing sides with respect to amendments or additions to this Armistice Agreement. Such recommended changes should generally be those designed to insure a more effective armistice.

## C. NEUTRAL NATIONS SUPERVISORY COMMISSION

### 1. COMPOSITION

36. A Neutral Nations Supervisory Commission is hereby established.

37. The Neutral Nations Supervisory Commission shall be composed of four (4) senior officers, two (2) of whom shall be appointed by neutral nations nominated by the Commander-in-Chief, United Nations Command, namely, SWEDEN and SWITZERLAND, and two (2) of whom shall be appointed by neutral nations nominated jointly by the Supreme Commander of the Korean People's Army and the Commander of the Chinese People's Volunteers, namely, POLAND and CZECHOSLOVAKIA. The term "neutral nations" as herein used is defined as those nations whose combatant forces have not participated in the hostilities in Korea. Members appointed to the Commission may be from the armed forces of the

appointing nations. Each member shall designate an alternate member to attend those meetings which for any reason the principal member is unable to attend. Such alternate members shall be of the same nationality as their principals. The Neutral Nations Supervisory Commission may take action whenever the number of members present from the neutral nations nominated by one side is equal to the number of members present from the neutral nations nominated by the other side.

38. Members of the Neutral Nations Supervisory Commission shall be permitted to use staff assistants furnished by the neutral nations as required. These staff assistants may be appointed as alternate members of the Commission.

39. The neutral nations shall be requested to furnish the Neutral Nations Supervisory Commission with the necessary administrative personnel to establish a Secretariat charged with assisting the Commission by performing necessary record-keeping, secretarial, interpreting, and such other functions as the Commission may assign to it.

40. a. The Neutral Nations Supervisory Commission shall be initially provided with, and assisted by, twenty (20) Neutral Nations Inspection Teams, which number may be reduced by agreement of the senior members of both sides on the Military Armistice Commission. The Neutral Nations Inspection Teams shall be responsible to, shall report to, and shall be subject to the direction of, the Neutral Nations Supervisory Commission only.

b. Each Neutral Nations Inspection Team shall be composed of not less than four (4) officers, preferably of field grade, half of whom shall be from the neutral nations nominated by the Commander-in-Chief, United Nations Command, and half of whom shall be from the neutral nations nominated jointly by the Supreme Commander of the Korean People's Army and the Commander of the Chinese People's Volunteers. Members appointed to the Neutral Nations Inspection Teams may be from the armed forces of the appointing nations. In order to facilitate the functioning of the Teams, sub-teams composed of not less than two (2) members, one of whom shall be from a neutral nation nominated by the Commander-in-Chief, United Nations Command, and one of whom shall be from a neutral nation nominated jointly by the Supreme Commander of the Korean People's Army and the Commander of the Chinese People's Volunteers, may be formed as circumstances require. Additional personnel such as drivers, clerks, interpreters, and communications personnel, and such equipment as may be required by the Teams to perform their missions, shall be furnished by the Commander of each side, as required, in the Demilitarized Zone and in the territory under his military control. The Neutral Nations Supervisory Commission may provide itself and the Neutral Nations Inspection Teams with such of the above personnel and equipment of its own as it may desire; provided, however, that such personnel shall be personnel of the same neutral nations of which the Neutral Nations Supervisory Commission is composed.

## 2. FUNCTIONS AND AUTHORITY

41. The mission of the Neutral Nations Supervisory Commission shall be to carry out the functions of supervision, observation, inspection, and investigation, as stipulated in Sub-paragraphs 13c and 13d and Paragraph 28 hereof, and to report the results of such supervision, observation, inspection, and investigation to the Military Armistice Commission.

42. The Neutral Nations Supervisory Commission shall:

a. Locate its headquarters in proximity to the headquarters of the Military Armistice Commission.

b. Adopt such rules of procedure as it may, from time to time, deem necessary.

c. Conduct, through its members and its Neutral Nations Inspection Teams, the supervision and inspection provided for in Sub-paragraphs 13c and 13d of this Armistice Agreement at the ports of entry enumerated in Paragraph 43 hereof, and the special observations and inspections provided for in Paragraph 28 hereof at those places where violations of this Armistice Agreement have been reported to have occurred. The inspection of combat aircraft, armored vehicles, weapons, and ammunition by the Neutral Nations Inspection Teams shall be such as to enable them to properly insure that reinforcing combat aircraft, armored vehicles, weapons, and ammunition are not being introduced into Korea; but this shall not be construed as authorizing inspections or examinations of any secret designs or characteristics of any combat aircraft, armored vehicle, weapon, or ammunition.

d. Direct and supervise the operations of the Neutral Nations Inspection Teams.

e. Station five (5) Neutral Nations Inspection Teams at the ports of entry enumerated in Paragraph 43 hereof located in the territory under the military control of the Commander-in-Chief, United Nations Command; and five (5) Neutral Nations Inspection Teams at the ports of entry enumerated in Paragraph 43 hereof located in the territory under the military control of the Supreme Commander of the Korean People's Army and the Commander of the Chinese People's Volunteers; and establish initially ten (10) mobile Neutral Nations Inspection Teams in reserve, stationed in the general vicinity of the headquarters of the Neutral Nations Supervisory Commission, which number may be reduced by agreement of the senior members of both sides on the Military Armistice Commission. Not more than half of the mobile Neutral Nations Inspection Teams shall be dispatched at any one time in accordance with requests of the senior member of either side on the Military Armistice Commission.

f. Subject to the provisions of the preceding Sub-paragraph, conduct without delay investigations of reported violations of this Armistice Agreement, including such investigations of reported violations of this Armistice Agreement as may be requested by the Military Armistice Commission or by the senior member of either side on the Commission.

g. Provide credentials and distinctive insignia for its staff and its Neutral Nations Inspection Teams, and a distinctive marking for all vehicles, aircraft, and vessels, used in the performance of its mission.

43. Neutral Nations Inspection Teams shall be stationed at the following ports of entry:

| Territory under the military control of the United Nations Command | | Territory under the military control of the Korean People's Army and the Chinese People's Volunteers | |
|---|---|---|---|
| INCHON | (37°28′N, 126°38′E) | SINUIJU | (40°06′N, 124°24′E) |
| TAEGU | (35°52′N, 128°36′E) | CHONGJIN | (41°46′N, 129°49′E) |
| PUSAN | (35°06′N, 129°02′E) | HUNGNAM | (39°50′N, 127°37′E) |
| KANGNUNG | (37°45′N, 128°54′E) | MANPO | (41°09′N, 126°18′E) |
| KUNSAN | (35°59′N, 126°43′E) | SINANJU | (39°36′N, 125°36′E) |

These Neutral Nations Inspection Teams shall be accorded full convenience of movement within the areas and over the routes of communication set forth on the attached map (Map 5).

## 3. GENERAL

44. The Neutral Nations Supervisory Commission shall meet daily. Recesses of not to exceed seven (7) days may be agreed upon by the members of the Neutral Nations Supervisory Commission; provided, that such recesses may be terminated on twenty-four (24) hour notice by any member.

45. Copies of the record of the proceedings of all meetings of the Neutral Nations Supervisory Commission shall be forwarded to the Military Armistice Commission as soon as possible after each meeting. Records shall be kept in English, Korean, and Chinese.

46. The Neutral Nations Inspection Teams shall make periodic reports concerning the results of their supervision, observations, inspections, and investigations to the Neutral Nations Supervisory Commission as required by the Commission and, in addition, shall make such special reports as may be deemed necessary by them, or as may be required by the Commission. Reports shall be submitted by a Team as a whole, but may also be submitted by one or more individual members thereof; provided, that the reports submitted by one or more individual members thereof shall be considered as informational only.

47. Copies of the reports made by the Neutral Nations Inspection Teams shall be forwarded to the Military Armistice Commission by the Neutral Nations Supervisory Commission without delay and in the language in which received. They shall not be delayed by the process of translation or evaluation. The Neutral Nations Supervisory Commission shall evaluate such reports at the earliest practicable time and shall forward their findings to the Military Armistice Commission as a matter of priority. The Military Armistice Commission shall not take final action with regard to any such report until the evaluation thereof has been received from the

Neutral Nations Supervisory Commission. Members of the Neutral Nations Supervisory Commission and of its Teams shall be subject to appearance before the Military Armistice Commission, at the request of the senior member of either side on the Military Armistice Commission, for clarification of any report submitted.

48. The Neutral Nations Supervisory Commission shall maintain duplicate files of the reports and records of proceedings required by this Armistice Agreement. The Commission is authorized to maintain duplicate files of such other reports, records, etc., as may be necessary in the conduct of its business. Upon eventual dissolution of the Commission, one set of the above files shall be turned over to each side.

49. The Neutral Nations Supervisory Commission may make recommendations to the Military Armistice Commission with respect to amendments or additions to this Armistice Agreement. Such recommended changes should generally be those designed to insure a more effective armistice.

50. The Neutral Nations Supervisory Commission, or any member thereof, shall be authorized to communicate with any member of the Military Armistice Commission.

# ARTICLE III

## ARRANGEMENTS RELATING TO PRISONERS OF WAR

51. The release and repatriation of all prisoners of war held in the custody of each side at the time this Armistice Agreement becomes effective shall be effected in conformity with the following provisions agreed upon by both sides prior to the signing of this Armistice Agreement.

a. Within sixty (60) days after this Armistice Agreement becomes effective, each side shall, without offering any hindrance, directly repatriate and hand over in groups all those prisoners of war in its custody who insist on repatriation to the side to which they belonged at the time of capture. Repatriation shall be accomplished in accordance with the related provisions of this Article. In order to expedite the repatriation process of such personnel, each side shall, prior to the signing of the Armistice Agreement, exchange the total numbers, by nationalities, of personnel to be directly repatriated. Each group of prisoners of war delivered to the other side shall be accompanied by rosters, prepared by nationality, to include name, rank (if any) and internment or military serial number.

b. Each side shall release all those remaining prisoners of war, who are not directly repatriated, from its military control and from its custody and hand them over to the Neutral Nations Repatriation Commission for disposition in accordance with the provisions in the Annex hereto: "Terms of Reference for Neutral Nations Repatriation Commission."

c. So that there may be no misunderstanding owing to the equal use of three languages, the act of delivery of a prisoner of war by one side to the other side shall, for the purposes of this Armistice Agreement, be called "repatriation" in English, "song hwan" in Korean, and "ch'ien fan" in Chinese, notwithstanding the nationality or place of residence of such prisoner of war.

52. Each side insures that it will not employ in acts of war in the Korean conflict any prisoner of war released and repatriated incident to the coming into effect of this Armistice Agreement.

53. All the sick and injured prisoners of war who insist upon repatriation shall be repatriated with priority. Insofar as possible, there shall be captured medical personnel repatriated concurrently with the sick and injured prisoners of war, so as to provide medical care and attendance en route.

54. The repatriation of all the prisoners of war required by Sub-paragraph 51a hereof shall be completed within a time limit of sixty (60) days after this Armistice Agreement becomes effective. Within this time limit each side undertakes to complete the repatriation of the above-mentioned prisoners of war in its custody at the earliest practicable time.

55. PANMUNJOM is designated as the place where prisoners of war will be delivered and received by both sides. Additional place(s) of delivery and reception of prisoners of war in the Demilitarized Zone may be designated, if necessary, by the Committee for Repatriation of Prisoners of War.

56. a. A Committee for Repatriation of Prisoners of War is hereby established. It shall be composed of six (6) officers of field grade, three (3) of whom shall be appointed by the Commander-in-Chief, United Nations Command, and three (3) of whom shall be appointed jointly by the Supreme Commander of the Korean People's Army and the Commander of the Chinese People's Volunteers. This Committee shall, under the general supervision and direction of the Military Armistice Commission, be responsible for coordinating the specific plans of both sides for the repatriation of prisoners of war and for supervising the execution by both sides of all of the provisions of this Armistice Agreement relating to the repatriation of prisoners of war. It shall be the duty of this Committee to coordinate the timing of the arrival of prisoners of war at the place(s) of delivery and reception of prisoners of war from the prisoner of war camps of both sides; to make, when necessary, such special arrangements as may be required with regard to the transportation and welfare of sick and injured prisoners of war; to coordinate the work of the joint Red Cross teams, established in Paragraph 57 hereof, in assisting in the repatriation of prisoners of war; to supervise the implementation of the arrangements for the actual repatriation of prisoners of war stipulated in Paragraphs 53 and 54 hereof; to select, when necessary, additional place(s) of delivery and reception of prisoners of war; and to carry out such other related functions as are required for the repatriation of prisoners of war.

b. When unable to reach agreement on any matter relating to its responsibilities, the Committee for Repatriation of Prisoners of War shall immediately refer such matter to the Military Armistice Commission for decision. The Committee for Repatriation of Prisoners of War shall maintain its headquarters in proximity to the headquarters of the Military Armistice Commission.

c. The Committee for Repatriation of Prisoners of War shall be dissolved by the Military Armistice Commission upon completion of the program of repatriation of prisoners of war.

57. a. Immediately after this Armistice Agreement becomes effective, joint Red Cross teams composed of representatives of the national Red Cross Societies of the countries contributing forces to the United Nations Command on the one hand, and representatives of the Red Cross Society of the Democratic People's Republic of Korea and representatives of the Red Cross Society of the People's Republic of China on the other hand, shall be established. The joint Red Cross teams shall assist in the execution by both sides of those provisions of this Armistice Agreement relating to the repatriation of all the prisoners of war specified in Sub-paragraph 51a hereof, who insist upon repatriation, by the performance of such humanitarian services as are necessary and desirable for the welfare of the prisoners of war. To accomplish this task, the joint Red Cross teams shall provide assistance in the delivering and receiving of prisoners of war by both sides at the place(s) of delivery and reception of prisoners of war, and shall visit the prisoner of war camps of both sides to comfort the prisoners of war and to bring in and distribute gift articles for the comfort and welfare of the prisoners of war. The joint Red Cross teams may provide services to prisoners of war while en route from prisoner of war camps to the place(s) of delivery and reception of prisoners of war.

b. The joint Red Cross teams shall be organized as set forth below:

(1) One team shall be composed of twenty (20) members, namely, ten (10) representatives from the national Red Cross Societies of each side, to assist in the delivering and receiving of prisoners of war by both sides at the place(s) of delivery and reception of prisoners of war. The chairmanship of this team shall alternate daily between representatives from the Red Cross Societies of the two sides. The work and services of this team shall be coordinated by the Committee for Repatriation of Prisoners of War.

(2) One team shall be composed of sixty (60) members, namely, thirty (30) representatives from the national Red Cross Societies of each side, to visit the prisoner of war camps under the administration of the Korean People's Army and the Chinese People's Volunteers. This team may provide services to prisoners of war while en route from the prisoner of war camps to the place(s) of delivery and reception of prisoners of war. A representative of the Red Cross Society of the Democratic People's Republic of Korea or of the Red Cross Society of the People's Republic of China shall serve as chairman of this team.

(3) One team shall be composed of sixty (60) members, namely,

thirty (30) representatives from the national Red Cross Societies of each side, to visit the prisoner of war camps under the administration of the United Nations Command. This team may provide services to prisoners of war while en route from the prisoner of war camps to the place(s) of delivery and reception of prisoners of war. A representative of a Red Cross Society of a nation contributing forces to the United Nations Command shall serve as chairman of this team.

(4) In order to facilitate the functioning of each joint Red Cross team, sub-teams composed of not less than two (2) members from the team, with an equal number of representatives from each side, may be formed as circumstances require.

(5) Additional personnel such as drivers, clerks, and interpreters, and such equipment as may be required by the joint Red Cross teams to perform their missions, shall be furnished by the Commander of each side to the team operating in the territory under his military control.

(6) Whenever jointly agreed upon by the representatives of both sides on any joint Red Cross team, the size of such team may be increased or decreased, subject to confirmation by the Committee for Repatriation of Prisoners of War.

c. The Commander of each side shall cooperate fully with the joint Red Cross teams in the performance of their functions, and undertakes to insure the security of the personnel of the joint Red Cross team in the area under his military control. The Commander of each side shall provide such logistic, administrative, and communications facilities as may be required by the team operating in the territory under his military control.

d. The joint Red Cross teams shall be dissolved upon completion of the program of repatriation of all the prisoners of war specified in Sub-paragraph 51a hereof, who insist upon repatriation.

58. a. The Commander of each side shall furnish to the Commander of the other side as soon as practicable, but not later than ten (10) days after this Armistice Agreement becomes effective, the following information concerning prisoners of war:

(1) Complete data pertaining to the prisoners of war who escaped since the effective date of the data last exchanged.

(2) Insofar as practicable, information regarding name, nationality, rank, and other identification data, date and cause of death, and place of burial, of those prisoners of war who died while in his custody.

b. If any prisoners of war escape or die after the effective date of the supplementary information specified above, the detaining side shall furnish to the other side, through the Committee for Repatriation of Prisoners of War, the data pertaining thereto in accordance with the provisions of Sub-paragraph 58a hereof. Such data shall be furnished at ten-day intervals until the completion of the program of delivery and reception of prisoners of war.

c. Any escaped prisoner of war who returns to the custody of the detaining side after the completion of the program of delivery and reception of prisoners of war shall be delivered to the Military Armistice Commission for disposition.

59. a. All civilians who, at the time this Armistice Agreement becomes effective, are in territory under the military control of the Commander-in-Chief, United Nations Command, and who, on 24 June 1950, resided north of the Military Demarcation Line established in this Armistice Agreement shall, if they desire to return home, be permitted and assisted by the Commander-in-Chief, United Nations Command, to return to the area north of the Military Demarcation Line; and all civilians who, at the time this Armistice Agreement becomes effective, are in territory under the military control of the Supreme Commander of the Korean People's Army and the Commander of the Chinese People's Volunteers, and who, on 24 June 1950, resided south of the Military Demarcation Line established in this Armistice Agreement shall, if they desire to return home, be permitted and assisted by the Supreme Commander of the Korean People's Army and the Commander of the Chinese People's Volunteers to return to the area south of the Military Demarcation Line. The Commander of each side shall be responsible for publicizing widely throughout territory under his military control the contents of the provisions of this Sub-paragraph, and for calling upon the appropriate civil authorities to give necessary guidance and assistance to all such civilians who desire to return home.

b. All civilians of foreign nationality who, at the time this Armistice Agreement becomes effective, are in territory under the military control of the Supreme Commander of the Korean People's Army and the Commander of the Chinese People's Volunteers shall, if they desire to proceed to territory under the military control of the Commander-in-Chief, United Nations Command, be permitted and assisted to do so; all civilians of foreign nationality who, at the time this Armistice Agreement becomes effective, are in territory under the military control of the Commander-in-Chief, United Nations Command, shall, if they desire to proceed to territory under the military control of the Supreme Commander of the Korean People's Army and the Commander of the Chinese People's Volunteers, be permitted and assisted to do so. The Commander of each side shall be responsible for publicizing widely throughout the territory under his military control the contents of the provisions of this Sub-paragraph, and for calling upon the appropriate civil authorities to give necessary guidance and assistance to all such civilians of foreign nationality who desire to proceed to territory under the military control of the Commander of the other side.

c. Measures to assist in the return of civilians provided for in Subparagraph 59a hereof and the movement of civilians provided for in Subparagraph 59b hereof shall be commenced by both sides as soon as possible after this Armistice Agreement becomes effective.

d. (1) A Committee for Assisting the Return of Displaced Civilians is hereby established. It shall be composed of four (4) officers of field grade, two (2) of whom shall be appointed by the Commander-in-Chief, United

Nations Command, and two (2) of whom shall be appointed jointly by the Supreme Commander of the Korean People's Army and the Commander of the Chinese People's Volunteers. This Committee shall, under the general supervision and direction of the Military Armistice Commission, be responsible for coordinating the specific plans of both sides for assistance to the return of the above-mentioned civilians, and for supervising the execution by both sides of all of the provisions of this Armistice Agreement relating to the return of the above-mentioned civilians. It shall be the duty of this Committee to make necessary arrangements, including those of transportation, for expediting and coordinating the movement of the above-mentioned civilians; to select the crossing point(s) through which the above-mentioned civilians will cross the Military Demarcation Line; to arrange for security at the crossing point(s); and to carry out such other functions as are required to accomplish the return of the above-mentioned civilians.

(2) When unable to reach agreement on any matter relating to its responsibilities, the Committee for assisting the Return of Displaced Civilians shall immediately refer such matter to the Military Armistice Commission for decision. The Committee for Assisting the Return of Displaced Civilians shall maintain its headquarters in proximity to the headquarters of the Military Armistice Commission.

(3) The Committee for Assisting the Return of Displaced Civilians shall be dissolved by the Military Armistice Commission upon fulfillment of its mission.

# ARTICLE IV

# RECOMMENDATION TO THE GOVERNMENTS CONCERNED ON BOTH SIDES

60. In order to insure the peaceful settlement of the Korean question, the military Commanders of both sides hereby recommend to the governments of the countries concerned on both sides that, within three (3) months after the Armistice Agreement is signed and becomes effective, a political conference of a higher level of both sides be held by representatives appointed respectively to settle through negotiation the questions of the withdrawal of all foreign forces from Korea, the peaceful settlement of the Korean question, etc.

# ARTICLE V

# MISCELLANEOUS

61. Amendments and additions to this Armistice Agreement must be mutually agreed to by the Commanders of the opposing sides.

62. The Articles and Paragraphs of this Armistice Agreement shall remain in effect until expressly superseded either by mutually acceptable

amendments and additions or by provision in an appropriate agreement for a peaceful settlement at a political level between both sides.

63. All of the provisions of this Armistice Agreement, other than Paragraph 12, shall become effective at          hours on                1953.

Done at Panmunjom, Korea, at          hours on the       day of 1953, in English, Korean, and Chinese, all texts being equally authentic.

| | | |
|---|---|---|
| KIM IL SUNG<br>Marshal, Democratic<br>  People's Republic<br>  of Korea<br>Supreme Commander,<br>Korean People's Army | PENG TEH-HUAI<br>Commander, Chinese<br>  People's Volunteers | MARK W. CLARK<br>General, United States<br>  Army<br>Commander-in-Chief,<br>  United Nations<br>  Command |

## PRESENT

| | |
|---|---|
| NAM IL<br>General, Korean People's Army<br>Senior Delegate,<br>Delegation of the Korean People's<br>  Army and the Chinese People's<br>  Volunteers | WILLIAM K. HARRISON, JR.<br>Lieutenant General, United States<br>  Army<br>Senior Delegate,<br>United Nations Command Delegation |

# ANNEX

# TERMS OF REFERENCE
# FOR
# NEUTRAL NATIONS REPATRIATION
# COMMISSION
(See Sub-paragraph 51b)

# I

# GENERAL

1. In order to ensure that all prisoners of war have the opportunity to exercise their right to be repatriated following an armistice, Sweden, Switzerland, Poland, Czechoslovakia and India shall each be requested by both sides to appoint a member to a Neutral Nations Repatriation Commission which shall be established to take custody in Korea of those prisoners of war who, while in the custody of the detaining powers, have not exercised

their right to be repatriated. The Neutral Nations Repatriation Commission shall establish its headquarters within the Demilitarized Zone in the vicinity of Panmunjom, and shall station subordinate bodies of the same composition as the Neutral Nations Repatriation Commission at those locations at which the Repatriation Commission assumes custody of prisoners of war. Representatives of both sides shall be permitted to observe the operations of the Repatriation Commission and its subordinate bodies to include explanations and interviews.

2. Sufficient armed forces and any other operating personnel required to assist the Neutral Nations Repatriation Commission in carrying out its functions and responsibilities shall be provided exclusively by India, whose representative shall be the umpire in accordance with the provisions of Article 132 of the Geneva Convention, and shall also be chairman and executive agent of the Neutral Nations Repatriation Commission. Representatives from each of the other four powers shall be allowed staff assistants in equal number not to exceed fifty (50) each. When any of the representatives of the neutral nations is absent for some reason, that representative shall designate an alternate representative of his own nationality to exercise his functions and authority. The arms of all personnel provided for in this Paragraph shall be limited to military police type small arms.

3. No force or threat of force shall be used against the prisoners of war specified in Paragraph 1 above to prevent or effect their repatriation, and no violence to their persons or affront to their dignity or self-respect shall be permitted in any manner for any purpose whatsoever (but see Paragraph 7 below). This duty is enjoined on and entrusted to the Neutral Nations Repatriation Commission. This Commission shall ensure that prisoners of war shall at all times be treated humanely in accordance with the specific provisions of the Geneva Convention, and with the general spirit of that Convention.

## II

## CUSTODY OF PRISONERS OF WAR

4. All prisoners of war who have not exercised their right of repatriation following the effective date of the Armistice Agreement shall be released from the military control and from the custody of the detaining side as soon as practicable, and, in all cases, within sixty (60) days subsequent to the effective date of the Armistice Agreement to the Neutral Nations Repatriation Commission at locations in Korea to be designated by the detaining side.

5. At the time the Neutral Nations Repatriation Commission assumes control of the prisoner of war installations, the military forces of the detaining side shall be withdrawn therefrom, so that the locations specified in the preceding Paragraph shall be taken over completely by the armed forces of India.

6. Notwithstanding the provisions of Paragraph 5 above, the detaining side shall have the responsibility for maintaining and ensuring security and order in the areas around the locations where the prisoners of war are in custody and for preventing and restraining any armed forces (including irregular armed forces) in the area under its control from any acts of disturbance and intrusion against the locations where the prisoners of war are in custody.

7. Notwithstanding the provisions of Paragraph 3 above, nothing in this agreement shall be construed as derogating from the authority of the Neutral Nations Repatriation Commission to exercise its legitimate functions and responsibilities for the control of the prisoners of war under its temporary jurisdiction.

# III

# EXPLANATION

8. The Neutral Nations Repatriation Commission, after having received and taken into custody all those prisoners of war who have not exercised their right to be repatriated, shall immediately make arrangements so that within ninety (90) days after the Neutral Nations Repatriation Commission takes over the custody, the nations to which the prisoners of war belong shall have freedom and facilities to send representatives to the locations where such prisoners of war are in custody to explain to all the prisoners of war depending upon these nations their rights and to inform them of any matters relating to their return to their homelands, particularly of their full freedom to return home to lead a peaceful life, under the following provisions:

a. The number of such explaining representatives shall not exceed seven (7) per thousand prisoners of war held in custody by the Neutral Nations Repatriation Commission; and the minimum authorized shall not be less than a total of five (5);

b. The hours during which the explaining representatives shall have access to the prisoners shall be as determined by the Neutral Nations Repatriation Commission, and generally in accord with Article 53 of the Geneva Convention Relative to the Treatment of Prisoners of War;

c. All explanations and interviews shall be conducted in the presence of a representative of each member nation of the Neutral Nations Repatriation Commission and a representative from the detaining side;

d. Additional provisions governing the explanation work shall be prescribed by the Neutral Nations Repatriation Commission, and will be designed to employ the principles enumerated in Paragraph 3 above and in this Paragraph;

e. The explaining representatives, while engaging in their work, shall be allowed to bring with them necessary facilities and personnel for wireless communications. The number of communications personnel shall be limited to one team per location at which explaining representatives are in residence, except in the event all prisoners of war are concentrated in one location, in which case, two (2) teams shall be permitted. Each team shall consist of not more than six (6) communications personnel.

9. Prisoners of war in its custody shall have freedom and facilities to make representations and communications to the Neutral Nations Repatriation Commission and to representatives and subordinate bodies of the Neutral Nations Repatriation Commission and to inform them of their desires on any matter concerning the prisoners of war themselves, in accordance with arrangements made for the purpose by the Neutral Nations Repatriation Commission.

# IV

## DISPOSITION OF PRISONERS OF WAR

10. Any prisoner of war who, while in the custody of the Neutral Nations Repatriation Commission, decides to exercise the right of repatriation, shall make an application requesting repatriation to a body consisting of a representative of each member nation of the Neutral Nations Repatriation Commission. Once such an application is made, it shall be considered immediately by the Neutral Nations Repatriation Commission or one of its subordinate bodies so as to determine immediately by majority vote the validity of such application. Once such an application is made to and validated by the Commission or one of its subordinate bodies, the prisoner of war concerned shall immediately be transferred to and accommodated in the tents set up for those who are ready to be repatriated. Thereafter, he shall, while still in the custody of the Neutral Nations Repatriation Commission, be delivered forthwith to the prisoner of war exchange point at Panmunjom for repatriation under the procedure prescribed in the Armistice Agreement.

11. At the expiration of ninety (90) days after the transfer of custody of the prisoners of war to the Neutral Nations Repatriation Commission, access of representatives to captured personnel as provided for in Paragraph 8 above, shall terminate, and the question of disposition of the prisoners of war who have not exercised their right to be repatriated shall be submitted to the Political Conference recommended to be convened in Paragraph 60, Draft Armistice Agreement, which shall endeavor to settle this question within thirty (30) days, during which period the Neutral Nations Repatriation Commission shall continue to retain custody of those prisoners of war. The Neutral Nations Repatriation Commission shall declare the relief from the prisoner of war status to civilian status of any prisoners of war who have not exercised their right to be repatriated and for whom no other disposition has been agreed to by the Political Conference within one hundred and twenty (120) days after the Neutral Nations Repatriation Commission has assumed their custody. Thereafter, according to the application of each

individual, those who choose to go to neutral nations shall be assisted by the Neutral Nations Repatriation Commission and the Red Cross Society of India. This operation shall be completed within thirty (30) days, and upon its completion, the Neutral Nations Repatriation Commission shall immediately cease its functions and declare its dissolution. After the dissolution of the Neutral Nations Repatriation Commission, whenever and wherever any of those above-mentioned civilians who have been relieved from the prisoner of war status desire to return to their fatherlands, the authorities of the localities where they are shall be responsible for assisting them in returning to their fatherlands.

# V

## RED CROSS VISITATION

12. Essential Red Cross service for prisoners of war in custody of the Neutral Nations Repatriation Commission shall be provided by India in accordance with regulations issued by the Neutral Nations Repatriation Commission.

# VI

## PRESS COVERAGE

13. The Neutral Nations Repatriation Commission shall insure freedom of the press and other news media in observing the entire operation as enumerated herein, in accordance with procedures to be established by the Neutral Nations Repatriation Commission.

# VII

## LOGISTICAL SUPPORT FOR PRISONERS OF WAR

14. Each side shall provide logistical support for the prisoners of war in the area under its military control, delivering required support to the Neutral Nations Repatriation Commission at an agreed delivery point in the vicinity of each prisoner of war installation.

15. The cost of repatriating prisoners of war to the exchange point at Panmunjom shall be borne by the detaining side and the cost from the exchange point by the side on which said prisoners depend in accordance with Article 118 of the Geneva Convention.

16. The Red Cross Society of India shall be responsible for providing such general service personnel in the prisoner of war installations as required by the Neutral Nations Repatriation Commission.

17. The Neutral Nations Repatriation Commission shall provide medical support for the prisoners of war as may be practicable. The detaining side shall provide medical support as practicable upon the request of the Neutral Nations Repatriation Commission and specifically for those cases requiring extensive treatment or hospitalization. The Neutral Nations Repatriation Commission shall maintain custody of prisoners of war during such hospitalization. The detaining side shall facilitate such custody. Upon completion of treatment, prisoners of war shall be returned to a prisoners of war installation as specified in Paragraph 4 above.

18. The Neutral Nations Repatriation Commission is entitled to obtain from both sides such legitimate assistance as it may require in carrying out its duties and tasks, but both sides shall not under any name and in any form interfere or exert influence.

# VIII

# LOGISTICAL SUPPORT FOR THE NEUTRAL NATIONS REPATRIATION COMMISSION

19. Each side shall be responsible for providing logistical support for the personnel of the Neutral Nations Repatriation Commission stationed in the area under its military control, and both sides shall contribute on an equal basis to such support within the Demilitarized Zone. The precise arrangements shall be subject to determination between the Neutral Nations Repatriation Commission and the detaining side in each case.

20. Each of the detaining sides shall be responsible for protecting the explaining representatives from the other side while in transit over lines of communication within its area, as set forth in Paragraph 23 for the Neutral Nations Repatriation Commission, to a place of residence and while in residence in the vicinity of but not within each of the locations where the prisoners of war are in custody. The Neutral Nations Repatriation Commission shall be responsible for the security of such representatives within the actual limits of the locations where the prisoners of war are in custody.

21. Each of the detaining sides shall provide transportation, housing, communication, and other agreed logistical support to the explaining representatives of the other side while they are in the area under its military control. Such services shall be provided on a reimbursable basis.

# IX

# PUBLICATION

22. After the Armistice Agreement becomes effective, the terms of this agreement shall be made known to all prisoners of war who, while in the custody of the detaining side, have not exercised their right to be repatriated.

# X

## MOVEMENT

23. The movement of the personnel of the Neutral Nations Repatriation Commission and repatriated prisoners of war shall be over lines of communication as determined by the command(s) of the opposing side and the Neutral Nations Repatriation Commission. A map showing these lines of communication shall be furnished the command of the opposing side and the Neutral Nations Repatriation Commission. Movement of such personnel, except within locations as designated in Paragraph 4 above, shall be under the control of, and escorted by, personnel of the side in whose area the travel is being undertaken; however, such movement shall not be subject to any obstruction and coercion.

# XI

## PROCEDURAL MATTERS

24. The interpretation of this agreement shall rest with the Neutral Nations Repatriation Commission. The Neutral Nations Repatriation Commission, and/or any subordinate bodies to which functions are designed or assigned by the Neutral Nations Repatriation Commission, shall operate on the basis of majority vote.

25. The Neutral Nations Repatriation Commission shall submit a weekly report to the opposing Commanders on the status of prisoners of war in its custody, indicating the numbers repatriated and remaining at the end of each week.

26. When this agreement has been acceded to by both sides and by the five powers named herein, it shall become effective upon the date the Armistice becomes effective.

Done at Panmunjom, Korea, at 1400 hours on the 8th day of June 1953, in English, Korean, and Chinese, all texts being equally authentic.

NAM IL
General, Korean People's Army
Senior Delegate,
Delegation of the Korean People's
  Army and the Chinese People's
  Volunteers

WILLIAM K. HARRISON, JR.
Lieutenant General, United
  States Army
Senior Delegate,
United Nations Command
  Delegation

# *Appendix B*

(Maximum effort at any one time during the war)

## UNITED STATES
(Approximately ten times the effort of all others)

Seven Army divisions
One Marine division
Army and corps headquarters, logistical and support forces
One tactical air force and complete supporting complement
One combat cargo command, air
Two medium bombardment wings
U.S. Seventh Fleet, including fast carrier task group, blockade and escort forces, amphibious force, reconnaissance and anti-submarine units, supply and repair units
Military sea transport services

## UNITED KINGDOM

Two army brigades of five infantry battalions, two field artillery regiments, one armored regiment
Far East naval forces including one aircraft carrier, two cruisers, eight destroyers and supporting units, with Royal Marine detachment

## CANADA

One army brigade of three infantry battalions, one artillery regiment, supporting armored, anti-tank, and service forces
Three destroyers
One air transport squadron

## TURKEY

One army brigade of about 6,000 men

## AUSTRALIA

Two infantry battalions
One fighter squadron
One air transport squadron
One aircraft carrier, two destroyers, one frigate

## THAILAND

One regimental combat team of about 4,000 men
Two corvettes
One air transport squadron

## PHILIPPINES

One regimental combat team of about 5,000 men

## FRANCE

One infantry battalion
One patrol gunboat

## GREECE

One infantry battalion
One air transport squadron

## NEW ZEALAND

One artillery regiment
Two frigates

## THE NETHERLANDS

One infantry battalion
One destroyer

## COLOMBIA

One infantry battalion
One frigate

## BELGIUM

One infantry battalion

## ETHIOPIA

One infantry battalion

## UNION OF SOUTH AFRICA

One fighter squadron

## LUXEMBOURG

One infantry company

In addition, Denmark furnished a hospital ship; Sweden, Norway and Italy hospital units; India a field ambulance unit; the British Commonwealth countries furnished their own medical facilities; and the United States provided medical services to all allied forces as required.

# *Appendix C*

## CASUALTY TOLL OF THE KOREAN WAR, JUNE 25th, 1950 TO JULY 27th, 1953

| Country | Dead | Wounded | Missing (and unrepatriated as of Dec. 23, '53) | Total |
|---|---|---|---|---|
| Republic of Korea* (military and civilian) | 415,004 | 428,568 | – | – |
| United States** | 29,550 | 103,492 | 3,486 | 136,528 |
| United Kingdom*** | 670 | 2,574 | 118 | 3,362 |
| Turkey**** | 717 | 2,246 | 167 | 3,130 |
| Canada | 309 | 1,203 | 32 | 1,544 |
| Australia | 265 | 1,351 | 36 | 1,351 |
| France | 288 | 818 | 18 | 1,124 |
| Thailand | 114 | 794 | 5 | 913 |
| Greece | 169 | 543 | 2 | 714 |
| Netherlands | 111 | 589 | 4 | 704 |
| Colombia | 140 | 452 | 65 | 657 |
| Ethiopia | 120 | 536 | 0 | 656 |
| Belgium-Luxembourg | 97 | 350 | 5 | 452 |
| Philippines | 92 | 299 | 57 | 448 |
| New Zealand | 31 | 78 | 0 | 109 |
| South Africa | 20 | 0 | 16 | 36 |
| Totals | 447,697 | 543,893 | 4,011 | 151,728 |

Communist China—900,000 dead and wounded estimated by U.S. Def. Dept.

North Korea—520,000 dead and wounded estimated by U.S. Def. Dept. No reliable estimate of civilian casualties.

* ROK Defense Ministry refuses to release its military casualty tabulation. This estimate issued at United Nations, New York. No reliable figures on missing. Military casualties about one-fifth above totals.

** U.S. figures as of Jan. 1, 1954 revision by U.S. Defense Department after approximately 3,950 casualties previously listed as missing were declared dead. More than 85% of U.S. wounded returned to duty after treatment.

*** Source of U.K. and other Commonwealth casualties, British Commonwealth Forces, Korea.

**** Source of all other U.N. component casualties, respective delegations to United Nations General Assembly.

# *Index*

Acheson, Dean, 12, 13, 27, 74, 80, 94, 135, 136, 162, 164, 166, 206 f., 241
Almond, Gen. Edward M., 60, 66 f., 86, 95, 108, 133
Armistice, slow progress of, 205 ff.; agreement texts, 310 ff.
Attlee, Clement, 10, 117 f.

Baillie, Hugh, 117
Bevin, Ernest, 107
Bradley, Gen. Omar, 94, 164, 171, 244
Briggs, Ellis O., 271
Brodie, Gen. Thomas, 130
Brownell, Herbert, 244
Bryan, Gen. Blackshear M., 269
Burke, Adm. Arleigh A., 204

Casualties, number of, 216 f., 337
Chang Chun San, Col., 209
Chang Pyong San, Gen., 204
Chiang Kai-shek, 27, 153, 162, 227, 248
China, troops offered by, 27; MacArthur on, 91 ff.; intransigence of, 102; peace terms of, 120; Russia fails, 179
Choi Duk Shin, Gen., 261
Chou En-lai, 202, 258, 262; threat by, 76 f.; peace terms of, 120 f., 135 f.; part played by, 251, 252 f., 254
Chunchon, 9, 147, 149, 191
Church, Gen. John H., 19, 21, 40
Clark, Gen. Mark W., 276, 280; takes command, 228; clashes with Rhee, 228 f.; clashes with Van Fleet, 248; renews prisoner proposal, 249 f.; welcomes proposals, 253; consults Rhee, 261, 264; faces dilemma, 267 ff.; castigates Rhee, 270, 272
Collins, Gen. J. Lawton, 59, 116, 134
Craigie, Gen. L. C., 204

Daniel, Adm. John C., 253
Dean, Gen. William F., 28, 36 f.
den Ouden, Col. M. P. A., 143
Doyle, Adm. James H., 114
Dulles, John Foster, 9, 304

E C A, 3, 5 f.
Eisenhower, Gen. Dwight D., 151, 228, 263, 304; on Korea, 236, 243; visits Korea, 244 f.; on expanding ROK forces, 245; charges Truman neglect, 247; cancels Formosa's neutralization, 248; reassures Rhee, 264 f.; Rhee rebuffs, 265; calls Rhee's bluff, 274
England, 95, 136, 234 f.

Formosa, 6, 13, 27, 103, 121, 153, 171, 248
Freeman, Col. Paul, 144

Geneva Convention, 220, 223
Gromyko, Andrei, 202
Gross, Ernest A., 12

Hamhung, 82, 91, 102, 113
Han River, 28, 129, 148, 189 f.
Harrison, Gen. William, 260, 261; as chief negotiator, 229, 236; walks out of meetings, 237; on U. N. terms, 238; reassures Communists, 277 ff.
Harvey, Capt. Maurice, 188
Hodes, Gen. Henry I., 204
Hsieh Fang, Gen., 204
Hungnam, 82, 112 ff.

Inchon, 56 ff., 130 f., 142
India, 16; proposes repatriation plan, 240, 241 f.; accepted as neutral commissioner, 259 f.

Johnson, Louis, 13
Joy, Adm. C. Turner, 204, 205, 207, 208, 211, 224, 227, 229

338